That Most Distressful Nation

THAT MOST DISTRESSFUL NATION

The Taming of the American Irish

by Andrew M. Greeley

Foreword by Daniel P. Moynihan

Chicago/Quadrangle Books/1972

Library of Congress Catalog Card Number: 74–182501
International Standard Book Number: 8–8129–0246–7

Grateful acknowledgment is made to the following for permission to reprint copyrighted materials: The Macmillan Company, for "Easter 1916" by William Butler Yeats; John Murray, for "Sunday in Ireland" by John Betjeman; Random House–Alfred A. Knopf, for "The Sweetness of Nature," and "The Midnight Court," by Bryan Merryman.

Foreword
by Daniel P. Moynihan

Would it be fair to say of American Irish history, as Oscar Wilde said of Niagara Falls, that it would be more impressive if it flowed the other way?

One could get this impression from *That Most Distressful Nation: The Taming of the American Irish,* the most recent of Andrew M. Greeley's many works. It is all there in the title: a past of heroic or at least colossal travail; a present shading from lace-curtain respectability to *le confort bourgeois* and yet further to the higher indulgences with which the American well-to-do have experimented of late. But the pleasures of the rich and the ease of the middle class are less than heroic either to experience or to contemplate. They bespeak a tamed people, and such, Greeley will argue, is the condition of the American Irish today.

There is, to be sure, a residuum of bronze-age *hauteur* in the very notion that settling down to one woman, a steady job, and offspring in college is in some profoundly sad way a diminishment of man's estate. Or at least something no gentleman would endure (and there were, of course, no ladies in that not so remote period). Still, we have Greeley's judgment that this is what has happened.

> The American Irish had the shortest way to come of any of the immigrant groups—for all the impoverishment of the Famine, the Atlantic crossing, and the early years in the slums. With the exception of the Jews, they have achieved the most remarkable success of any immigrant group. The

only thing they have lost is their explicit sense of distinction as a group and their consciousness of a heritage—and, necessarily, any consciousness of goals for the future.

This is both a statement and an interpretation of fact. It must rest in the first instance on census data and its equivalent, but beyond this, as in all of Greeley's work, one is asked, what does the data signify? In this instance Greeley aligns himself solidly with J. H. Plumb, whose Saponeskow Lectures given at the City College of New York in 1968 on *The Death of the Past*[1] have established more clearly than any recent writing that "The sense of the past has usually been linked in human consciousness with a sense of the future," and that this connection has been especially dynamic in the Western Christian world. Allow the one to wither or foreshorten, and the other will follow suit. Although it risks the absurd, or rather the stereotype, there is an Irish sensibility even in this passage of Greeley at his most cosmopolitan; for what is he saying but that the world always cheats you, even as it appears at long last to smile with favor and reward? What indeed has been the profit of winning a share of this world and losing one's immortality in the process?

Let it be. What of the data? I question them somewhat. Let that stand as a mark of respect. Few American sociologists working in this or an allied field have anything like Greeley's command of the available information, nor yet of the uses to which it can be put. His study with Peter Rossi of *The Education of American Catholics,* although it appeared only in 1966, has become a classic instance of the capacity—one is tempted to say tendency—of careful survey research to demolish previous understandings of what the world is like and what goes on in it. In demonstrating the extraordinarily weak influence of Catholic education on the religious practices of those who experienced it, Greeley and Rossi sounded what has been almost a dominant theme of American social research since; that is to say, the extremely limited capacity of formal institutions to influence patterns of behavior in directions different from the influence derived from the primary reference groups of family and

---

1. J. H. Plumb, *The Death of the Past* (London: The MacMillan Company, 1969), p. 11.

community. This to many has been a most disappointing development, casting doubt, as it does, on all manner of enthusiasms from
St. Ignatius Loyola High School to Project Head Start to the Voice
of America.

In another view, it is just as profoundly an optimistic finding,
the secular equivalent, almost, of the Christian's "good news."
There are limits, it appears, to the power of the state. We never
did get, as Raymond A. Bauer has shown us, that New Soviet
Man, and we may yet evade the even more ambitious improve-
ments awaiting us in the meliorist decades ahead. There is all the
more reason, then, for scholars to turn to the consideration of these
primary groups so long neglected in favor of more exciting adven-
tures in social planning. Kenneth Boulding has reminded us how
little we have learned of the family in recent generations. Greeley
has repeatedly made the same point with respect to ethnic groups.

My concern with his data about the success of the American
Irish in a sense confirms his point. I don't think we know enough
to make any statement about which is "second" among immigrant
groups. That American Jews are first none will question, or none
ought, although there is *no* census data as such on the subject, re-
flecting a long taboo in American government on the subject of
religion. (One recalls the account of the first race for what was to
become the America's Cup. Queen Victoria came to watch. On
being informed that rounding the Isle of Wight, or wherever, the
America was clearly first, the Queen asked who was second.
"There is no second, Ma'am," a courtier replied.) We will skip
second place and examine the evidence for third. We are faced
with census data that show American Chinese to have the highest
social-economic status in the land, and that Japanese-Americans
follow them. Surely there are similarly defined groups who would
also place ahead of the Irish in these terms. Supposing there were
a large number of persons who still thought of themselves as Scots?
Would not they show to advantage as against their Celtic neighbors? And what of German Americans? Surely. . . . And yet one
grants Greeley a larger definition of success, having something to
do with an impact on American society in line with the liberal,
democratic tradition of the nation.

Greeley brings solid research to the question he terms "one of the great myths of 'pop' social science in the United States . . . that the Catholic population in general and the Irish Catholic population in particular is conservative." (In this he shares the view first put forth by William V. Shannon in *The American Irish,* published in 1963.)[2] One is pained to see the honorable term "conservative" used to comprehend a range of attitudes that are neither conservative nor liberal, but merely vulgar, bigoted, and selfish. But, given these terms, the American Irish do score better, that is to say, more liberal—and one must be quite explicit about values in these matters—than just about any identifiable group save American Jews. (One has the impression that if the German as against Polish distinction were analyzed more rigorously with respect to Jews, the Catholic Irish might land right in the middle of the group, or rather between the two groups. In his study *Why Can't They Be Like Us?,* for example, Greeley showed that in affiliation to the Democratic party the Irish came just between the two. The highest pro-Democratic scores were scored by *Polish* Catholics and Polish Jews, a finding that ought to stir some curiosity, but won't.)

Perhaps the issue of relative success need not be too long pursued. The results of such inquiry can only be mischievous. If such work is to be done, at very least the findings should be published in Latin, or, if that is thought to give an undue advantage to clerics such as Greeley, it would probably be best to reduce the whole matter to sets of differential equations. It is not a subject we need know too much about.

But this bit of folk wisdom—that there are things one will be well advised not to know too much about—has been allowed to suppress an altogether different impulse which is to learn a lot more about ethnicity. This sense of tribal difference has been a kind of secret knowledge we have held in common for centuries, but rarely dared to acknowledge in more than suggestive detail. Schoolboys teach it to one another, but they will find little of it in their school-

---

2. William V. Shannon, *The American Irish* (New York: MacMillan, 1963).

books, nor have American scholars done much to make it a subject no textbook can ignore. Little by way of formal instruction suggests to the American student, at whatever level, the uniqueness of the American experience, with its fantastic compounding of ethnic groups, which is to say the experience of the incredible migration that in a flash, almost, filled the near empty continent of North America with the most diverse population ever in history to establish and seek to perpetuate a single polity. If the society that resulted did not exist it would be impossible to invent it, and if it had not kept itself together for a number of centuries it would seem risky to predict that it could last another generation. And yet it has and will. This is what Greeley's work is about.

That is to say, it is about ethnicity—in his case, about the ethnic history of the American Irish. Just as any study of "race" in the American experience probably should begin with American Indians, so the American Irish are the logical place to begin a consideration of ethnicity in American life and, also, of course, to begin the discussion of whether the two categories are really distinct. The Catholic Irish were the first group of "different" immigrants to arrive in large numbers, to settle in large cities, and to make obvious that they would not necessarily either change their ways nor yet stay out of sight. Nothing could be quite the same thereafter. Nothing was, especially as a succession of other groups, similarly disposed, followed in their wake. Whether the Negro American is simply the most recent of such groups, or rather the next most recent preceding the Puerto Ricans, is, as I state, an unresolved question.

I have contended elsewhere that the twentieth-century Negro experience in the city is best understood in the context of the nineteenth-century Irish experience rather than that of the Jews, which seems to me to have been profoundly different, if only in degrees of previous urbanization, but which generally has been the implicit model for social interventions on behalf of the black newcomers. Logically this would be true also of the Puerto Rican experience, that is to say, the Irish pattern, *mutatis mutandi,* has persisted.

Under the admirable direction of Dr. George Hay Brown, the

Bureau of the Census has begun to give us at least little bits of information on this subject. A recent report broke down the American population into ethnic categories.[3]

In these terms the American Irish account for some 16 million people, roughly 8 per cent of the population. There are, however,

RACE AND ETHNIC ORIGIN	TOTAL*
Total	202,848
RACE	
White	177,626
Negro	22,810
Other races	2,412
ETHNIC ORIGIN	
English, Scotch, Welsh	31,006
French	5,189
German	25,661
Irish	16,325
Italian	8,733
Polish	4,941
Russian	2,132
Spanish origin	8,956
Central or South American	501
Cuban	626
Mexican	5,023
Puerto Rican	1,450
Other Spanish origin	1,356
Other ethnic origin†	84,689
Not reported	15,216

*Numbers in thousands. Noninstitutional population.

†Includes about 20 million Negroes, as well as many persons reporting more than one origin.

---

3. U.S. Bureau of the Census, "Selected Characteristics of Persons and Families of Mexican, Puerto Rican and other Spanish Origin: March 1971," Series P-20, No. 224, October 1971, Table 1.

100 million persons (including Negroes) who either report other ethnic origins or are not reported. It would seem reasonable to estimate that roughly 65 per cent of these 100 million are of mixed European ancestry. Some of these still regard themselves as having an "ethnic" identity; others simply think of themselves as Americans. The latter are presumed products of the melting pot, unless one adds the "English, Scotch, Welsh" whom the melting-pot American is presumedly supposed to resemble after the removal of impurities.

The "English, Scotch, Welsh" may be lumped together, but the Irish must be enumerated separately. Not even the Bureau of the Census, that least hyperbolic of institutions, declines to note that the Irish are different from the other three major groups of the British Isles, different even from the Celtic Scotch and Welsh, albeit that in almost all superficial characteristics the four groups resemble one another closely, and that they differ from one another far less than they differ from persons, of whatever ancestry, living outside the British Isles. Yet we know that there is a sense in which this is not so of the Irish: their history has made them different from the "English, Scotch, Welsh." Does this difference persist in the United States? A scholar such as Greeley argues that it does, even when all memory of the events that made for it has vanished. This argument seems to me to clash with his evident disapproval of the view held, as he asserts, by many, that there is no need to know such history, that society can be seen as "a giant Markov model in which all one needs to know of the past is contained in the present. . . ." But both contentions can be accepted. The past is present: it can only be that. But an unexamined past, an historical memory that has accommodated itself to events, will almost certainly leave out a great deal that an ethnic group needs to know if it is to understand its own experience. Similarly, the relevance of that experience for other groups is bound to be diminished in the absence of a specific analytic effort to find such relevance.

On then with the rediscovery of the Irish experience, now all but lost to sentiment, vulgarity, clericalism, and indifference. Thomas N. Browne has taught us what we need to know to under-

stand this evanescence. Irish enthusiasm, including Irish nationalism, in late nineteenth-century America was a device whereby the
immigrants staked their claim to be Americans. A curious logic, to
be sure, but one understood at the time, as the "Fighting Irish of
Notre Dame" testify even to this moment. But once the claim was
acknowledged the original assertion lost much of its meaning. It
never, on the other hand, became dysfunctional. Not for a century
has it been to anyone's disadvantage to be Irish in America—which
is not true of all groups—but neither has it mattered much, and so
the whole thing faded. Vulgarians took over, whose rather sad St.
Patrick's Day gaieties in the South Bostons of the land are recorded
with increasing impatience by the local press, and this, in turn,
hastened the departure of those of sensibility and self-respect. A
decade ago, writing with Nathan Glazer *Beyond the Melting Pot,*
I visited the headquarters, in a once splendid Fifth Avenue museum,
of the American Irish Historical Society. It was empty alike of
scholars and antiquarians, and clearly had been so for years. The
Society had been established for honorable purposes by mostly
competent men but was no longer of any use. (More then is the
wonder and pleasure of its recent revival.) On, to repeat, with the
reconstruction of the Irish experience.

It has been, of course, an experience until recently of sustained
defeat. A thousand years of it in Ireland, two thousand years in
Europe. "Camelot," Greeley reminds us, "was, after all, a Celtic
City," to which one adds the thought that very likely it *was* a city,
but the time came when nobody believed that anymore, and for
sure when no one could locate the ruins. Defeat made for ugliness
in people, as it has to do. Surely there has not been a crucifixion
scene in many years as heart rending as that which appeared recently
on the front page of the *New York Times* of a Catholic girl hanging
to a lamp post in Northern Ireland, her head shaved, boiling tar
poured over and dripping from it. This was the wedding shower
she had received from the Catholic ladies of Londonderry because
of her intent to marry a British soldier. (But the damage done to the
Irish by defeat is as nothing to that inflicted on the British through
victory. The plain barbarity of British acts in Northern Ireland in
1971 and now 1972 is scarcely imaginable save as one considers

what they have done to themselves since Cromwell. In all else generous and brave: in this thing, hideous.)

Defeat also made for dullness. It appears settled, for example, that the IQ of the Irish in Ireland is a full standard deviation behind that of the English in Ireland. The implications of such a gap for the number of genuinely clever persons that will appear in one group as against the other are greater than might be supposed. Perhaps it is merely that defeat made for flight, and that the bright ones left. No one seems to know, but what remains is . . . well, what remains. A decent quiet country.

The Irish resistance to British rule provided, along with the Polish experience in yet more complicated circumstances, a model of sorts for the colonial wars of liberation that have taken up so much of modern history. One could wish that those who followed, or repeated, the model might have gone on to learn from the Irish how to establish a democratic society in the aftermath of colonial rule. It stands, as Greeley notes, as an achievement of a high order, one that has now persisted for half a century, such that Eire must be ranked among the most stable of the world's democracies. If the Irish have distinguished themselves in that respect, nothing of the sort could be said of their role in what most of us would still regard as the fateful struggle of the Western democracies (and of the Soviet Union) with Nazi Germany. But in this Eire forecast the distinct disengagement of former colonial peoples from the struggles of their previous masters, no matter how mortal, much less how moral. A prophetic people.

Greeley argues that they have achieved much at the individual level in the United States, and obviously this is true enough in a general sense. Still there is his reservation that they have done so only on condition of having put aside much of their tradition. Even those who might judge that nothing of over-much value was lost might agree that forsaking that tradition *was,* rather, the price of admission to wherever it is you have got when, for the second time, you have arrived in America. Even those who would not pay it had it paid, symbolically, for them. (I can recall as a young assistant secretary in the subcabinet of John F. Kennedy that just about every White House aide I knew, apart from O'Brien, O'Donnell, and Dungan, would assert with a near-desperate need to believe that the President was not really a Catholic in the sense that he believed all those things, that he was really more like a Unitarian. As for his brother, well, there could be no arguing his religious convictions, but then part of his value to the President lay in not being excessively refined.)

It is, or ought to be, clear that there is no possibility—not the most remote—that a distinctive Irish identity can be re-created in the United States. Any who question this need only observe the indifference of the vast proportion of the American Irish to the onset of near civil war in Ulster. Some few persons of decent purpose and fair-minded understanding have tried to summon some response, but none has been forthcoming. Alone among intellectuals, Graham Greene has spoken out, but he is, of course, an Englishman. (The idea of forming a committee of university professors to sign one of the full-page advertisements—for ourselves—in the *New York Times* "News of the Week in Review," if it has occurred to anyone, has been mercifully set aside. Outside the Catholic institutions there simply are not enough Irish Catholic professors to fill up a page.) But there is no need for the re-creation of a distinctive ethnic identity. *It is enough to hope that the Irish experience, as that of others, may become part of the American sensibility.* It is something we need to know about ourselves, something we need to teach, and which we must first learn.

It will not be easy. Greeley notes that the City College of New York has now established separate departments of Afro-American, Asian, and Puerto Rican studies, which will evolve into a full-fledged School of Ethnic Studies, and also a Department of Jewish studies which will remain within the liberal arts faculty. Will no other groups be included? There is no reason to think this will happen unless some good reason is offered. There are good reasons for including Irish history in a School of Ethnic Studies, of which the most important is that the Irish, despite a long period of awkwardness in the end, opted to assert that their experience in America was not that of losers but of winners. This assertion occurred well before it was anything like the reality Greeley says has of late come to pass, and it may indeed have been something of a self-fulfilling prophecy. But be that as it may, it disqualified the Irish for the not altogether unrewarded role of victim. Simultaneously they did not develop an intellectual tradition strong enough to command the interest even of themselves, and certainly not of others. Hence no Department of Irish Studies, saving of course those that concentrate on the work of Joyce and Yeats, and this is understood to be a matter altogether distinct from the doings of the Mayor of Chicago or his varied predecessors.

If this happens it will be a loss to our understanding of American history. Greeley quotes Arthur Mann that "It is the fashion for intellectuals to write the biographies of politicians, and in doing so, they are apt to criticize the politicians for not having the skills of intellectuals. I often wonder what would happen if politicians should write the biographies of intellectuals; presumably they would criticize intellectuals for not having the skills of politicians." This was written some while ago. With more politicians adopting dimly to weakly understood "intellectual" postures, it is indeed likely that future intellectuals will be even more disapproving of the tradition of working-class politics, innocent alike of self-deception or of theory, whose prime concern was governance. To govern, as Greeley notes, the prime problem is to collect enough power in one place so that decisions can be made. The critical problem of the cities, he writes, "is not so much corruption as it is powerlessness." Given the temptations of those who do manage to collect power, one would suppose that the Irish urban political tradition of acquiring and exercising it for rather strictly limited purposes would be more appreciated by liberal intellectuals than it has been. The opposite has been the case.

What baffles and sometimes outrages the critics of Mayor Richard J. Daley of Chicago, as Joseph Epstein recently noted in *Commentary,* is that he lacks social vision. Glazer and I made much the same point, not quite so sharply, a decade ago, referring to this general political tradition. We argued then, and would today, that it is hard enough to govern in the here-and-now, much less the future. Still the critics persist.

Recently a *New Yorker* article referred to Mayor Daley's Chicago as a "totalitarian state within America." The author of this passage obviously thinks just that, but one is troubled by the impression that what really bothers him is that the government of Chicago is *not* totalitarian. It wields great power for the limited purposes of government traditionally defined, and seems utterly indifferent to everything else that goes on. Consider, for the moment, the prospect of a Chicago alderman detecting political subversion in the score of a string quartet, or an abstract impressionist painting, or a Picasso bronze. In a curious way Eugene McCarthy, surely the most intellectual political figure of national stature to appear since Woodrow Wilson, was rarely understood to be advocating, as repeatedly he did, *limits* to government power. That there might be much in common between the Mayor of Chicago and the former senior Senator from Minnesota is a thought that one fears would give pain to them both, but I would suggest there is, if only in the fact that the now dominant intellectual tradition in America seems incapable of comprehending either man, and prefers to twist both to caricatures of what it disapproves in the one case and approves in the other. In a life largely spent at the political levels of government, I have found myself growing more concerned about this phenomenon primarily because it seems to me to involve the perpetuation of seriously inadequate understandings of the conditions in which government succeeds. I have found myself, for example, near to pleading with the Irish politicians who helped bring about—or so they feel, and they were there—the decision by Roosevelt to choose Harry S. Truman over Henry Wallace for the vice-presidency in 1944, to somewhere record what they did. Otherwise it will be altogether ignored, or depicted by their cultural enemies as yet another instance of big-city bosses involved in matters they did not understand and did not deserve to influence. I have had no success. They know their history will be written by their enemies, and either are resigned or content that it should be.

There is something rather sad in this, although the gentlemen involved are not much given to self-pity. It involves the acceptance of a thoroughly debased judgment of themselves and their tradition, that reminds one of the way in which middle and late nineteenth-century cartoonists, English for the most part, but such as Thomas Nast here in this country, gradually transformed the physiognomy of the symbolic Irishman from something recognizably human to something distinctly beastlike. L. Perry Curtis, Jr., in his recent study *Apes and Angels: The Irishman in Victorian Caricature,* has shown this with great effect. He writes:

> The gradual but unmistakable transformation of Paddy, the stereotypical Irish Celt of the mid-nineteenth century, from a drunken and relatively harmless peasant into a dangerous ape-man or simianized agitator, reflected a significant shift in the attitudes of some Victorians about the differences between not only Englishmen and Irishmen, but also between human beings and apes.[4]

This occurred, of course, in the context of the Darwinian debate over evolution, but it was largely, or so one would suppose, a case of science put to the uses of politics. (It is interesting to note that in the United States the Negro on most occasions was depicted as having the same prognathous characteristics as the Celt, but that, on some occasions, such as one cartoon I have seen that followed the Draft Riots in New York City in 1862, both black and white upholders of the Union shared the precise "advanced" facial features associated with the Anglo-Saxon, while the Irish were to the condition of . . . The Hairy Ape. (Although, of course, O'Neill christened him "Yank.")

We submit to this condition at a cost. In the largest measure the cost is to our understanding of our own past as a nation, but there will be a price paid also in our understanding of the world. The spell of Marxism, as Greeley writes, is still very much upon us, but political reality round and about the world is bound up increasingly with the resurgent experience of ethnicity. On any continent, in all but a tiny handful of singular nations, ethnic, racial, and religious divisions—all partaking of common characteristics—have become the locus of profound political conflict. Despite some efforts by Marxist theorists, that set of doctrine has no better explanation for this phenomenon than does traditional American liberalism. And yet, failing to understand it, we clearly fail to comprehend our times,

---

4. L. Perry Curtis, Jr., *Apes and Angels: The Irishman in Victorian Caricature* (Washington, D.C.: The Smithsonian Institution, 1971).

and have that much less a prospect of mastering them. And so, to repeat, the saliency of ethnic history comes to us at this time with special force.

In 1963 Nathan Glazer and I published *Beyond the Melting Pot,* a study of the major ethnic groups of New York. Liberalism was then much in thrall to the idea that ethnicity was vulgar—an affair of Tammany Hall and balanced tickets—and that the correct course of public policy was to eradicate ethnic identity as much as could be done by official decree. New York pioneered in laws that would forbid officials to know anything about the race, color, creed, or national origin of, say, the students at CCNY. Glazer and I contended that whatever the laws, ethnicity persisted, and was seen by many as something of value. The book was not received with excessive generosity.

Last year we issued a new edition in which we surveyed events of the 1960s. This time it was we who were less than generous. We would have preferred the decade be tried over again. To be sure, the ethnic reality had come to be more widely perceived, but we felt it had also been seriously misinterpreted.

We posited two models of ethnic relations, for convenience termed Northern and Southern. In the North there are many groups; coalitions form and reform; positions in the pecking order shift; there is a rhetoric of civility and celebration. ("While we cannot yet establish that there was a Chinese member of Columbus' crew, it was of course the case that he navigated with a compass developed in China so that in every legitimate sense it may be claimed . . .") In the Southern model there are two groups; no coalitions are possible; positions are fixed, one group being on top and the other on the bottom; there is a rhetoric of threat and abuse. We felt the latter model, with local variations, was the one being legitimized and encouraged in New York, and that, while this served the interests of some individuals, it could be immensely destructive to the life of the city. We felt that the Northern model had been a social invention of some consequence, bringing stability to situations that seemed hopeless. By contrast, the Southern model is fundamentally instable.

Donald L. Horowitz has since offered a general theory of ethnic differentiation, distinguishing between vertical, that is to say, hierarchical systems, which would be our Southern model, and horizontal ones, which would correspond to the New York experience. The former is a caste situation: Winner and Loser. The latter may be thought of as a big poker game with many players and no permanent outcomes.

There will be consequences to the way we chose to understand the ethnic experience. To date most academic institutions have opted to study ethnicity as a form of caste. It can be that, and in many parts of the nation and of the world, it is. But there is another reality, which by and large has been ours in the North, and we should study it also. This is the style of ethnic relations that seeks accommodation. We ignore it at genuine peril.

There is evidence we are awakening to this situation. The Higher Education Act of 1971 that has, as I write, passed the Senate, authorizes a new program for the "development of ethnic heritage curriculum materials by institutions of higher education for use in the nation's elementary and secondary schools." The report of the Senate Committee on Education and Public Welfare reads:

> This program has two basic purposes: to aid elementary and secondary school students in learning about their own heritages and to assist them in learning about the heritages of other citizens. The program is meant to provide children of different ethnic backgrounds a sense of positive identification with the American past and also to provide them with an intellectual understanding of the nature of American society as a pluralistic society.
>
> The ethnic studies program thus has these two distinct yet closely interrelated objectives. As Professor Rudolph Vecoli of the University of Minnesota stated in testimony before the committee:
>
>> Personal identity is rooted in history. An individual's view of his relationship to the past can be a source of a positive ego identity drawing strength from his family and ethnic group origins or if it is one which denigrates his background it can undermine his sense of worth and self-respect. And it has been well said that a person who cannot respect himself cannot respect others.
>
> The Committee has come to the conclusion that the curriculum in our elementary and secondary schools all too fre-

quently does not provide this source of positive identity, rather it serves to alienate and confuse far too many of our youth. The basic reason for this is that many schools have fostered a shame or at least an uneasiness among their students about their ethnic heritages. They have done this in reliance on the "melting pot" theory, the idea that differences between the many diverse groups in the United States would eventually be melted down to conform with the characteristics of the predominant group.

The only problem with this theory is that it didn't happen that way in the past and it isn't happening that way now. But we are paying now for its past and present influence in American life by a feeling of alienation from society felt by many citizens and by a mood of intolerance of any diversity in our society.

The Committee believes this theory must be discarded and we ought to recognize instead what has always existed in our country: an amazing mosaic of diverse groups, each with its own characteristics but each lending strength to the unified whole. And we ought to take pride in this unique American achievement of the successful formation of a new country from these widely different nationality, racial, and religious groups.

There are, of course, difficulties in achieving this goal: most states and the federal government make it illegal to know anything about the ethnic, racial, or religious identity of job applicants, employees, students, tenants, or whatever. This can make for considerable awkwardness now that an increasing number of groups demand to know. A certain institutional schizophrenia has developed, which may or may not stabilize. Thus at CCNY recently the administration issued directions for an ethnic census, which among other instructions stated that "Identification of Italian-Americans will be done visually and by name." In no circumstances was anybody to be asked whether they regarded themselves as Italian-American, nor was the information gathered to be used for any other than the purposes mandated by the federal government. Otherwise the college would be violating state regulations. Ethnicity is not only a complex subject, it can be a silly one. The directive concluded with a stern warning that "No person is to be counted as having more than one identity." This suggests a lack of administrative skill. (Absent a ready supply of Italian applicants, for example, could not the quota—it is coming to that, of course—be filled by appointing a Swede to the Enrico Fermi chair in physics?) Agility will help, and so will a measure of good humor.

It would be getting on to thirty years ago that, as a freshman at CCNY, I was having lunch with a friend, a Rabbi's son from Brooklyn, who was engrossed in an article describing the admissions practices of well-known colleges and universities.

The proportion of Jewish students in each was somehow (probably inaccurately) calculated, and the institution was judged to be "tolerant" in that degree. My friend reported the more notable outcomes. An Ivy League university was found to be 5.4 per cent "tolerant." Something such. A fashionable girls' school turned out to be 2.2 per cent "tolerant." This was the general range of scores.

"Are we listed?" I asked. "What about that!" he exclaimed, with a sense of distinction both of us came to treasure. "We are!" "How do we do?" Deadpan now, he replied, "87 per cent 'tolerant.' "

One would hope we might learn to be at least that tolerant of some of the excesses of enthusiasms that assert themselves as issues of ethnic studies arise, just as we ought to learn to be more accepting of our own various perceptions of what has greatest priority. All this work is important. It is scarcely begun.

Preface

I met with Napper Tandy, and he took me by the hand,
Saying, "How is old Ireland and how does she stand?"
"She's the most distressful country that ever yet was seen
"They are hanging men and women for the wearing of the green."

I care not for the Thistle and I care not for the Rose.
When the bleak winds round us whistle, neither down nor crimson
shows,
But like hope to him that's friendless, when no joy around is seen
O'er our graves with love that's endless blooms our own immortal green.
"The Wearing of the Green," Irish revolutionary song

The whole race . . . is madly fond of war, high-spirited and quick to battle, but otherwise straightforward and not of evil character. And so when they are stirred up they assemble in their bands for battle, quite openly and without forethought, so that they are easily handled by those who desire to outwit them; for at any time or place and on whatever pretext you stir them up, you will have them ready to face danger, even if they have nothing on their side but their own strength and courage. On the other hand, if won over by gentle persuasion they willingly devote their energies to useful pursuits and even take to a literary education. Their strength depends both on their mighty bodies, and on their numbers. And because of this frank and straightforward element in their character they assemble in large numbers on slight provocation, being ever ready to sympathize with the anger of a neighbour who thinks he has been wronged.
STRABO, speaking of pre-Christian Celts,
quoted by Myles Dillon and Nora K. Chadwick in *The Celtic Realms*

As a pilgrim father that missed th' first boats, I must raise me claryon voice again' th' invasion iv this fair land be th' paupers and arnychist iv effete Europe. Ye bet I must—because I'm here first. . . . As I told ye I come a little late. Th' Rosenfelts an' th' Lodges bate me be at least a boat lenth, an' be th' time I got here they were stern an' rock bound thimsilves. So I got a gloryous rayciption as soon as I was towed off th' rocks. Th' stars an' sthripes whispered a welcome in th' breeze an' a shovel was thrust into me hand an' I was pushed into a sthreet excyvatin' as though I'd been born here.

MR. DOOLEY

May you be in Heaven a half-hour before the Divil knows you're dead.

Traditional Irish toast

O ne of my friends who read an early draft of this book observed that it was likely to offend both the Irish and the non-Irish, the former because they would think that it was anti-Irish and the latter because they would consider it much too pro-Irish. "There is," he said (not exactly coining a new phrase), "something in it to offend everyone."

On the whole, this was a not unwelcome observation, for I am saying to American society, "You've tried to turn us into lower-middle-class WASPs and, damn it all, you haven't succeeded." On the other hand, I am saying to the American Irish, "Why did you let them turn you into lower-middle-class WASPs?"

If anyone thinks this is a contradiction, they simply do not understand the Irish. We are a stubborn, perverse, wrongheaded, paradoxical people, and if you are going to write about us in an adequate way, then you must write in a stubborn, perverse, wrongheaded, and paradoxical fashion.

If, on the whole, I am satisfied with the thought that there will be something in this book to offend everyone, I am dismayed by the thought that it will be taken too seriously by the overacculturated American Irish and not nearly seriously enough by the mainline WASP and WASH liberal intellectuals and journalists. I have had too much experience with the propensity of certain kinds of successful but semi-literate American Irishmen who interpret every sentence with stubborn, serious literalness to think they would not submit this book to the same mindless parsing. I have also had too much experience with a certain kind of American liberal to think that he will listen to anyone who is not at every moment somber, serious, self-important, and dull.

This is a very serious book, so serious that I have done all that I can to make it hilarious.

Most of the material was written originally for this volume, but some of the chapters have already appeared in journals. The final chapter first angered the literal-minded, overacculturated Irish in the *New York Times Magazine* of St. Patrick's Day week, 1971. The chapters on Beverly were xeroxed from the *Critic* before they were circulated among the highly irate citizens of that charming community. The chapter on the Irish and the blacks appeared in *Dissent,* a journal for which Michael Harrington and I seem to be the only Irish contributors. Finally, part of the chapter on the Irish as politicians appeared in the *New Republic,* whereupon it was promptly denounced by another Irishman as a defense of Richard Daley, which it really wasn't. I wish to thank the editors of these journals for permission to reprint the articles.

I must also thank, in the order of their appearance, Professor Morris Janowitz for suggesting this book, and Emanuel Geltman of Quadrangle Books—the latter being at least as Irish as I am, if not more so—for accepting the suggestion. William McCready helped with the chapter on the Irish personality, which is acknowledged by his joint authorship of that chapter. His wife, Nancy, is responsible for the anonymous "Irish poem" with which the book ends. Dr. Melvin Kohn of the National Institute of Mental Health made available some of the statistical data. Ellen Sewell served as research assistant and Patrick Bova as librarian. Virginia Quinn and Julie Antelman struggled through the typing of the manuscript while managing to keep reasonably straight faces most of the time. Peter Rossi and Daniel Patrick Moynihan, the latter an acknowledged Irishman and the former, I suspect, a crypto one, launched me and my horse, Rosinante, on our ethnic quest.

All these people are prepared to take credit for whatever praise the book receives. Since I am going to vigorously resist these pretensions, I had better absolve them from most of the blame—and let them go with only a light penance.

I also wish to thank Father Sean O'Connor, S. J., of County Galway and Eoin McKiernan of the Irish American Cultural Institute for persuading me of the importance of the Gaelic language and the Gaelic literary heritage.

And of course I am grateful to Mr. Moynihan for gracing this volume with his Foreword.

Finally, I wish to thank all of those American Irish who have shaped, plagued, bedeviled, and enriched my life. It's a terrible thing to be Irish until you consider the alternatives!

A. M. G.

Contents

That Most Distressful Nation

1.

"The Irish Don't Count"

Afriend of mine, one of the rare specialists in Irish Studies in American academe, had for several years proposed summer programs in his field to be held at his college. Each year he had received a routine refusal. Finally he went to Washington to discover what changes in his proposal were necessary to make it acceptable. He sat in the office of a prominent bureaucrat of the Office of Education where the conversation was pleasant and the bureaucrat was polite. As one hour turned into two, my friend grew irate. "There are programs in Mexican Studies, Scandinavian Studies, Jewish Studies, and, of course, Black Studies that the Office of Education is financing. Why not a program in Irish Studies?" he demanded, pounding the desk. The bureaucrat lost his veneer of professional patience and pounded back. "The Irish," he shouted, "don't count!"

And that settled that.

One also notices that the City College of New York offers courses in Chinese Studies, Black Studies, Puerto Rican Studies, and Jewish Studies. The Italians, who are a substantial part of the New York population, apparently haven't made a sufficient contribution to world culture to rate a program of their own.[1] And as for the Irish, well, what the hell is there to study about them? The new interest in ethnicity has made the study of ethnic groups fashionable, but why

---

1. To the Italian-American Civil Rights League: I'm being ironic. I am well aware of Michelangelo, Raphael, Dante, Columbus, Marconi, and Manzoni.

should anyone study the Irish? Everyone knows everything worth knowing about them and they don't count anymore, anyhow, because they are nothing more than lower-middle-class WASPs.

The revival of interest in ethnicity is presently in a period of sustained pause, owing to a white nativist backlash. It is all right, of course, for blacks to be different, and probably all right for Jews to be different, but it is not all right for anyone else to be different. Both the *National Observer* and the *Christian Science Monitor* responded to an article of mine in the *New York Times Magazine* about the disappearance of the Irish by commenting that it was a good thing that ethnic diversities were disappearing because they interfered with social harmony. (These comments, incidentally, were delivered with characteristic WASP humorlessness, completely missing the point of the article.) Some kinds of black militants, perhaps feeling threatened because they don't have a complete monopoly on the mass media, have renounced the new interest in ethnicity as a white racist cop-out. A substantial segment of American liberalism is no more capable of disagreeing with black militants, say, than were American Dominicans capable of disagreeing with Thomas Aquinas before the Second Vatican Council. Political leaders are less interested in ethnic groups now, since it has developed that it is not quite so easy to turn the ethnic vote from one party to another. Funding agencies, public and private, are beginning to discover that white ethnics may not be a problem after all; indeed, they may not even be racists and hawks. Hence there is no "good" the professional do-gooders can do for them.

It is quite possible, then, that after a brief burst of interest American scholarship and American journalism will forget about ethnic diversity and pretend once again that we are a melting pot, that all the white immigrant groups are being homogenized into one pleasant, charming, Anglo-Saxon mass.

It is unlikely that this ethnicity will disappear that easily, however, if only because considerable numbers of young scholars have found, for both personal and professional reasons, that it is a vast and fascinating subject, well worth the focus of their academic careers. It must be emphasized that these young scholars are beginning almost from scratch, because for the past three decades their predecessors have done their best to pretend that there is no ethnic diversity in American society, and that whatever still exists is rapidly vanishing. About some ethnic groups, of course, we know more than others. There is an emerging social science literature on Italian-Americans. A brilliant doctoral dissertation has been done at the University of Chicago on the Greeks. Nothing has been written of any consequence about the Poles since W. I. Thomas and Florian Znaniecki's *The Polish Peasant in Europe and America*[2] of a half-century ago—save a doctoral dissertation by Znaniecki's daughter, Helena Lopata. The German-Americans disappeared from sight at the time of the First World War, though a substantial historical literature exists before that time.

About the Irish we know next to nothing. The chapter on the Irish in *Beyond the Melting Pot,* by Nathan Glazer and Daniel Patrick Moynihan,[3] is the only attempt I know of by a social scientist to say anything meaningful about the American Irish. And Glazer and Moynihan limited themselves to the Irish of New York City who, I have argued with Mr. Moynihan in a decade-long debate, are not necessarily typical. To my knowledge, this book, then, is the first attempt to write about the Irish experience in the United States from a sociological point of view.

We know practically nothing about the American Irish. At first, this seems like an absurd statement, for of course everybody knows about them: they are the most pushy and obnoxious of the immigrant groups. They came first, and managed after several generations to become respectable, conservative, lower-middle-class members of American urban society. They drink too much, they are racist, and their political ethics leave much to be desired. They had too many children and accepted everything their clergy told them. They insisted on keeping their own schools, and during the Joseph McCarthy era became superpatriot anti-communists. At the present time they may be assumed to be strong supporters of American militarism (after all, wasn't Cardinal Spellman the "military vicar," and

---

2. W. I. Thomas and Florian Znaniecki, *The Polish Peasant in Europe and America* (Boston: Richard G. Badger–Gorham Press, 1918).

3. Nathan Glazer and Daniel Patrick Moynihan, *Beyond the Melting Pot* (Cambridge, Mass.: Harvard-MIT Press, 1963).

so, too, isn't his successor, Cardinal Cooke?). What more needs to be said about the Irish, save perhaps that after the Vatican Council it looks like they are settling down to become good Protestants?

But I repeat my previous assertion: We don't know anything about the Irish. Worse still, most of the Irish don't know anything about themselves. Paddy, the gorilla with a shillelagh in one hand and a pint of booze in the other, was a caricature of nineteenth-century cartoons. The conservative, lower-middle-class racist hawk is a caricature of twentieth-century liberals, and the barroom Irish of such journalists as Pete Hamill, Joe Flaherty, and Jimmy Breslin are self-caricatures, which seem to entertain and amuse WASPs and Jews in New York City. (And if any book review editor turns this volume over to one of those characters to review, I'll either revive the *clan-na-gael* or find out whether the Mafia takes contracts on Micks.)

There is little serious history and practically no sociology about the American Irish. Literature, of course, we have in copious amounts, but most of the Irish novelists were desperately ashamed of their heritage and deeply involved in working out the painful ambivalences of their relationships with the Roman Church. Only the *New Yorker* writer J. F. Powers seems to have been able to match the ability of Jewish writers to be critical yet sympathetic towards his ancestral heritage. Recent young novelists like Tom McHale are still angry at the Catholic Church. Unquestionably they have reason, but that anger gives a very distorted view of the Irish experience. Even James T. Farrell, whose *Studs Lonigan* is indispensable (whatever its literary merit) for understanding the sociology of the Chicago Irish, rarely displays compassion or sympathy for his heritage. Literature without compassion or sympathy may be powerful, funny, or both, but it does not contribute to balanced understanding of an ethnic heritage. To make matters worse, the Irish novelists, and indeed the rest of the alienated intelligentsia and quasi-intelligentsia, have frequently assumed that the only way to break into the intellectual elite is to affect completely the stereotypical judgment about Irish morals and life. The Jewish intellectual did not make this mistake; instead of becoming a WASP, he in fact frequently seems almost too insistent that the

WASP become Jewish. The Irish, for all their political skills, never quite figured that one out.

Thus the best one has on the subject of the American Irish is a number of stereotypes, frequently superficial at that. Obviously, there is some plausibility in a stereotype or it never would exist in the first place, but the stereotype of the Irish drunk, or the Irish conservative, or the Irish Catholic member of the Church Belligerent do not even begin to cope with the reality of the complex Irish-American experience.

Of necessity, this book is exploratory. When faced with the reality that there is relatively little known about the American Irish, there are two things a sociologist can do: he can delay publication for a decade or so until there is an established body of theory and empirical data, and then write *the* definitive work on the American Irish, or he can write a book which reports the rather meager existing data and raises questions for future research. I have chosen to do the latter. Why? First, I wanted to do it; second, Quadrangle Books wanted me to do it; and, third, it seemed on the whole to be a very Irish thing to do. Whether it is a sociological volume or simply a volume by a sociologist will depend on how the reader defines his terms. Wherever I can find empirical data, I will use it; wherever I can't, I intend to use whatever resources I can get my hands on—surmise, conjecture, personal experience, introspection, and, when the occasion arises, poetry. I choose to do it this way partly because I think it is better to produce an incomplete book at the right moment than a complete book at the wrong moment, and because increasingly I am persuaded that this pursuit of reality with no holds barred is the only appropriate posture for social scientists.

Let me make clear some of the social science assumptions that create the context of the present volume:

1. I assume with Milton Gordon[4] that acculturation can take place without assimilation; that is to say, an ethnic group can acquire many of the behavioral traits of the larger society without

---

4. Milton Gordon, *Acculturation in American Life* (New York: Oxford University Press, Inc., 1964).

losing either its sense of identity or its desire to interact with other members of the group when such interaction is possible, particularly in more intimate social relationships.

2. I further assume with Moynihan and Glazer that ethnic groups are frequently political, economic, and social interest groups which will continue to exist whether or not they pass on much of their cultural heritage, because it is in their self-interest to do so.

3. I also assume that an ethnic group serves as a carrier of cultural tradition, at least for some members of the group. With the Irish, for example, the Catholic Church, problems with alcohol, and a predilection for politics seem to be passed on as part of the Irish cultural heritage.

4. I further believe that for some members of ethnic groups a component of their personal identity is the ethnic self-definition, with or without any particular conscious interest in the cultural heritage.

5. I am convinced that certain ethnic traits can be passed on through the early childhood socialization process, whereby a child learns role expectations in relation to parents, siblings, cousins, aunts and uncles, close friends. Indeed, with my colleague Peter Rossi, I think this may be the most important aspect of ethnic heritage, and it is no less important because it can occur without conscious concern for such transmission on the part of parents or children.

6. I contend that while ethnic groups as such came into existence in the United States, the history and the culture of the old country play a role—the precise nature of which is yet to be defined—in the values and structure of the American ethnic groups. The American Irish are not the Irish Irish, yet they do have something in common.

7. Finally, in addition to the cultural heritage, I assume that the status of an ethnic group at present is a result of the principal reasons for migration, the state of American society at the time of immigration, and the experience the ethnic group has had with both its successors and predecessors since immigration began.

Two additional points must be made. (1) The Irish, like all other human groups, are pluralistic; vast amounts of diversity exist within the Irish-American community (if one can even call it a community). Hence, even with elaborate statistical resources available, one is still speaking of means and averages, not of universes. In the more impressionistic data on which I must rely, I am dealing with tendencies and trends and not with universals.

(2) While ethnic characteristic may make some people different from other people, they do not make them all that different. There are some Irishmen, for example, who have much more in common with some Jews than either do with fellow Irishmen or fellow Jews. We will note later that the Jews and the Irish are the most politically liberal of the white ethnic groups in the United States, but, of course, there are many conservative Irish and some conservative Jews, and on some political and social issues there are both Jews and Irishmen who have more in common with political conservatives than they do with the majority of their own respective groups. All generalizations in this book, therefore, must be assumed to be preceded by the adjective "some," or "many," or "most"; no generalization should be preceded by "all."

I set down these detailed qualifications because I think it is important to make the ground rules under which one proceeds quite precise at the beginning. I don't want anyone to turn the *clan-na-gael* loose on me!

2

Historical Background

We know their dream; enough
To know they dreamed and are dead;
And what if excess of love
Bewildered them till they died?
I write it out in a verse—
MacDonagh and MacBride
And Connolly and Pearse
Now and in time to be,
Wherever green is worn,
Are changed, changed utterly:
A terrible beauty is born.

W. B. YEATS,
"Easter 1916"

Well, the last fire is trodden down,
Our dead are rotting fast in lime,
We all can sneak back into town,
Stravague about as in old time,

And stare at gaps of grey and blue
Where Lower Mount Street used to be,
And where flies hum round much we knew
For Abbey street and Eden Quay

And when the devil's made us wise
Each in his own peculiar hell
With desert hearts and drunken eyes

We're free to sentimentalize
By corners where the martyrs fell.
DERMOT O'BYRNE,
"A Dublin Ballad—1916"

Occasionally, a gifted sociologist such as Robert Nisbet is concerned about the relationship between sociology and history, but most sociologists are quite unconcerned about history. For them, society is conceived of as a giant Markov model in which all one needs to know of the past is contained in the present. When the typical American sociologist is told that the political party structure in the United States is, to a considerable extent, the result of three phenomena—the rural-urban difference at the time of the Revolutionary War, the North-South difference that produced the Civil War, and the influx of Catholic immigrant groups, particularly after 1830—he may observe that the information is interesting but of little pertinence for his analysis of the contemporary social structure of American politics.

Because of this disinterest in history, sociology has yet to develop the tools to enable it to judge how much of a group's historical past is relevant to its present situation. It is frequently asserted, for example, that the impact of slavery on the black family has contributed considerably to the problems of the black community today. Fortunately for this particular problem, Professor Herbert Gutman's as yet unpublished research demonstrates clearly that the black family was remarkably stable under slavery, and that if there has been any crisis in some black families, it was more the result of the Great Depression, the collapse of Southern agriculture, and massive migration to the North. Once again, however, one is faced with the problem of articulating and measuring such a possible relationship.

Similarly, one can assert, as Professor James Q. Wilson does, that the informal and roundabout style characteristic of Irish police sergeants may well be derived from the Penal times in Ireland (as may be that infuriating trait the Irish have of answering one question

11

with another[1]). This simply suggests that two types of behavior, one characteristic of ancestors and one of descendants, seem to have certain similarities, which is, at best, a very low level of argumentation. How valid is my argument that the persistent quest for respectability among the American Irish is a result of six centuries of second-class citizenship under the British occupation? What impact did the Famine have, not so much on the attitudes of the Irish who fled from it, but on their descendants who survived the Great Depression? It is not only impossible to answer such questions, it is difficult to know how to ask them.

I begin with the assumption that history is important, that the cultural, political, social, and economic experiences of the past tend to persist, and that the more we know of the history of an ethnic group the better we are able to understand its present situation. If one is unable to do more than speak of plausibilities and similarities between the past and the present, one is still in better shape for knowing something of the past than nothing. If my assumption that ethnic heritage is passed on through early childhood experiences of role expectations is correct, then the past is very important indeed.

How purely Celtic is the inheritance of the American Irish is an unanswerable question, for there were pre-Celtic groups in Ireland before the Celtic invaders appeared in the sixth century B.C., and many immigrant groups arrived periodically after that. The Danes, the Normans, the English all contributed bits to the Irishman-in-formation. G. K. Chesterton once remarked, "Some countries conquer other countries, the Irish conquered nations."

Historians are unable to separate out ethnic stocks very well; it is altogether possible that the Celtic clans made only a small contribution to the Irish gene pool. But the cultural context of the subsequent history of Ireland seems to have been established primarily by those interesting people who arrived in that heavily forested island some six centuries before Christ. When one reads contemporary descriptions of the Gaels, one is struck by how contemporane-

---

1. Franklin Roosevelt is reported to have said to Mayor James Walker, "Jimmy, why do you Irish always answer a question by asking another?" To which Walker responded, "Do we, now?"

ous they sound. Stereotypes they may have been, but they are strikingly like current stereotypes.

Thus a gentleman named Strabo, relying upon the work of a predecessor called Posidonius, says this of the Celts:

> To the frankness and high-spiritedness of their temperament must be added the traits of childish boastfulness and love of decoration. They wear ornaments of gold, torques on their necks, and bracelets on their arms and wrists, while people of high rank wear dyed garments besprinkled with gold. It is this vanity which makes them unbearable in victory and so completely downcast in defeat. In addition to their witlessness they possess a trait of barbarous savagery which is especially peculiar to the northern peoples, for when they are leaving the battle-field, they fasten to the necks of their horses the heads of their enemies, and on arriving home they nail up this spectacle at the entrances to their houses. Posidonius says that he saw this sight in many places, and was at first disgusted by it, but afterwards, becoming used to it, could bear it with equanimity.[2]

And Diodorus, apparently a student of Posidonius, too, has a few things to say about the culture of the Celtic inhabitants of Gaul.

> Physically the Gauls are terrifying in appearance, with deep-sounding and very harsh voices. In conversation they use few words and speak in riddles, for the most part hinting at things and leaving a great deal to be understood. They frequently exaggerate with the aim of extolling themselves and diminishing the status of others. They are boasters and threateners and given to bombastic self-dramatization, and yet they are quick of mind and with good natural ability for learning. They have also lyric poets whom they call Bards. They sing to the accompaniment of instruments resembling lyres, sometimes a eulogy and sometimes a satire. They have also certain philosophers and theologians who are treated with special honour, whom they call Druids.[3]

This stereotype sounds frighteningly familiar. Surely the Irish must have changed since the sixth century, B.C. If only Strabo and Dio-

---

2. Myles Dillon and Nora K. Chadwick, *The Celtic Realms* (New York: New American Library, 1967), p. 7.
3. *Ibid.*, p. 9.

dorus didn't sound quite so much like Jimmy Breslin and Joe Flaherty!

The Celts, so far as we can figure out, began their expansion from Central Europe; and by the third century B.C. they held sway from Asia Minor to Scotland and Valencia. Although there was no central Celtic kingdom, there was a single culture which one of the experts described in terms that seem hauntingly modern:

> We are told that the Gauls were valiant, quarrelsome, cruel, superstitious and eloquent: their art also is full of contrasts. It is attractive and repellent; it is far from primitiveness and simplicity; it is refined in thought and technique, elaborate and clever, full of paradoxes, restless, puzzlingly ambiguous; rational and irrational; dark and uncanny—far from lovable humanity and transparence of Greek art. Yet it is a real style, the first great contribution by the barbarians to European art, the first great chapter in the everlasting contacts of southern, northern and eastern forces in the life of Europe.[4]

There are strong similarities between the culture of the Celts and Hindu India. Both apparently found their roots in Indo-European language and social structure. Celtic religion with its Brahmin-like class of Druids, Celtic legal structure, poetry, and family organization are similar enough to that of India to assume a common heritage.[5] Their religion, incidentally, was a fertility cult centering around the worship of the Earth Mother. As in India the Earth Mother was surrounded by a wide variety of colleagues and consorts. The Druids' sacred oath has a Hindu counterpart, and there is a common belief in immortality and reincarnation.

The Celts, then, were barbarians by Roman standards but eminently civilized by the standards of those who had preceded them in the plains and hills and marshes of Central Europe. They were no match for the Romans in organizational abilities or for the fierceness of the succeeding barbarian tribes. Under the pressure of Roman, Teutonic, and Gothic invasion the remnants of the Celts retreated to such extremities of Europe as Brittany, Wales,

---

4. *Ibid.*, p. 17.
5. *Ibid.*, p. 10.

the Isle of Man, the highlands of Scotland, and the forests and bogs of Ireland.

When I stand on Irish soil today, with most of the forests and bogs gone, I have the illusion that I am not in Europe. The faces around me are not European, they are American (at least from that part of America I know best). Even physically Ireland seems to be not of Europe. Such an impression may only be a trick of an imagination trained to expect leprechauns lurking around the next corner.

Quite apart from a romantic imagination, many of the cultural forces which shaped Western Europe were experienced not at all, or only slightly, by Ireland. Neither the Romans nor the Teutons ever got around to invading that country; nor were the Muslims a serious threat. Ireland, indeed, played a role in the Carolingian Renaissance, but as a sender of culture, not a receiver. Despite the conquest of parts of Ireland by some of the Norman knights of Henry II, those few made only a shallow imprint on Irish culture. The Crusades left Ireland untouched. There never was a unified kingdom under an absolute monarch, at least never one of native origin. As a matter of fact, the first national government that enjoyed both legitimacy and effectiveness was the Irish Free State government of the early 1920's, and it governed only part of Ireland. The Renaissance and the Enlightenment may have touched Dublin through the Anglo-Irish culture of men like Swift and Goldsmith, but Anglo-Irish was not Irish; and what happened in Dublin had little effect on the rest of the country. United Ireland and the Revolution of '98 was only a pale shadow of the French Revolution. The Act of Union afterwards effectively squelched the beginnings of industrial development everywhere except in Belfast. The Young Ireland Movement of 1848 had something in common with the other revolutionary movements of the same year, but it was very short-lived and, like all the other attempts, unsuccessful.

It is possible, of course, to make too much of this. Ireland is, in fact, a part of Europe. It was influenced by Christianity (though, as we shall see later, the Irish have always had their own particular brand of it—not infrequently disturbing to Rome). The

British occupation since the time of Henry II imposed upon the country a British version of European culture—including the language. The frequent and always unsuccessful alliances between the Irish and those other traditional enemies of the English, the French, have kept Ireland in contact with the French version of European culture. Thus the proclamation of the Easter Rising in 1916 was very much in debt to the ideology of the French Revolution as reflected through the United Irish Movement of '98 and the Young Ireland Movement of '48. Nevertheless, the standardized image of European political and cultural history that we acquired in our high school and college textbooks is a record of events which have little meaning or at least different meanings for Ireland than for either England or the continent. Ireland is Europe, all right, but either not quite or just barely.

THE STRUGGLE FOR FREEDOM

One of the most striking themes of Irish history is the elusive quest for unity. Ancient Ireland was divided into some forty clans, each one of which occupied a bit of territory and was presided over by a king. These kings were organized into four kingdoms, Munster, Leinster, Connacht, and Ulster, and the four were presided over by a shadowy king with no power. Even the heads of the four kingdoms frequently had no control over what the lesser kings did. Without Roman influence—particularly their principle of territorial administration—clan rule, with its attendant disorder, feuding, and general chaos, continued unabated well into the Christian era. Apparently one of the reasons that Adrian IV "gave" Ireland to King Henry of England was that he believed Henry could reform the Irish Church so that bishops might become territorial rulers rather than be assigned to specific clans.

One has the impression when reading Irish history that the feuds among the kings and the clans were at least as important as resisting foreign invaders, and that despite frequent heroism and occasional military genius, the Irish propensity for doing battle with other Irishmen instead of with the enemy was very often responsible for snatching defeat from the jaws of victory. Even the last of the Irish revolts in 1916 was begun with a split in the revolutionary forces. One faction, led by Owen MacNeill, refused at the last minute to join in the seizure of the General Post Office by Pierce and Conway, thereby assuring a military defeat of the Easter Rising despite the symbolic victory.

But the Irish never stopped rebelling. Adrian IV, good English pope that he was, presented Ireland to Henry II in 1156, and conquest in earnest began in 1170. English-Norman rule never really penetrated too deeply into the culture or structure of Irish life. The Normans themselves were rather quickly assimilated. At the end of the Middle Ages, with the accession of the Tudors in England, a more determined attempt was made to bring Ireland under control—an attempt which went on for 450 years before the English finally gave it up as a bad job.

The first revolt was that of Silken Thomas, the Earl of Kildare, in 1537; it was followed by the revolt of Hugh O'Neill, Earl of Tyrone, in 1595. The Rebellion of 1641 was followed by that of Owen Roe O'Neill in 1649 and that of Patrick Sarsfield in 1689. Ireland was free of rebellion for another century, but then there came Wolfe Tone and the United Irishmen in 1798 and Robert Emmet in 1803. During the Famine there was the Young Ireland rising of 1848 and after it the Fenian rising of 1867. The final chapter began on Easter Monday in 1916 with the seizure of the General Post Office, final, that is to say, if one forgets about Ulster, that province where Bernadette Devlin and the Provisional IRA act to keep up the tradition of rebellion.

Nor were these rebellions mere scuffles in the street. On the contrary, especially after the Reformation they became bloody, total wars in which reprisals and counterreprisals, atrocities and counteratrocities were almost taken for granted. Oliver Cromwell can easily be described as the first practitioner of genocide in modern history. In the decade of Cromwell's invasion more than half the population of Ireland died—about three-quarters of a million people, somewhat less, be it noted, than the number that died in the Great Famine two centuries later.

17

Rebellion, atrocity, repression, misery, famine, penal legislation, sullen resentment, and then a whole new cycle all over again: this was the history of Ireland for at least half a millennium.

The English tried all kinds of strategies to bring the rebellious Irish subjects under control. Early on they dealt with the native chieftains. In the early centuries of occupation, an Irish parliament was allowed to exist under control of the British Crown. Then Cromwell and succeeding British kings (with the exception of the brief reign of Catholic King James II) systematically reduced the Catholic population to abject misery by massive land grabs used to reward English supporters and to establish a Protestant aristocracy in Ireland friendly to English policy. These "Anglo-Irish," in control of the Irish parliament in Dublin, passed a series of "Penal Laws" designed to further degrade the indigenous Catholic population by excluding them from all the political and social benefits of organized society, that is, education, political representation, religious expression, ownership of property. Finally, in 1800, an Irish Parliament, representing only the Protestant segment of the country and which still had to be bribed into submission, agreed to the permanent union of the two countries. The parliament in Dublin was dissolved and abolished to be integrated into the one at Westminster.

In the nineteenth century, particularly under the leadership of Gladstone, the policy was reversed. Penal Laws were gradually repealed, home-rule legislation was pushed (though not passed until 1914 and then suspended), and Irish peasants were given increased rights over their land and eventually accorded something like ownership in the 1880's. So satisfied were the English with the land reform and the consequent relative prosperity for the Irish peasant that they were astonished when the Irish still insisted on rebelling in the first part of the twentieth century. King George V, a humane and sympathetic man, was absolutely astonished at the Easter Rising, because he thought land reform had permanently settled "the Irish question."

But the Irish question was, of course, insoluble, for the English were absolutely convinced that their rule of Ireland was legitimate both legally and morally, and the Irish were equally convinced that it was both legally and morally illegitimate. Nicholas Mansergh summarizes it:

> The English invasions of Ireland were unending because the conquest was never complete. And all the while through the long years of adversity, pressure from without was consolidating within a core of resistance to the invader, which depended in the last resort, not upon destructible material forces, but upon a slowly maturing and finally indestructible conviction that Ireland should and would be free. Resistance and rebellion were always unavailing, for a poverty-stricken and ill-disciplined people, whose distaste for compromise left them disunited in many crises, could not hope successfully to challenge the resources of an island power whose heritage was the dominion of the sea. Yet in as much as manifestations of the will to resist kept alive the spirit of resistance, they were not barren of result. While the sporadic rebellions were wasteful of lives that could ill be spared, it may well be that nationalist historians are right in saying that, by such sacrifices alone, was Ireland enabled to nourish a tradition so vivid, so emotional, so fanatical as to resist the miasmata of failure and despair. . . . [T]he English rulers of Ireland, having failed while yet there was time to take the measures necessary to conciliate a not-unfriendly people, were confronted at the last by an Irish ideal which, alien to their outlook yet fostered by their misrule, was to prove a source of strength more resilient, because it was more single-minded, than any which a great Empire could command.[6]

How explain the rebelliousness of the Irish? H. B. C. Pollard, an English police chief in Ireland during the Civil War, caricaturized only somewhat the fundamental English Protestant conviction that Irish Catholics were an inferior breed.

> Whether revolutionaries are aware of it or not, their morbid discontent with existing society, and their perfect willingness to embark on a course of action which will bring death and ruin to thousands, and even to themselves, in pursuit of a grand experiment or an inner vision, is not a wonderful self-sacrifice but merely a perverted form of self-gratification. The

---

6. Nicholas Mansergh, *The Irish Question 1840–1921* (Toronto: University of Toronto Press, 1966), pp. 20–21.

communist who talks glibly of shooting down the bourgeoisie is gratifying a perverted instinct with the prospect of a wholesale blood bath. The visionary who rushes to martyrdom for a cause gratifies once and for ever his masochistic propensity.

It has been said that the Irish derive keen pleasure from the woes with which they cause themselves to be afflicted; and pleasure in pain is typical—significantly typical—of many of the conditions which I have outlined above. And when it is understood in its true bearing on the psychology of revolution and of revolutionaries, it must destroy the fine illusions and the glamour that, to some minds, hung about the leaders of "the murder gangs." There is nothing particularly fine about a group of moral decadents leading a superstitious minority into an epidemic of murder and violent crime; yet this is what has happened of recent years in Ireland, it is what has happened time and again in the past, and it is what will happen again in the future; for the Irish problem is a problem of the Irish *race,* and is neither a by-product of politics nor of environment, but is rooted in the racial characteristics of the people themselves.[7]

The cycle of revolt, strife, and depression was such that culture, learning, science, and technology had little opportunity to develop in Ireland. Unquestionably there was a great culture centered mostly in the monasteries between the time of St. Patrick and the invasion of the Danes in the ninth century, and there always was a folk culture; but generation after generation of Catholic aristocracy was either destroyed in battle or fled the country in the wake of unsuccessful rebellion. The Protestant aristocracy (in later days called "the Ascendency"), however cultivated it may have been on occasion, had little influence on the rest of the country. Only in Belfast was there any industrial development, and the Act of Union cut short the economic and industrial development beginning in the south of Ireland. The Penal Laws and the persecution of Catholics, the repeated famines, the devotion of the best resources of the most gifted people to rebellion, all of these factors

---

7. H. B. C. Pollard, *Secret Societies of Ireland* (London: Philip Allan and Co., 1922).

guaranteed that Ireland would exist in a state of disorganized chaos while most of the rest of Europe was making an eventful entry into the modern world.

The myth of the slovenly, irresponsible, happy-go-lucky, and carefree Irish has caused most of us to assume that Ireland really did not have what it took to become a successful modern industrial nation. The Irish were too busy with their dreams and their drink, with their poetry and their feuding to ever become an effective modern state.

What this stereotype overlooks is the fact that the Irish who migrated to the United States yielded nothing to anybody—save perhaps the Jews—in their orientation towards achievement, and the Irish Republic, for all its problems, has been one of the most successful revolutionary countries of the twentieth century.

There are two important points that need to be made about the Republic. First of all, despite the intense factionalization of the period before the establishment of the Irish Republic, true democratic principles were established and maintained by the new government. The pro–Free State faction, led by William Cosgrave, accepted dominion status with Britain and finally prevailed over the anti–Free State faction led by Eamon de Valera. During the Civil War these two factions killed each other off in much greater numbers than the English had, yet de Valera and Cosgrave proved sufficiently adroit as politicians to keep extremists in line and to build a civilized and responsible democratic system. The present prime minister, John Lynch, continues that tradition of political astuteness by his adamant refusal to get involved in the Ulster conflict.

Michael Collins and the IRA defeated the British in the Black and Tan War through the tactics of terror, and the IRA has never abondoned those tactics in the half-century since 1921. The present war in Ulster continues the tactics of fifty years ago. Ironically, the IRA was probably responsible for Collins' death when he agreed to the compromise of the Irish Free State and the partition of the island. In the bloody civil war that followed, the "Free Staters" and the IRA killed each other with as much enthusiasm

21

as they had previously displayed against the Black and Tans. In the middle 1920s, "Dev," who had been allied with the IRA, decided that he could accomplish by electoral politics what the IRA could not accomplish by force of arms. He broke with the IRA, took the "oath" (with a mental reservation that only an Irishman could understand), and proceeded to end most of the ties with England that the IRA found objectionable.[8]

The uneasy truce between the "legion of the rearguard" and "Dev" was finally broken, and the IRA turned once again to its tactics of guerrilla terror, even though it ought to have been clear that it was not 1916 and that they did not have the active sympathy of most Irishmen. For four decades the IRA continued to struggle, raiding Ulster police posts, stealing large supplies of guns, bombing buildings, and robbing banks in both England and Ulster. The failure of the Ulster and British governments to respond to moderate Catholic elements in Ulster (such as those represented by Bernadette Devlin who, for all her socialist rhetoric, is hardly a terrorist) gave the IRA a new lease on life.

J. Bowyer Bell traces in meticulous detail the persistence of the IRA and makes two general conclusions:

> 1. Even though its tactics lost all hope of effectiveness fifty years ago, the IRA has stubbornly persisted in the style of the Easter Rising and the Black and Tan War.
> 2. No defeat, however shattering, has prevented the IRA from returning to the battle.

Bell is impressed with their persistence if not with their flexibility:

> What is special about the IRA is not the errors and defeats, which are legion, or the old successes, which are splendid; but the continuity, however futile such persistence may seem to the rational. Scorned or discounted, the IRA continues. Che Guevaras come and go, EOKA or FLOSY win or lose, the Irgun disappears or the Mau Mau is crushed or the Hungarian Freedom Fighters go into exile and the Algerians into office;

---

8. Thus earning a reputation for "cuteness," by which is meant not attractiveness but deviousness. Prime Minister Lynch is also said to be "cute."

but the IRA remained—generation after generation, dedicated to Tone, to physical force, and to the Ultimate Republic.[9]

Bell thinks this is admirable, and perhaps it is. Joe Cahill, the gentle-faced, soft-spoken killer with the cap, whom the U.S. Immigration Service would not permit into the country, is the lineal descendent of Michael Collins, and his calm discussion of the necessity of killing British soldiers is part of a half-century tradition.

Horrifying? I suppose it depends on one's tastes. I do not find Cahill or the IRA attractive, but then I have never lived under oppression. And I note that many of those Americans who are so ready to denounce the folly of the "outlawed Irish Republican Army" seem quite sympathetic to the Panthers, the Blackstone Rangers, Huey Newton, and Eldridge Cleaver. Would Leonard Bernstein have had a party for Joe Cahill?

However violent the IRA, it still can be said that, with the possible exception of India, Ireland is the only revolutionary country of the twentieth century that has been able to permit political opposition. More than that, when de Valera finally ousted Cosgrave in an election, the event was, so far as I know, the only time in modern history that a revolutionary government has been pushed from power by a peaceful, democratic election. De Valera's party has remained in control for most of the last four decades. However, on two occasions the opposition party has formed governments, and once, in a paradoxical twist that only the Irish could accomplish, the Fine Gael, the legitimate successor of the Free State party, proclaimed the existence of the Republic of Ireland, something which de Valera, ardent republican that he was and is, never quite managed.

It may well be argued that the Irish learned the skills of parliamentary democracy in the 120 years during which Irish representatives connived and obstructed the Union Parliament at Westminster. They also acquired from their British conquerors the techniques of running the civilized and legally restricted governmental structure. One can only say that for a country that had seen so much strife

9. J. Bowyer Bell, *The Secret Army—the IRA, 1916–1970* (New York: John Day, 1971), p. 378.

and violence, the Irish learned very quickly how to run a law-abiding, responsible democracy.

Secondly, much to the surprise of everyone, and almost without anyone noticing, the Irish Republic in the last decade seems to have actually solved its economic problems and begun an era of prosperity. Under the leadership of Prime Minister Sean Lemass and T. K. Whitaker of the Department of Finance, the Republic instituted an essentially Keynesian five-year economic plan that was fantastically successful. Oliver MacDonagh summarizes the results of the efforts of Whitaker and Lemass:

> The success of the first program astonished friend and foe alike. The growth rate of 1959–64, the period of the first program, was 4 instead of 2 per cent. In the same years, the GNP rose by nearly 25 per cent and exports by more than 40 per cent. Investment was almost doubled, despite the fact that savings also increased. The social revolution was no less dramatic. The population of the Republic had fallen, in an almost unbroken line from 6.5 million in 1851 to 2.8 million in 1961. But in 1961–66 it actually increased by 2.3 per cent, while the net emigration dropped to 16,000, about one-third of the level of the preceding decade. Still more significant was the change in the structure of the population revealed by the census of 1966. The largest increase was in the 20–24 age group, which had grown by nearly 25 per cent. The 10–14 and 15–19 groups also showed remarkable increases. In effect, this meant, if current trends continued, that the proportion of those reaching maturity who would be absorbed in the Republic was 75 per cent, not far short of double the proportion who remained at home in the years 1950–59. Moreover, the marriage rate was bound to change dramatically. The extraordinarily low rate of 5.5 per thousand, a long-established factor in Irish society, would probably increase by 2.0 per thousand in the coming decade. The renewal of life and hope might be discerned even in the face of the country. Not merely in the urban areas as a whole, but also in no less than a quarter of the countryside, the population increased by over 7 per cent in 1961–66. In the remaining rural areas, the decline was reduced to 4 per cent, a no less remarkable achievement. The fundamental explanation was industrial growth, planned development radiating outward from the selected centers, and the systematic reorganization of agriculture and tourism. In few other Western nations

would these statistics seem even especially encouraging, but in the Republic they proclaimed a "miracle."[10]

The second five-year plan is apparently as successful as the first. One need only try to find a parking place in Dublin today to realize that the assets and liabilities of economic progress have come to Ireland. Irish scholars tell me that there are a number of reasons for the success of the five-year plan. Whitaker and his staff apparently are brilliant economists. Lemass, though a participant in the Easter Rising, was capable of looking forward to economic growth instead of backward to the heroics of the quarrels at the time of "the trouble" and the Civil War. In addition to the economic and political correlates of prosperity, my Irish friends tell me, there was also a shift in the morale of the Irish people. For the first time they began to believe that economic progress was possible for their country, and that they, the Irish, could practice the skills of the modern industrial and financial world with as much intelligence and proficiency as anyone else. The tragic figure of John Fitzgerald Kennedy, I am informed, played an important part in the resurgence of Irish confidence. "If he could make it, why can't we?" was apparently a widespread attitude in Ireland during the first five-year plan. Oddly enough, Kennedy may have been more important to the Irish Irish than to the American Irish, since the latter had no doubt about their abilities to make money.

Ireland was part of the first generation of modern revolutionary countries, along with Turkey and Mexico. It can be said with no exaggeration that Ireland was the most successful of the revolutionary nations. Unlike the others, it did not have a population problem, owing to that peculiar method of birth control, the late marriage, and the fact that its surplus population could migrate to England and the United States. Nevertheless, the ability of the Irish Republic to produce political democracy and economic prosperity in a relatively short period of time after independence suggests that Ireland could have been one of the great and strong

---

10. Oliver MacDonagh, *Ireland* (Englewood Cliffs, N.J.: Prentice-Hall, 1969), p. 133.

nations of the modern world if it had achieved its freedom, say, one hundred years earlier. The question is, of course, academic, but it still must be conceded that tranquility and prosperity (along with, it must be confessed, a certain dullness) came rather quickly and almost rather anticlimactically after a half-millennium of strife and misery.

It also must be remembered that the American Irish fled, most of them, for their lives from a nation that had been under oppression for almost a thousand years. They had virtually no political or legal rights; abject poverty was a matter of course for them, and conflict and rebellion were endemic, and education and industrial development was effectively prohibited. The very fact that they were Irish Catholic meant they were marked as permanently inferior. The cultural traditions of their past, including their language, were systematically extirpated, and their most gifted leaders were hanged, shot, imprisoned, or exiled. The memories of these events may have faded from the minds of the American Irish. (Which of my American Irish readers, for example, ever even heard of Owen Roe O'Neill, and how many know what happened to Parnell, or how many are aware that there was another Michael Collins besides the astronaut?) The results of such a tragic heritage are not easily eliminated. To lament, as some Catholic self-critics have, that the Irish in the United States have not produced as impressive a cultural and intellectual community as the Jews, let us say, is to forget completely what the history of Ireland has been since that generous English pope presented it to his friend Henry II. What ought to be surprising about the American Irish is not that they have not been quite as socially and financially successful as the Jews, but that they have been successful at all. And what is astonishing is not that their intellectual and cultural contributions are limited, but that they have any time for the arts at all. Nor is it surprising that the Irish political style is pragmatic and suspicious of ideology; under the circumstances, it is astonishing that there is enough trust remaining from their heritage that they are capable of politics at all.

There are four aspects of the Irish experience that have had a special influence on the American Irish. They are the Gaelic past, the Catholic religion, the Penal Laws, and the Great Famine. We shall postpone for the next two chapters the subjects of Catholicism and the Celtic heritage and conclude this chapter with some comments on the impact of the Penal Laws and the Famine.

THE PENAL LAWS

The Penal Laws began in Elizabethan times, were reinforced during the reign of Cromwell, and developed to their fullest after the triumph of William of Orange at the Battle of Boyne in 1691. They represent the most savage, the most repressive legislation that the modern world has ever seen. The land of Ireland was confiscated from the Catholics. Between the time of Elizabeth I and William of Orange, the British government took twelve million acres out of a total of fifteen million cultivatable acres in Ireland. Catholics, four-fifths of the population, owned one-seventh of the land.

In the early 1700's the most repressive of the Penal Laws were enacted. All priests were required to register their names and their parishes under penalty of being branded with a red-hot iron; they were required then to swear allegiance to the House of Stuart or suffer banishment. Unregistered priests were to be castrated, though the London government refused to go along with this extreme form of barbarism. In 1719 all bishops were banished from Ireland under penalty of being hanged, drawn, and quartered; friars and monks were also banished. Public crosses, which were widely venerated by the Irish people, were destroyed. Catholic chapels were not permitted to have belfries, towers, or steeples. Catholic pilgrimages were banned under pain of flogging. Catholics were forbidden to sit in Parliament, to vote for members of Parliament, or to be members of grand juries (the local government bodies). They were forbidden to send their children abroad for education or to have schools of their own. A reward of ten pounds was promised for the apprehension of Catholic schoolmasters. Education at Trinity College in Dublin was reserved for Protestants. Catholics were forbidden to marry Protestants, and death was decreed for any priest who performed such a marriage. All marriages were civilly invalid unless they were performed by a minister of the Church of Ireland. Catholics were excluded from the legal profession; they could be neither barristers, nor solicitors, nor magistrates, nor judges. They could not be members of municipal corporations. They could not serve in the army or the navy; they could not bear arms; they could not wear swords on ceremonial occasions. They could not own a horse worth more than five pounds; any Protestant seeing a Catholic with a more valuable horse could compel him to sell it for five pounds. Catholics might not acquire land from Protestants; a Catholic landowner could not deed his estate as a whole; no Catholic could hold a lease for more than thirty years, but a Catholic who became a Protestant could inherit his father's whole estate. Lord Chancellor Bowes summarized the whole thing beautifully when he said, "The law does not suppose any such person to exist as an Irish Roman Catholic." His successor, John Fitzgibbon, the Earl of Clare, called Catholics "the scum of the earth." Wolfe Tone, the Protestant revolutionary, described the Penal Laws as "that execrable and infamous code, framed with the art and the malice of demons, to plunder and degrade and brutalize the Catholics."

Dean Swift, no lover of the Catholics by any means, commented, "The rise of our rents is squeezed out of the very blood, and vitals, and clothes, and dwellings of the tenants, who live worse than English beggars." Bishop George Berkeley commented that the Irish peasant was "more destitute than savages, and more abject than negroes. . . . The very savages of America are better clad and better lodged than the Irish cottagers throughout the fertile counties of Limerick and Tipperary."

There was no restraint of any sort on the landlords' power to get the highest rents possible. Resulting from the increase of population, the shortage of land was acute, and rents constantly moved up. Even though he paid his rent, the peasant had no guarantee against eviction to make room for another willing to pay more. As much as they hated the "rack-renting," they hated the tithes even more. The peasants' tithes provided vast sums of money for the Protestant Church of Ireland, which served very few people. In 1753, for example, out of sixty-seven Protestant parishes in

County Clare, sixty-two had no Protestant church and most had no parson or curate; nonetheless, the peasants contributed to the support of those parishes.

There were still more Penal Laws. No Catholic was permitted to have more than two apprentices. No Catholic was permitted to manufacture or sell books or newspapers, or to grant mortgages. No Catholic priest, even if he was registered, was allowed to move one step outside his parish. A Catholic wife who became a Protestant was permitted to live apart from her husband and make him support her. Catholic orphans were brought up as Protestants. Protestants were forbidden to take Catholic apprentices. A Protestant landowner lost his civil rights if he married a Catholic, and a Protestant heiress who married a Catholic forfeited her inheritance.

Writing in 1780, Arthur Young observed:

> The cottages of the Irish, which are all called cabbins, are the most miserable looking hovels that can well be conceived. . . . A landlord in Ireland can scarcely invent an order which a servant, labourer, or cottier dares to refuse to execute. . . . Disrespect, or anything tending towards sauciness, he may punish with his cane or his horsewhip with the most perfect security. A poor man would have his bones broken if he offered to lift a hand in his own defense.[11]

And Edward Wakefield noted, "Landlords of consequence have assured me that many of their cottier's would think themselves honoured to have their wives and daughters sent for to the bed of their master—a mark of slavery which proves the oppression under which such people must live."[12]

In other words, the state of the Irish in the 1700s was not very much different from that of the slaves in the southern part of the United States at the same time. The survival of the Irish under such circumstances is quite surprising. They must have astonished their British and Anglo-Irish overlords, who thought that the "Final Solution" to the Irish problem shouldn't have taken so long.

---

11. Giovanni Costigan, *A History of Modern Ireland* (New York: Pegasus, paperback, 1970), p. 94.
12. *Ibid.,* p. 94.

Interestingly enough, much of the Penal legislation also affected the Ulster Presbyterians, who were as ready to join revolts as their Irish Catholic enemies well into the nineteenth century. The rising of the United Irishmen in 1798, for example, was a truly national affair, with the Presbyterian farmers of the North, the Catholic peasants of the South led by their priests, and the Anglo-Protestant disciples of the French Revolution, such as Wolfe Tone in Dublin, banding together in common cause against England. By the late nineteenth century, however, while the alliance between the left-wing Protestants and the southern Catholics continued, the Ulster Presbyterians had opted out of the coalition.

There are many different ways to survive under such a repressive regime. The Irish Catholics, like the blacks of the American South, proved adept at developing modes of accommodation while retaining an independence of spirit. The aforementioned propensity of the Irish to answer a question by asking one, is most likely a product of the Penal times. It is plausible that the informal, round-about, casual, and frequently implicit and unspoken Irish political style is a legacy from those Penal times, too. The fundamental distrust of official structures and disregard for official laws that allegedly characterizes so many Irish politicians (and which unquestionably, in fact, has characterized such worthies as Mayor Hague and Alderman Prendergast) likewise may be traced to behavior patterns acquired during the Penal time. So, since both the law and the Establishment are out to get you, the best thing to do is get them first.

Many of the Penal Laws were unenforceable, and no serious attempts were made to enforce others. Nevertheless, the Irish Catholics spent their lives in a country where it was presumed that they had no right to exist.

While there were no organized revolts between the enactment of the Penal Laws at the beginning of the 1700s and "the '98," there was, nonetheless, "agrarian revolt," as Irish Catholic vigilante groups rose up to protect what little was left to their countrymen. The Whiteboys began as a protest against tithing; the Oakboys against forced labor on the roads; the Steelboys to fight against evictions; and after them came the Ridgeboys, the Peep o'Day

Boys, the Thrashers, Caravats, Shanavests, Rockites, Ribbonmen, and the Defenders. Most of these secret vigilante groups were relatively harmless. Few people were killed, but houses were destroyed, hayracks burned, and cattle killed. Since these groups were secret societies, they were officially condemned by the Catholic Church; members were excommunicated, though it is unlikely that the parish priests were very opposed to their activities. The Molly Maguires, who appeared in the coal fields of West Virginia, must certainly be viewed as an adaptation on the American scene of the Whiteboys and similar groups of the eighteenth century.

A final means of adaptation to the Penal Laws was emigration to France and Spain to fight in the army and to America to begin a new life. Those most likely to migrate to America before 1800, however, were not Irish Catholics but Ulstermen, who disliked the Anglican ascendency in Dublin as much as the Catholics. Perhaps as many as a half-million "Scots-Irish" migrated to the United States and became an implacable enemy to British rule in the colonies. Interestingly enough, these Ulster migrants defined themselves as Irish, and used the term "Scots-Irish" (which was given to them by others in America) only to distinguish themselves from the "Famine Irish" who came after 1848. Also, in this pre-revolutionary migration were some south-of-Ireland Protestants, mostly of Celtic rather than Anglo-Saxon ancestry. Most of them were shopkeepers and artisans who had become Protestants during the Penal years; they were probably in good enough financial condition to attempt migration during the famines of the eighteenth century. Periodically, the Irish Catholic leadership lamented the fact that the Protestants, be they Ulstermen or converts, were better able to take advantage of the opportunity to migrate than the Irish Catholics; but of course they also had more opportunity to develop the self-confidence necessary even to begin to think about changing their situation than did the oppressed and miserable Irish Catholics. It was only the incredible crisis of the Great Famine that forced migration on many of them as the only alternative to death. Beginning with the campaign of Daniel O'Connell and the resultant first Catholic Emancipation Act of 1829, the British government slowly and reluctantly repealed the Penal Laws, though it was only with the Wyndham Act of 1903 that the last disabilities against Irish Catholic land ownership were eliminated. A measure of the reluctance of the British government to remove the penal legislation was that the price set for Catholic emancipation in 1829 was that O'Connell agree that the property qualification for voting be raised from forty shillings to ten pounds. Potential Catholic voters were thereby reduced from 200,000 to less than 10 per cent of that. With such a history of extreme repression, it is indeed surprising not that the Irish hated the English, but that after their final liberation in the 1920s the hatred died so quickly. While it is presumably unwise to say so publicly in modern Ireland, an occasional Irishman will lament the fact that the British made such an absolute mess of the Union of 1800. Some sort of federation of independent states in the British Isles might have made a good deal of economic, social, and political sense, of benefit to all concerned. But both the Anglo-Irish ascendency in Dublin and the British public and government in London were absolutely assured of the moral and religious superiority of Protestant rule; that freedom be given to Irish Catholics was as inconceivable from Dublin Castle to Westminster to the English voter as freedom for blacks was inconceivable in the American South.

Among the more interesting phenomena of Penal Ireland were the "hedge schools," illegal and informal schools in which teachers and students met, frequently out of doors, so that some sort of education would be imparted to Irish Catholic children. The hierarchy, clergy, and laity of Ireland feared that the official school system was nothing more than an attempt on the part of the Ascendency to convert the children of Irish Catholics. This unquestionably helped to shape the mentality that led to a separate parochial school system in the United States.

There were three basic strains that characterized the Irish nationalist organizations in the nineteenth century after Daniel O'Connell: the parliamentary group, seeking constitutional home rule towards the end of the century under the leadership of Charles Parnell; the land reformers, such as Michael Davitt's Land League;

and the secret revolutionary organizations, such as the Fenians and the Irish Republican Brotherhood (IRB). These groups sometimes cooperated and sometimes squabbled with one another. The Sinn Fein, which was the political base of the revolt of 1916–23, stood somewhere between Parnell on the one hand and the IRB on the other. The founder of the Sinn Fein, Arthur Griffith, conceived of the union of Ireland and Great Britain much like the dual monarchy of Austria-Hungary. But, after the events of the Easter Rising, the Sinn Fein and the Irish Volunteers became the Irish Republican Army and were swept irresistibly toward open revolt. The IRB, a small, secret society, had written the scenario for revolt before 1900, and the stupidity of the British government in thinking that land reform would ultimately placate the militant minority that the IRB represented seems, in retrospect, quite incredible. Even more stupid, however, was the bloody suppression of the Easter Rising of 1916, which drove the overwhelming majority of the Irish people, who had in the relative prosperity of the first decade-and-a-half of the twentieth century little taste for armed revolt, into the arms of the IRB. These events, stirring, complicated, tragic, and often futile, took place in Ireland after the immigrants had arrived on the shores of the United States. As a matter of fact, one can say that instead of being shaped by the post-Famine political events, the American Irish helped shaped the events. Without the financial and political support of the American Irish, it is questionable whether the revolt which began in 1916 would have been successful. Eamon de Valera, after all, was born in Brooklyn.

THE FAMINE

The Easter Rising was a failure that became a success because the British military government under the incredibly inept General Maxwell executed a handful of the leaders of the revolution. Perhaps a legal case could have been made for these killings, but no legal case will excuse the British government from the deaths of millions of Irish Catholics from the famines at the time of Cromwell to those in the middle of the nineteenth century. As we have already noted, perhaps three-quarters of a million Catholics died in the famine of the middle seventeenth century; 1741 was called by the Irish "the year of the slaughter," with over 400,000 deaths from famine. But these were minor events compared to the Great Famine at the end of the 1840s. In 1841 the population of Ireland was over eight million; by 1851, at the normal rate of increase, it should have been over nine million; in fact, it was only 6.5 million. In the space of a decade Ireland lost 2.5 million people, probably less than half by migration. In other words, between 1847 and 1850 somewhere between one million and 1.5 million Irish Catholics died while the British government barely lifted a finger to save them. Indeed, it continued to export agricultural products from Ireland and to clear tenants off the land. The Potato Famine, then, was one of the great disasters of modern Western Europe.

It is estimated that the population of Ireland was about four million in 1800, which meant that in the years between 1800 and 1840 the population had more than doubled, and some British observers described Ireland as the most densely populated country in Europe. These people lived always on the edge of famine, depending on the success of one highly unpredictable crop, the potato, for their existence. When the crop prospered, there was work and food aplenty (or at least enough); but when it failed, disaster was almost inevitable. The British government did not create the blight that destroyed the potato crop in the 1840s, certainly, but it did force upon Ireland the kind of political and economic subjection that made some sort of disaster practically inevitable.

The state of pre-Famine Ireland was described sympathetically by three Frenchmen: Gustave de Beaumont and his friend, Alexis de Tocqueville, and Duvergier de Hauranne.

De Beaumont:

> I have seen the Indian in his forests and the Negro in his chains, and thought, as I contemplated their pitiable condition, that I saw the very extreme of human wretchedness; but I did not then know the condition of unfortunate Ireland. There is

no doubt that the most miserable of English paupers is better fed and clothed than the most prosperous of Irish laborers.

De Tocqueville remarked that the wrongs done the people in Clare are retained "with a terrifying exactitude of local memory."

> Whatever one does, the memory of the great persecutions is not forgotten. Who sows injustice must sooner or later reap the fruits. . . . All the rich Protestants whom I saw in Dublin speak of the Catholics with extraordinary hatred and scorn. The latter, they say, are savages . . . and fanatics led into all sorts of disorders by their priests.

Duvergier de Hauranne wrote that there were in Ireland "two nations," the conquerors and the conquered.

> There is nothing between the master and the slave, between the cabin and the palace. There is nothing between all the luxuries of existence and the last degree of human wretchedness.[13]

The fact that there existed within Ireland two nations, one the oppressor and the other oppressed, is clear when one ponders that between 1845 and 1850, when more than a million Irishmen were dying, two million quarters of wheat a year were shipped out of Ireland. In the Poor Law Act of 1847 it was stipulated that no peasant with a holding of a quarter-acre or more was eligible for relief—thus forcing people to sell their land. Lord John Russell, the Prime Minister of England, responding to an appeal from Lord Clarendon, Viceroy in Ireland, wrote: "The state of Ireland for the next few months must be one of great suffering. Unhappily the agitation for Repeal [of the Penal Laws] has contrived to destroy nearly all sympathy in this country." Later, Clarendon told Russell, "I don't think there is another legislature in Europe that would disregard such suffering as now exists in the west of Ireland, or coldly persist in the policy of extermination."

The permanent head of the Treasury, Sir Charles Trevelyan, observed smugly: "The poorest and most ignorant Irish peasant

---

13. The three Frenchmen are quoted in Costigan, *op. cit.,* pp. 91, 103, 105.

must, I think, by this time have become sensible of the advantage of belonging to a powerful community like that of the United Kingdom, the establishments and pecuniary resources of which are at all times ready to be employed for his benefit." At another point he wrote, "The Irish problem [referring to overpopulation] being altogether beyond the power of man, the cure had been applied by the direct stroke of an all-wise Providence in a manner as unexpected and as unthought of as it is likely to be effectual." Finally, when a million people were dead, Sir Charles was moved to some compassion: "It is hard upon the poor people that they should be deprived of knowing that they are suffering from an affliction of God's providence."

Sir Charles Wood, Chancellor of the Exchequer, and Trevelyan's boss wrote to an Irish landlord: "I am not at all appalled by your tenantry going. That seems to me a necessary part of the process. . . . We must not complain of what we really want to obtain." And Sir Robert Peel benignly observed, "The time has come when it is not any longer necessary to pet Ireland. We only spoil her by undeserved flattery and by treating her to everything for which she herself ought to pay." Nassau Senior, Professor of Economics at Oxford, on whom the governmental leaders depended for economic advice, was quoted as saying that he feared the famine of 1848 would not kill more than a million people, and that would scarcely be enough to do much good. The London *Times* rejoiced at the thought that soon the native Irishman would be "as rare on the banks of the Liffey as a red man on the banks of the Manhatten."

Sir Charles Trevelyan, always eager to see things from the moral point of view, reflected, "The great evil with which we have to contend is not the physical evil of the famine, but the moral evil of the selfish, perverse and turbulent character of the people."

All through the Famine, according to Cecil Woodham-Smith, cartoons were published "week after week depicting the Irishman as a filthy, brutal creature, an assassin and a murderer, begging for money, under a pretence of buying food, to spend on weapons."

And Lord Tennyson, that darling of Victorian poetry, commented, "The Kelts are all made furious fools. They live in a horrible island and have no history of their own worth the least notice. Could not anyone blow up that horrible island with dynamite and carry it off in pieces—a long way off?"[14]

The island was not carried a long way off, but many of its people were; and not all of them made it safely to other shores. Thousands, perhaps tens of thousands, died either on the passage from Ireland or shortly after arriving in the New World. At Grosse Isle, near Detroit, for example, there is a plaque which reads, "In this secluded spot lie the mortal remains of 5,294 persons who, flying from pestilence and famine in Ireland in the year 1847, found in America but a grave." The North Atlantic crossing of the Irish emigrants was not as bad as the middle passage by which black slaves were brought to the United States, but it was bad enough, and those who survived could only look to a slight improvement. In Mrs. Woodham-Smith's words:

> The Irish famine emigration is unlike most other emigrations because it was of a less-civilized and less-skilled people into a more-civilized and more-skilled community. Other immigrations have been of the independent and the sturdy in search of wider horizons, and such emigrants usually brought with them knowledge and technical accomplishment which the inhabitants of the country in which they settled did not possess. The Irish, from their abysmal poverty, brought nothing, and this poverty had forced them to become habituated to standards of living which the populations amongst whom they came considered unfit for human beings. Cellar dwellings, whether in English towns or the cities of North America, were almost invariably occupied by the Irish. Poverty, ignorance and bewilderment brought them there, but it must not be forgotten that cellar dwellings resembled the dark, mud-floored cabins in which over half the population of Ireland had been accustomed to live under British rule.[15]

Many of the ships were called "coffin ships," not inappropriately. For example, the bark *Elizabeth and Sarah* was a small craft of 330 tons and carried 276 people to the promised land across the

---

14. The Englishmen—Lord Clarendon, Sir Charles Trevelyan, Sir Charles Wood, Mrs. Woodham-Smith, Sir Robert Peel, and Lord Tennyson—are quoted in Costigan, *op. cit.*, pp. 185–187.

15. Cecil Woodham-Smith, *The Great Hunger* (New York: Harper & Row, 1963), p. 207.

ocean. It was supposed to have carried twelve thousand gallons of water, but it had only a little more than eight thousand in leaky casks. The captain was required by law to distribute seven pounds of food to each passenger weekly, but no distribution was ever made. There were thirty-six births, thirty-two of which were to be shared among the 276 passengers; there was no sanitary convenience of any kind. The trip took eight weeks, and forty-two persons died during the voyage. The wonder is that more did not succumb.

The Grosse Isle way station in Canada was an incredible center of human misery.

> On May 26 thirty vessels, with 10,000 emigrants on board, were waiting at Grosse Isle; by the 29th there were thirty-six vessels, with 13,000 emigrants. And "in all these vessels cases of fever and dysentery had occurred," wrote Dr. Douglas [medical officer in charge of the station]—the dysentery seems to have been infectious, and was probably bacillary dysentery. On May 31 forty vessels were waiting, extending in a line two miles down the St. Lawrence; about 1,100 cases of fever were on Grosses Isle in shed, tents, and laid in rows in the little church; an equal number were on board the ships, waiting to be taken off; and a further 45,000 emigrants at least were expected.[16]

One ship, the *Agnes,* arrived at Grosse Isle with 427 passengers, of whom only 150 were alive after the fifteen-day quarantine. After the quarantine the emigrants were crammed into steamers for transportation to Montreal, a trip of two or three days during which death claimed up to half of those aboard.

In 1847, 100,000 emigrants left Ireland for Canada. Seventeen thousand, it is estimated, died en route and at least fifty thousand more died in Canada itself. Thousands more died in the United States, but the disaster there was less severe.

It took perhaps a century for Ireland to recover from the effects of the Famine. By the early 1860s the population of the country was close to its 1800 level of four million. Through a combination of late marriage and continued emigration, the population was contained at that level, with only marginal increases or decreases

---

16. *Ibid.,* p. 220.

for another century. It was only with the economic gains and development plans of the 1960's that sustained population increase began.

The descriptions of the Famine recorded by contemporary observers—corpses lying in the fields, the streets "black with funeral processions," tenant farmers being packed into ships so that the lords would not have to pay poor taxes on them, emaciated men, women, and children struggling down the lanes on their way to death, frantic riots for food, occasional murders of the gentry, and (heaven save us) even a splendid state visit from Queen Victoria—can only begin to give a picture of the unspeakable horrors of such a disaster, one which the British political leadership viewed with some complacency because it helped to solve the problem of overpopulation in Ireland.

Was England guilty of genocide in the 1840s? Surely not in quite the same sense of Adolf Hitler; the British government did not directly execute the victims of starvation and fever. But British political and economic policies made the disaster certain catastrophe, and British leadership viewed the sufferings of the Irish people with little compassion and, in some cases, satisfaction. The mass murder of populations in modern times comparable with that of the famines of the 1840s, such as the liquidation of the Jews and the mass murder of civilians in the Soviet Union before and during the Second World War, did indeed make the Great Famine pale by comparison. There is one big difference, however. Those who managed to live through the extermination camps were hailed as heroes and encouraged by a world that acknowledged the inhumanity of what had happened to them. There was no such solace for the survivors in Ireland or for those who emigrated abroad. The Irish immigrants were unwelcome, unwanted, and despised. Worse than that, their sufferings were tucked under the rug of world history, to be forgotten even by their own descendants. When Cecil Woodham-Smith's *The Great Hunger* was published, the critical reaction was callous. No one, of course, denied the truth of her story or tried to defend the policies of the British government, but precious few reviewers seemed to be aware that there was in the United States a substantial population descended from those who fled for their lives at the time of the Famine. It is not that Mrs. Woodham-Smith ignores the connection:

> It is a matter of history that the Irish political record has some black spots. Irish emigrants, especially of the famine years, became, with rare exeptions, what their transatlantic environment made them, children of the slums, rebuffed, scorned by respectable citizens and exploited by the less respectable. The Irish were the most unfortunate emigrants and the poorest, they took longest to be accepted, longest to become genuinely assimilated, they waited longest before the opportunities the United States offers were freely available to them.
>
> The story of the Irish in the New World is not a romantic story of liberty and success, but the history of a bitter struggle, as bitter, as painful, though not as long-drawn-out, as the struggle by which the Irish at last won the right to be a nation.[17]

There seems to be a grudging reluctance on the part of American intellectuals to face the horrors of the Famine, the perils of the North Atlantic crossing, and the inhuman experiences of the emigrant Irish. Indeed, one finds precious little compassion for the Irish either in contemporary accounts of the early years of immigration or in present reflections upon those years. I am unaware of a single American intellectual who ever bothered to try to understand the present state of the American Irish in terms of their past experiences. The Irish have never been an approved object of sympathy or understanding in the American republic. It is perhaps just as well, because at this point in time we are capable of declaring ourselves able to do without the intellectuals' compassion, sympathy, and understanding; we made it in spite of their hatred and oppression. There lurks in the Irish psyche, I am convinced, a profound skepticism about the fashionable compassions of the American liberal do-gooder. We are inclined to think their compassions are just a bit phony, and we wonder where they were when we needed their help. We also find it just a bit ironic when they demand that we feel guilty for what their ancestors did to the

---

17. *Ibid.*, p. 269.

blacks and the American Indians. They do not seem to display much guilt for what happened to us at the hands of their ancestors here and in Europe.

However deeply felt and generally widespread this skepticism toward liberals is among the Irish, any recollection of the famine itself exists, if at all, deep in the unconscious of the American Irish. Many of us had grandparents, many more of us had great-grandparents who fled during those years or shortly thereafter. The story of the Famine, the crossing of the Atlantic and the fever on board ship, and the misery of the slum tenements of New York and Boston are neither part of our family traditions nor of the history we are taught, certainly not in the public schools, nor in the parochial schools. This seems to me to be an astonishing phenomenon. One wonders if by the year 2000, Jews will have forgotten Hitler's extermination camps. That the rest of the world would want to forget is understandable, but that Jews would let them forget it seems very unlikely. Yet the Irish have cooperated, one might almost say enthusiastically, in blotting out the memory of the Great Famine. Perhaps it is too horrible to remember; perhaps we were so eager to become Americans that we quickly shed the memories of a non-American past; perhaps we so wanted to prove ourselves capable of respectability that we thought it expedient to dismiss the injustices which had been visited upon our predecessors. Maybe part of the price of acceptance into American society was that we forget the past. In any case, we have forgotten it.

But that does not mean that its effects do not linger with us. No one would argue that the effects of the slave trade and slavery could be overlooked in an effort to understand American blacks—not even if blacks themselves wanted to forget. There is little difference in the history of the blacks and the Irish until the 1860s. Both lived in abject misery, the victims of political oppression and economic exploitation. The principal difference is that the Irish, having white skins, were eventually given a chance to "earn a place" in American society; the blacks were not permitted to do so. Just as no reasonable student of American blacks can think that the contemporary situation can be understood merely in terms of what happened since 1865, neither should any serious student of the American Irish assume that their history began at the same time.[18] I am not arguing that the Irish have had it worse than the blacks; most certainly they have not. I am saying something of much more limited import: the past histories of both groups cannot be ignored—even if the groups themselves would prefer to ignore their own histories.

We can conclude this sketchy account of the history of Ireland by saying that whatever comparisons might or might not be made with other groups, the Irish came to this country with a history of a thousand years of misery, suffering, oppression, violence, exploitation, atrocity, and genocide. Their country was given no opportunity to develop intellectually or economically. Their aristocracy was repeatedly liquidated or exiled. Their culture and even their language was systematically eliminated. They were thought of as an inferior people, and like all oppressed peoples began to half believe it themselves. Like all such peoples they were torn between the desire for respectability and savage resentment of their oppressors. If anyone thinks that the twin themes of respectability and resentment are not part of the heritage of the American Irish, he simply does not know the American Irishman very well.

---

18. A monumental history of Irish Catholicism is being prepared under the direction of Patrick A. Corish of St. Patrick's College, Maynooth, Ireland.

3.

The American Irish and the Celtic Heritage

Long, long ago, beyond the misty space
   Of twice a thousand years,
In Erin old there dwelt a mighty race,
   Taller than Roman spears;
Like oaks and towers they had a giant grace,
   Were fleet as deers,
With wind and waves they made their 'biding place,
   These western shepherd seers.

Great were their deeds, their passions and their sports;
   With clay and stone
They piled on strath and shore those mystic forts,
   Nor yet o'erthrown;
On cairn-crowned hills they held their council-courts;
   While youths alone,
With giant dogs, explored the elk resorts,
   And brought them down.[1]

It has been a long time since Finn MacCool and his band of heroes (or cutthroats, depending on your point of view) roamed the forests with their wolfhounds—a hell of a long time. There is little enough of awareness of the Celtic tradition even in Ireland and practically no awareness of it among the American Irish. And yet when one begins to poke around the ruins of the heritage, one

---

1. Thomas D'Arcy McGee, "The Celts," in *The Penguin Book of Irish Verse,* ed. Brandan Kennelly (Middlesex: Penguin Books, 1970), p. 253.

43

is not so sure. Maybe Finn and the Finians are still abroad in the land, though they may be lurking on the other side of the threshold of consciousness.

The Irish cultural tradition, only less ancient in Europe than the traditions of Greece and Rome, was badly battered during the years of English domination. The conquering power decided that everything Irish was barbaric and uncivilized, and they almost succeeded in stamping out the language, which was one of the principal bearers of the tradition. The Irish themselves lost confidence in the worth of their own heritage, and most Irish-Americans are unaware of its existence. It is difficult to say precisely what the Celtic elements are that still survive even in Ireland. In the early drafts of this book, I had not planned to discuss the impact of the Celtic tradition on the American Irish because I did not think there was any such impact. However, my colleague Emmet Larkin has pointed out to me that most of the Famine migration came from areas of Ireland where the Irish language was the first language of most people and the only language of many. Furthermore, as I tried to learn more about the Gaelic tradition, I discovered that there were a number of elements in that tradition which seemed to explain some aspects of the behavior and culture of the American Irish.

Any attempt to outline in a few pages the dimensions of the Celtic heritage is bound to be inadequate, and any speculation about the Celtic remnants in contemporary America is necessarily tenuous. Yet it seems to me that someone must begin such speculation.

Eoin MacNeill, the great historian of Irish culture (and one of the leaders of the Easter Rising), has insisted that the term "tribal" is not an accurate one to describe Irish social structure,[2] but as D. A. Binchy notes, "tribe" is just about the only word we have available in English to translate the Irish *tuath*, "a very small area, roughly corresponding to the modern barony" under the rule of a

---

2. For a discussion of MacNeill's point, see his *Phases of Irish History* (Dublin and Sydney: Gill and Son), pp. 290–299.

king or *ri* (from the same Indo-European root as the Latin *rex*).[3] In addition to ruling his tiny kingdom, the king might be an "over king," which meant that other leaders gave him hostages and paid him tribute. In his turn, the over king would be subordinate to the highest king known to the laws, the king of a province. Occasionally some provincial king would claim to be "high king" (*ard ri*) of the whole country, but there was little ground in the laws and not much hope in practice of his exercising authority over the whole country. It is to be noted, incidentally, that the over kings ruled subordinate kings but had no direct power over those lesser kings' subjects.

Under the king were the nobility, who owned the land collectively as families, not individuals. Indeed, the extended family was the basic social unit; individual rights came from membership in the family, which consisted of "the descendents of a common great grandfather, four generations. . . . It was the normal property-owning unity, and it was also the unit for the purpose of dynastic succession."[4]

Beneath the nobles in the pyramid were the "professional men"—the brehons who interpreted the law, the druids who were religious leaders, the "prophets" who foretold the future (the Irish word is *fáith,* which is from the same root as the Latin *vates*), and the poets who were apparently of two groups, the popular bards and the more scholarly *fili.* It was into this "professional class" that the Christian clergy were later to fit as replacement for the druids and the prophets—a fit that was not always a comfortable one, as Binchy remarks.[5]

Finally, came the common man, who was most likely to be free (slavery was rare), with his rights clearly specified by law. In Binchy's words:

> Then, as always, he did the chores: he tilled the soil, paid his taxes in the shape of food rent to the king, and usually stood

---

3. D. A. Binchy, "Secular Institutions," in Myles Dillon, *Early Irish Society* (Cork: Mercier Press, 1954), p. 54.

4. Myles Dillon, "Celtic Religion and Celtic Society," in Joseph Raferty, *The Celts* (Cork: Mercier Press, 1964), p. 69.

5. Binchy, *op. cit.,* p. 57.

> in a quasi contractual relation known as clientship to a neighboring nobleman, who in return, for a fixed render of provisions and a certain amount of boon work (or unpaid labor) advanced him stock to graze his land and guaranteed him a limited protection against the violence of other powerful neighbors.[6]

There were no such things as cities in Celtic society; indeed, there were not even towns. It was from the ninth-century Danish savages that the Irish learned about towns, and even then they tended to be centers for the Danes and later the Normans and the Anglo-Irish. The Irish kept to the countryside. (Even now they will tell you in the west that Dublin is not Ireland and that Cork really isn't either. Only the western cities of Limerick and Galway have some claim to the title. For the purists, only the Irish-speaking countryside—the so-called *Gaeltach*—is *really* Irish.)

Thus, Celtic Ireland was "at once tribal, rural, hierarchical, and familiar."[7]

> There was little scope for the development of those political, administrative and judicial institutions which characterize the state as we know it today. The *tuath* was a small unity both in extent and population, hence there was no need for any intermediate bodies between the ruler and his subjects. Further, it contained no cities or walled towns, and it is a commonplace of history that the structure of our modern society is based on the city and the marketplace; the very words we use—politics, civilization, and so on—are a reminder of the urban roots of the society we live in.[8]

But the most striking phenomenon in Irish society—and one that has important implications for an understanding of the American Irish and their political style—is that ancient Ireland had, as Sean O'Connor has put it to me, a system of law without law enforcement. The legal structure was entirely customary. In Kathleen Hughes's words:

---

6. *Ibid.*, p. 58.
7. *Ibid.*, p. 59.
8. *Ibid.*

How, then, was order maintained? Law was based on custom, and was declared through a special class of legal specialists, but, with one or two exceptions where the king had authority to execute it in special cases, it was privately enforced. There were no crimes against the state, only injuries to private persons, which must be met by compensation adjudged according to the injury received and the status of the injured party. Irish law had a well-developed surety system. Guarantors were taken to ensure the performance of customary obligations: each kin-group had, for example, its representative who guaranteed the duties to which his kinsmen were bound, and the king kept a "man of pledge for base clients" permanently in his household. When a man made an extraordinary contract he gave some treasure in pledge for its fulfilment, and if it was of major importance he also took guarantors who pledged themselves to see that the contract was maintained. If anyone failed to fulfil his contract his guarantors were liable, and failure meant loss of status with its rights to compensation and other privileges. The man who did not keep faith was degraded and lost his honour-price.[9]

The king was not interested in law enforcement; there was only the most rudimentary form of state, and one obtained one's rights ultimately by force or threat of force. But it does not follow that either law or lawyers were lacking. On the contrary, there was an elaborate and detailed structure of laws and a powerful and learned legal class—the brehons. In Binchy's words:

> The main interest of Irish law for the student of early institutions is that it shows how a legal system based not on state sanctions but on the power of traditional custom, formulated and applied by a learned professional caste, could function and command obedience. . . . They showed remarkable ingenuity in devising methods of procedure which would compel the average citizen of the *tuath* to keep the rules. Perhaps, indeed, their very success hindered the evolution of public justice by diminishing the need for it.[10]

One of the methods for keeping order was the combination of surety and honor described in the quotation from Kathleen Hughes.

9. Kathleen Hughes, *The Church in Early Irish Society* (London: Methuen & Co. Ltd.), pp. 4–5.
10. Binchy, *op. cit.,* p. 63.

If worse came to worst and the decisions of the brehons were not honored, the lawyers could turn to their allies, the bards, whose acid-tongued ridicule could bring even the most recalcitrant *ri* into line.

The Irish, of course, had no monopoly on either customary law or legal masters, but unlike common law, the brehon law never had a chance to develop into a modern, state-enforced legal system. A foreign law was imposed, and the Irish customary law was relegated to the bogs. Nevertheless it remained the custom of the people; and precisely because it had not developed but had been repressed, it survived longer than it otherwise might. Even in modern Ireland there persists a profound suspicion of the formal, state-enforced legal system.

It is tempting to make the obvious comparisons between the picture of Celtic Ireland that we have outlined and the political and legal behavior of the American Irish. Personal loyalty, informal arrangements, tight family structures, ridicule, boycott, and great love of legal learning combined frequently with little concern for the enforcement of the letter of the law, a fondness for legal contention and argument, suspicion of formal governmental regulations, indirect and circuitous ways of accomplishing one's purposes —all these are characteristic both of the American Irish and the Celtic tradition.

Obviously, the relationship is a complicated one. The skills described in the previous paragraph would have been necessary to survive a thousand years of foreign rule even if they were not part of the tradition. They also happened to be the skills that were appropriate for British parliamentary politics when the Irish Catholics began entering such politics in the early nineteenth century. At this stage in the development of our understanding, it is probably enough to say that much can be found in the Gaelic tradition that is consonant with the behavior of the contemporary American Irish.

Another aspect of the tradition was the extraordinary importance of poets and poetry. The bards were masters of words and stories. In the words of Kenneth H. Jackson:

> The Celtic poet and sage was a functionary in society, and was an essential part of the aristocratic structure of that

society. His prime duty was to praise and celebrate his chief and his chief's family in panegyric verse (which was traditionally what "poetry" meant above all to the Celt), to preserve and recite his genealogy, and in all other such ways to further his fame; hence the necessity for his existence as a court official. He was free to travel and eulogise other lords, and for all such praises, whether of his own patron or another, he expected a due reward—a sword or horse or richly jewelled brooch or the like. In fact the early Laws gave him a legal right to this, and they also laid down the size of the retinue with which he might travel and which he might impose on the hospitality of his host—twenty-four men, in the case of the highest class of poet, the *ollam*. This man's rank was very high in law, equal to that of a petty king, but the poets were all protected by an unwritten but nevertheless mighty sanction, the fear of satire. In a heroic aristocracy as described, glory and good reputation were essentially necessary, and the satires of the poets were dreaded because they could sing a man's dispraises all through Ireland and destroy his fame and standing.[11]

I am not qualified either to comment authoritatively on the quality of Irish poetry or to detail the substantive themes of the tradition, but Robin Flower, after describing an encounter in the 1930's with an old man in the west who was able to repeat vast amounts of Irish poetry, comments:

> I listened spellbound and, as I listened, it came to me suddenly that there on the last inhabited piece of European land, looking out to the Atlantic horizon, I was hearing the oldest living tradition in the British Isles. So far as the record goes, this matter in one form or another is older than the Anglo-Saxon Beowulf, and yet it lives still upon the lips of the peasantry, a real and vivid experience, while, except to a few painful scholars, Beowulf has long passed out of memory. To-morrow this too will be dead, and the world will be the poorer when this last shade of that which once was great has passed away. The voice ceased, and I awoke out of my reverie as the old man said: "I have kept you from your dinner with my tales of the *fiana*." "You have done well," I said, "for a tale is

---

11. Kenneth Hurlstone Jackson, *The Oldest Irish Tradition: A Window on the Iron Age* (Cambridge: Cambridge University Press, 1964), pp. 26–27.

better than food," and thanked him before we went our several ways.

In such memories, and in an odd quatrain still surviving from the byplay of the schools, the tradition of the poets is still alive in the spoken tongue. And in the great manuscripts written in the schools of poetry and history and law we can see them busy at their task of preserving the old tradition which their order had been instituted to guard. They stood firmly over the ancient ways and had but small capacity of adapting themselves to the change of times. Their existence was bound up with that of the aristocratic order which they served, and with it they fell. But their memory and their influence lived after them and, if the spoken Irish of to-day is perhaps the liveliest, the most concise, and the most literary in its turns of all the vernaculars of Europe, this is due in no small part to the passionate preoccupation of the poets, turning and re-turning their phrases in the darkness of their cubicles and restlessly seeking the last perfection of phrase and idiom.[12]

It is interesting to compare the translated Irish poetry with the more familiar Anglo-Irish verse. The Celtic poets, most of them anonymous, have nothing to fear from such a comparison. There is sensitivity to nature and religious faith of the highest order, for example, in the following verses of the king, Suibhne (Sweeney), driven mad by the sight of his people slain in battle. This was written in the twelfth century from eighth-century material:

> Over the plain of Moyra
>   Under the heels of foemen
> I saw my people broken
>   As flax is scutched by women.
>
> But the cries I hear by Derry
>   Are not of men triumphant;
> I hear their calls in the evening,
>   Swans calm and exultant.
>
> I hear the stag's belling
>   Over the valley's steepness;
> No music on earth
>   Can move me like its sweetness.

12. Robin Flower, *The Irish Tradition* (Oxford: Clarendon Press, 1947), pp. 105–106.

> Christ, Christ hear me!
>   Christ, Christ of Thy meekness!
> Christ, Christ love me!
>   Sever me not from Thy sweetness![13]

And there is bitterness in the anonymous lament of the old woman of Beare:

> The Old Woman of Beare am I
> Who once was beautiful.
> Now all I know is how to die.
> I'll do it well.
>
> Look at my skin
> Stretched tight on the bone.
> Where kings have pressed their lips,
> The pain, the pain.
>
> I don't hate the men
> Who swore the truth was in their lies.
> One thing alone I hate—
> Women's eyes.
>
> The young sun
> Gives its youth to everyone,
> Touching everything with gold.
> In me, the cold.[14]

But the Gaelic poet could also be witty and ribald. One of the more printable stanzas of the late eighteenth-century poem, "The Midnight Court" by Bryan Merryman, has this recommendation:

> Down with marriage! It's out of date;
> It exhausts the stock and cripples the state.
> The priest has failed with whip and blinker,
> Now give a chance to Tom the Tinker,
> And mix and mash in Nature's can
> The tinker and the gentleman!
> Let lovers in every lane extended

---

13. Stanzas 3–6 of "The Sweetness of Nature," trans. Frank O'Connor, in *The Penguin Book of Irish Verse,* ed. Brendan Kennelly (Middlesex: Penguin Books, 1970), pp. 54–55.
14. "The Old Woman of Beare," trans. Brendan Kennelly, in *Penguin Book of Irish Verse, op. cit.,* pp. 62–63.

Struggle and strain as God intended
And locked in frenzy bring to birth
The morning glory of the earth;
The starry litter, girl and boy
Who'll see the world once more with joy.
Clouds will break and skies will brighten
Mountains bloom and spirits lighten,
And men and women praise your might,
You who restore the old delight.[15]

Merryman also had some things to say about clerical celibacy, which no doubt helped to get the first English translation of the poem banned in Ireland. The interested reader had better find the poem for himself. Sacred or profane, the Irish-speaking poets had something to say, and they knew how to say it well.

Even a cursory reading of translations of Irish poetry makes it clear that we are dealing with a creative and imaginative tradition of the highest order. A love of words and skill at poetic imagery are obvious even to the tourist in Ireland.[16] The storytelling ability of both the native Irish and their American cousins, whether in novels and short stories or in "tall tales," hardly needs mention. But are writers like F. Scott Fitzgerald, J. F. Powers, John O'Hara, Flannery O'Connor, Elizabeth Cullinan, and Tom McHale lineal descendants of the bards? Are they really the cousins of Flower's poetry-reciting farmer, Cross's tailor, and those bearers of the Celtic tradition, the bards? More research will be needed to answer these questions; however, the skeptical reader should peruse first *The Tailor and Ansty* and then the wisdom of Mr. Dooley before he concludes that nothing of the tradition of the bards survived in the New World.

Another element in the Celtic heritage is the comic tradition.

---

15. Bryan Merryman, "The Midnight Court," trans. Frank O'Connor, in *ibid.*, pp. 107–108.

16. For one of the best descriptions of the talk of an Irish peasant, see Eric Cross, *The Tailor and Ansty* (Cork: Mercier Press, 1942). Interestingly enough, this book was banned as obscene after its publication. (The ban was later lifted.) By contemporary American standards, the tailor's sexual attitudes were quite mild. Frank O'Connor, in his introduction to the book, argues that the Irish-speaking countryman had a robust and healthy attitude toward sexuality, and that prudery and puritanism came only when English replaced Irish and the Celtic tradition languished.

Vivian Mercier[17] argues that the Irish comic inheritance is archaic, that it is in direct touch with its primitive roots in the pre-literate past, that it is more archaic than any modern Western literary tradition. Mercier does not explicitly trace this persistence of an archaic tradition to the arresting of literary development by foreign invasion, but there seems to be no better explanation for it. It is precisely the archaism which gives the Irish comic tradition its strength and its interesting combination of absurdity and playfulness.

> . . . like Homer or Aristophanes, he [the Gaelic writer] seems to believe in myth and magic with one half of his being, while with the other half he delights in their absurdity. . . . the same basic . . . material may become a fierce and noble hero-tale or an uproarious burlesque; similarly, an edifying saint's legend may become an anti-clerical satire, through quite small alterations and amplifications.[18]

Mercier then quotes with approval the words of Huizinga on the play-spirit of the primitive society: " 'Belief in the sanctities is a sort of half-belief, and goes with scoffing and pretended indifference.' "[19] He adds:

> It would be hard to frame a sentence which more accurately defines the ambivalence toward myth and magic—and sometimes toward Christian rites and accounts of miracles—shown by comic literature in Gaelic.[20]

The Anglo-Irish literature of Swift and others absorbed much of the archaism of Gaelic literature:

> Its contact with the play-spirit of an archaic civilization has enabled it to play with words, with ideas, with taboos, in a mood of abandon which has won the fascinated if somewhat apprehensive admiration of most of the literate world.[21]

There are two elements in this play-spirit: the fantastic and the grotesque. "The humour of other cultures besides the Irish displays one or the other of these emphases, but I doubt whether both

---

17. In these paragraphs I rely heavily on Vivian Mercier's book, *The Irish Comic Tradition* (Oxford: Oxford University Press, 1962).
18. *Ibid.*, p. 8.
19. *Ibid.*, p. 9.
20. *Ibid.*, p. 9.
21. *Ibid.*, p. 10.

types of humour have been simultaneously fostered to the same degree by any other people."[22] The fantastic, while it is often wild and occasionally sublime, is usually one step away from parody and fun-poking. "Behind the bards and the hagiographers, who endlessly strive to outdo each other in their accounts of heroic deeds and saintly miracles, there lurks the figure of the sceptic and/or parodist. Anyone who knows the contradictions of the Irish mind may come to suspect the sceptical parodist is but the bard or the hagiographer himself in a different mood."[23]

The great, noble, godlike Irish heroes have a habit of being caught in scatological or obscene situations. Mercier quotes from the Ulster Cycle a description of the embarrassing fate the great Cuchulain suffered after shooting off his big mouth:

> . . . and Cuchulain said: "I swear by the god by whom the Ulstermen swear, unless a man is found to fight with me, I will shed the blood of everyone who is in the fort."
> "Naked women to meet him!" said Conchobar.
> Then the women of Emain go to meet him with Mugain, the wife of Conchobar Mac Nessa, and bare their breasts before him.
> "These are the warriors who will meet you today," said Mugain.
> He covers his face; then the heroes of Emain seize him and throw him into a vessel of cold water. That vessel bursts round him. The second vessel into which he was thrown boiled with bubbles as big as the fist therefrom. The third vessel into which he went, he warmed it so that its heat and its cold were rightly tempered.[24]

One can hear the howls of obscene laughter around the peat fire at that one, and the voices saying (in Gaelic, of course), "Good enough for him! Two pots boiling! Sure, he must have been a hot one!"

Nor are the "holy saints" immune from mockery, as is evidenced by the many versions of the famous dialogue between St. Brendan and the monk Scuthian. To test his virtue, the monk habitually slept between two beautiful girls. Mercier recounts the story:

---

22. *Ibid.*, p. 11.
23. *Ibid.*, p. 12.
24. *Ibid.*, p. 13 .

Now two maidens with pointed breasts used to lie with him every night, that the battle with the Devil might be the greater for him. And it was proposed to accuse him on that account. So Brenainn came to test him, and Scothin said: "Let the cleric lie in my bed tonight," saith he. So when he reached the hour of resting the girls came into the house wherein was Brenainn, with their lapfuls of glowing embers in their chasubles; and the fire burnt them not, and they spill [the embers] in front of Brenainn, and go into the bed to him. "What is this?" asks Brenainn. "Thus it is that we do every night," say the girls. They lie down with Brenainn, and nowise could he sleep with longing. "That is imperfect, O cleric," say the girls; "he who is here every night feels nothing at all. Why goest thou not, O cleric, into the tub [of cold water] if it be easier for thee? 'Tis often that the cleric, even Scothin, visits it." "Well," says Brenainn, "it is wrong for us to make this test, for he is better than we are." Thereafter they make their union and their covenant, and they part *feliciter*.[25]

The grotesque and macabre components of the play-spirit are also strongly sexual. The "wake games"—those bizarre forms of jolliness with which the Irish celebrated death—involved kissing, mock marriages, and gross phallic symbolism as well as "playing tricks on the corpse." Similarly, ridicule of marriage and sex ran through much of the wedding celebrations. Weddings were frequented by masked *crossans* (cross bearers) with grotesque bellies and phalluses as part of their costumes. The clergy managed to clean up the wakes and weddings—more or less—but, as one can tell from an occasional Clancy Brother ballad, the Irish are still laughing behind the back of the priest at the absurdity of both sexual union and death. If one lives very close to the forces of life and death, maybe laughing at them is one way to survive. In any event, it is the way the Irish apparently chose.

Irish comedy is savage. There was no fate worse than having the poets turned loose on you. The bards were satirists and parodists who ridiculed and attacked even the highest in the land. They delighted in stirring up trouble and making things difficult for any king who was reluctant to defend his honor in battle. "The bardic system throve on a constant diet of tribal warfare and cattle raids."[26]

---

25. *Ibid.*, p. 43.
26. *Ibid.*, p. 136.

The poets loved to play with words, to deliver neat and witty epigrams, to engage in wild flights of fantasy; but they were testy, easily angered men, and when they turned their fury on you, you were in great trouble indeed. The later masters of Irish wit and parody and satire, such as Swift, Joyce, and O'Casey, came by their savagery legitimately. And so have the lesser lights:

> "Essex," said Queen Elizabeth, as the two of them sat at breakwhist in the back parlour of Buckingham Palace, "Essex, me haro, I've got a job that I think would suit you. Do you know where Ireland is?"
> "I'm no great fist at jobraphy," says his Lordship, "but I know the place you mane. Population, three million; exports, emigrants."[27]

Vivian Mercier concludes his study with the insistence that comedy is at the center of the Irish literary tradition.

> The Irish comic tradition, then, is not something peripheral, not an interesting bypath for the literary dilettante. On the contrary, one may even claim its right to be considered the central tradition of Irish literature. . . .

> Even the gods are comic; if "they kill us for their sport," we, like Homer, can win a sort of victory by laughing at them in our turn. As I have said before, no aspect of life is too sacred to escape the mockery of Irish laughter. By the fullest exercise of this great human gift the Irish have remained true to one of the deepest impulses of all mankind.[28]

So no matter how serious or grotesque their lives were, they must still laugh at them, and the joke might be scatological and obscene, perhaps, but a joke it remained. This is a dangerous and frequently savage perspective, but it is still one that helps man keep his sanity —and one that curiously enough can easily co-exist with Christian faith.

---

27. Percy French, *Prose, Poems and Parodies of Percy French,* ed. Mrs. De Burgh Daly (Dublin: Talbot Press, 1930), p. 174.
28. Mercier, *op. cit.,* p. 248.

But did the comic tradition cross the Atlantic? In some of the Irish-American writers there can be no doubt that it remained alive. Edwin O'Connor's *The Last Hurrah* is as fantastic a book as one could imagine, and James Michael Curley's reply (*I'd Do It Again*) is even more fantastic. The not sufficiently noticed works of Edward R. F. Sheehan are models of pure Celtic fantasy—combined with the sexuality that apparently got lost when the tradition went into English (though not for Joyce). Flannery O'Connor is an unquestioned master of the macabre and grotesque that can exist alongside profound faith. J. F. Powers' Father Urban may not be Irish but his "mort" is not dissimilar from the fate of poor Cuchulain. Young Tom McHale, in his *Farragan's Retreat,* serves up a gross mixture of the fantastic, the grotesque, the blasphemous, the satirical, and the tragic, which indicates that even the younger generation are not immune from the tradition. And Mr. Dooley could have attended the bardic schools. Finally, one need only read the Foreword to this book to see that at least one Irish statesman (Mr. Moynihan is now probably old enough to be called that) is still capable of laughter—probably too capable of it for his own good.

I should like to think that Chapter 15 of this book, "The South Side Irish Since the Death of Studs," is part of the tradition in the sense that it pokes fun at something one dearly loves.[29] How attenuated the tradition is in me was obvious when I read Mercier's book. We have all become dreadfully civilized, and when civilization comes, the play-spirit takes flight, to be replaced by sober, serious, respectable (I almost added "Protestant") dullness.

The American Irish have become very respectable and hence very serious. If you are serious, you can't laugh at important things, and certainly you can't laugh at yourself. There was a time when if you made fun of an Irishman he might poke you in the mouth or, more likely, make fun back at you. Now, he broods on his offended dignity and carefully analyzes every word you said with deadly literalness. So even the Irish cannot understand the flights of word-play and fantasy in which someone like Mr. Moynihan engages.

---

29. Maybe this whole book is.

That the deadly serious reformers and journalists of Cambridge, Chevy Chase, and Midtown wonder "what he really means" is understandable, but that he and the few others like him who still remain are not understood by the Irish is a sad sign of the time.

The Irishman who can no longer laugh at life and death, too, has ceased to be Irish. Bad luck for him.

Someone ought to turn the poets loose on him.

Finally, the Celtic tradition was an heroic one. Not only were many of the great poetic works about legendary heroes, but the most admired behavior in the land was modeled after theirs. This heroic culture did not have an opportunity to develop a philosophical, administrative, or scientific perspective as did its sister cultures of Athens and Rome; it was frozen in time by foreign conquest. But peculiarly enough, it was kept alive in the peasant society (whence came most of the American Irish) by the very foreign conquest that had prevented its further development. The Irish heroes were proud men, and they had something to be proud of. Theirs was a full, rich tradition, particularly gifted in song and story, and though it was a rural culture, MacNeill notes that "it was probably as high a development of rural life as any country had produced in any age."[30] MacNeill notes that the Irish nobility may have been "the most intensely proud class of men that ever existed.[31] Not only had they built a great culture, not only had their culture become cosmopolitan with the addition of Greek and Roman learning and Christian belief; the Irish nobles had not been conquered by the Romans, they were untouched by the Germans, they even managed to drive back the Danes after a century and a half of fierce battles. Yet their very success was their downfall. "Two thousand years of unbroken sway may suffice to set pride above prudence in the tradition of any class. . . . when the Irish nobles were scattered over Europe, the nobility of their bearing and the distinction of their manners won admiration for them in every land but one."[32]

> This intense pride is blazoned on the pages of our medieval literature, in annals, genealogies, stories, poems. . . .

---

30. MacNeill, *op. cit.*, pp. 353–354.
31. *Ibid.*, p. 354.
32. *Ibid.*, p. 355.

> Too much pride blinded the native rulers of Ireland to the
> insecurity of their state, and made them careless of their safety,
> and neglectful of the measures it required. Glorying in the
> long vista of their past, they did not look before them. They
> were conservative, inadaptable, unproviding. Herein lay the
> fatal weakness of medieval Ireland.[33]

Again we are faced with a parallel between what seems to be
frequent behavior among the American Irish (particularly in their
early years in this country) and the Celtic heritage. Nor will anyone
who has encountered an argumentative and slightly tipsy Irishman
at a cocktail party think that the tradition is entirely dead. As a
matter of fact, many American Irish may not even need a drink to
become victims of that "fierce pride that is their undoing."

A parallel is not a proven theory, but it is worth noting that the
Celtic heritage lasted a long time. At the time of the Famine there
might well have been two million Irishmen whose first language
was Irish. The famous "hedge schools" of the penal times (so called
because in warm weather they were held on the sunny side of
the hedge to avoid detection by the British) were frequently taught
in Irish. They heavily emphasized poetry and often insisted on
mastery of Greek and Latin. Such mastery shocked British observers
who thought it was foolish for an inferior people to bother with
such useless learning, but it impressed teachers at the continental
colleges which some of the hedge school graduates were able to
attend.[34]

Even though the Irish language was dying out in the middle of the
nineteenth century, and the Gaelic heritage with it, still the language
was strong in the west of Ireland where most of the ancestors of the
American Irish came from. It is therefore quite likely that the immigrants who arrived between 1850 and 1900 bore remnants of that
heritage. (Curiously enough, I know of no American Irishman who
has any memory of Irish being spoken in his family's past; repression of the memory of this "inferior" language must have been most
effective.) A tradition which was two thousand years in its develop-

---

33. *Ibid.,* p. 355.
34. For details about the hedge schools, see P. J. Dowling, *The Hedge
Schools of Ireland* (Cork: Mercier Press, 1968).

ment and which survived more than six hundred years of oppression ought to have had some vitality left in it even during its dying days. More research on this is surely needed; it seems possible that some traces of the old tradition did cross the Atlantic in the years after the Famine.

The American Irish may be—or at least may have been—good storytellers, good lawyers, good politicians, good talkers, but few of them have known why they were good at those things and still fewer cared. Today the American Irish could not care less about their Celtic past, even though it may still lurk in their unconscious minds.

Irish culture was shaped by more than the Celtic heritage. From the Danes (who, by the way, were defeated and assimilated after two centuries of conflict) the Irish learned about towns, ports, and roads. From the Normans they learned about more elaborate social structures. From the Anglo-Irish they learned English and the arts of parliamentary politics (indeed, learned the latter all too well, from the Anglo-Irish point of view). Most recently they learned from the English how to run a civil, two-party (or perhaps two-and-a-half party) democracy with an unarmed law-enforcement agency. From the English, too, they learned how to use planning as a means of building economic prosperity. Most of these influences also have had their impact on the American Irish, although it is difficult to sort them out. But the Celtic heritage was the raw material with which those forces worked. If the American Irish ever become interested in understanding themselves—and I doubt that they will —they will have no choice but to face their Celtic past.

It is not certain yet that the desperate attempts of the Irish government to keep the Gaelic language and cultural heritage alive will be successful. I began my study of the Celtic heritage with the feeling that the attempts were quaint but foolish. I will admit that I have changed my mind. Even a very superficial contact with the Celtic tradition persuades me that it is eminently worth saving. I still doubt that it can be saved, and that is a great loss for everyone —the native Irish, the American Irish, and the rest of the world.

And so:

Stony seaboard, far and foreign,
  Stony hills poured over space,
Stony outcrop of the Burren,
  Stones in every fertile place,
Little fields with boulders dotted,
Grey-stone shoulders saffron-spotted,
Stone-walled cabins thatched with reeds,
Where a Stone Age people breeds
  The last of Europe's stone age race.[35]

---

35. From John Betjeman, "Sunday in Ireland," in *A Book of Ireland,* ed. Frank O'Connor (London and Glasgow: William Collins Sons and Company, 1959, Fontana Books, 1971), p. 28.

4.

The Church

Against all Satan's spells and wiles,
Against false words of heresy,
Against the knowledge that defiles,
Against the heart's idolatry,
Against the wizard's evil craft,
Against the death wound and the burning,
The choking wave, the poisoned shaft,
Protect me, Christ, till Thy returning.

Christ be with me, Christ within me,
Christ behind me, Christ before me,
Christ beside me, Christ to win me,
Christ to comfort and restore me,
Christ beneath me, Christ above me,
Christ in quiet, Christ in danger,
Christ in hearts of all that love me,
Christ in mouth of friend and stranger.

"The Breastplate of St. Patrick"
Translated from the Irish by
Frances Alexander 1820–95

There was one thing the Irishman did have, whether he was scheming rebellion, dying of famine, fighting fever on the ship, struggling to make it through the slums of New York City, or attending the wake of a man like my grandfather who died working in the sewers at the age of forty-five. That was his religion.

The Irishman clung to his religion as though it were all he had, and frequently it was.

One of the most striking aspects of American Irish Catholicism is its papalism. Nowhere in the Catholic world, with the possible exception of some of the offices of the Roman Curia, has the cult of papal personality been so strong as it is in the United States, and while the disastrous reign of Paul VI has freed many Catholics from this cult—and made not a few of them contemptuous of the papacy—it is certainly true that in the hierarchy and many of the older clergy, loyalty to the papacy is at the very core of the Catholic world-view. One need only experience the servility with which most American bishops deal with the apostolic delegate to understand the strength of this papalism. The Irish remember that a pope turned them over to the tender mercies of the English. They know also that the papacy was frequently willing to give the English government considerable control over Irish ecclesiastical affairs. They are aware of the papal condemnations of many Irish freedom organizations (including the Fenians). They may even recall that an Irish ecclesiastical tradition grew up relatively independent, and flourished in the early Middle Ages when Rome was a city torn by the factional quarrels of noble families with the pope as a pawn. The Irish bishops seem a good deal more jealous of their own prerogatives and the independence of their tradition than do their American counterparts.[1] It is not that the Irish hierarchy, clergy, and laity are in any sense anti-papal or that the pope couldn't count on their support.[2] I think, rather, that the Irish Church is less con-

---

1. Part of the unwritten legend about the late Archbisop "Willy" O'Brien of Chicago recounts his visit with Cardinal Stritch to the home of an Irish bishop. "Willy's" secretary had told him that in Ireland every bishop considered himself a pope within the limits of his own diocese. O'Brien noted that the bishop sat at the head of the table, demoting Cardinal Stritch to his right hand. Conversation was dominated by the bishop, his staff seconding every statement, thus allowing the Cardinal little time to get a word in edgewise. "Willy" stage-whispered to his secretary across the table, "Jawn, you were right. This bastard does think he's the pope."

2. One of the jokes during the Vatican Council was that the members of the Roman Curia got on the train to go to Trent in northern Italy because they viewed the Council as nothing more than a continuation of that counter-Reformation assembly. The comeback crack was, "And the Irish hierarchy flew to Nicaea."

cerned about Rome and feels quite capable of going its own way. Irish-American Catholicism seems to feel deeply inferior vis-à-vis Rome, Irish Irish Catholicism seems to feel just a trifle superior.

Perhaps with cause, since Irish Catholicism is very ancient. In one of the periodic conflicts over the daying of Easter which raged between Ireland and Rome, St. Columbanus could proudly claim that his calendar was more ancient in origin than the Roman calendar. The stance the Irish took in these controversies with Rome and their efforts at reform was that they were the conservatives defending the tradition against Roman innovation.

The best of modern scholarly efforts conclude that St. Patrick was an historical figure and that his *Confession* and *Letter* are authentic.[3] All other material about him are later legends, frequently composed to support the claims of superiority of his see of Armagh.[4]

There were territorial dioceses and territorial bishops in Ireland from the time of St. Patrick, but the predominant ecclesiastical organization was the monastery and the *paruchia,* or confederation of monasteries extending far beyond the boundaries of the individual kingdoms. Either the bishop became a minor functionary of the abbey, responsible for ordaining priests, or he became a member of the staff of the king. In either case, unless he also happened to be

---

3. For a review of the "Patrick question," see Ludwig Bieler, "St. Patrick and the Coming of Christianity," in Patrick J. Corish, *A History of Irish Catholicism,* Vol. I, No. 1 (Dublin: Gill and Son, 1967).

4. Even today Ireland is the only country in the world which has two primates. The Archbishop of Dublin is the Primate of Ireland, and the Archbishop of Armagh (Patrick's successor) is the Primate of All Ireland. Dublin also has two cathedrals within walking distance of one another—the lovely Norman Christ's Church and the austere, Gothic St. Patrick's. The former was at one time staffed by a cathedral chapter of Irish religious while the latter was staffed by a cathedral chapter of Anglo-Norman seculars. Since both chapters claimed the right to elect the Archbishop, there was frequent conflict between the two, which first the papacy and then the English government had to worry about. Both cathedrals were taken over by the Church of Ireland (Anglican) during the Reformation and were never reclaimed by the Irish Republic. Most of the Catholic cathedrals are little more than nineteenth-century parish churches—with the exception of a massive gray monstrosity recently erected in Galway. Rumor has it that the Anglican bishop of Galway was willing to return the ancient cathedral, a small but attractive Gothic gem, to his Catholic colleague, since there were not enough Anglicans in Galway to use it; but the Catholic bishop was not interested in such a deal. Ireland may have become Christian under Patrick, but it was not a Christianity free from rivalry and contentiousness.

the abbot of the monastery, he had little power. Eventually many of the territorial bishops did become abbots, and the monastery system was for all practical purposes the church structure of Ireland—much to the horror of strict Roman canonists. There were a number of reasons for this development: the lack of cities and towns which could be diocesan centers, the personal rather than territorial Irish approach to fealty, and the custom of holding land as a family group rather than as individuals. The system worked rather well in Ireland, but it was a constant source of shock to English and continental observers. One of the reasons why Pope Adrian IV "gave" Ireland to his English relatives was that he hoped for a reform of the Irish ecclesiastical structure that would bring it into line with the practices of the rest of the Church.

Christianity was able to adapt rather easily to the Irish social structure. Priests and Monks replaced druids and prophets. Greek and Latin learning appealed to the Irish hunger for knowledge. The Church was able to moderate the constant tribal bickering (though not to eliminate it). Much of the artistic effort that had gone into decorating armor and war chariots was put to more peaceful purposes. As Professor Kathleen Hughes remarks:

> The Christian church had embraced all that was congenial in heroic society, its honour and generosity, its splendour and display, its enthusiasm, its respect for learning: in so doing, she had shed some of her classical trappings, and had become a Celtic church. Her strength and weakness lay in her full adjustment to her environment.[5]

One Christian custom that the Church had difficulty in selling to the Irish was clerical celibacy. Apparently the Irish commitment to concubinage was so strong (and outlined in great detail in the customary law) that the Church had to be content, at least in the beginning, with bishops having only one wife. In later years, married men were ordained if they would promise not to live with their wives any longer. However, this regulation seems not to have been very effective, and later writers, like Columbanus, were willing to

5. Kathleen Hughes, *The Church in Early Irish Society* (London: Methuen & Co. Ltd.), p. 156.

permit the married cleric to live with his family so long as he did not cohabit with his wife. One suspects that these regulations were not always honored.

By no means all the higher clergy obeyed the laws of celibacy. Bishops and abbots had children, and many monasteries were passed from father to son. In addition, the abbots were also military and political leaders who engaged in battles with other monasteries, sacking and killing when they encountered opposition. One abbot-king, Feidilmid of Cashel (820–847), terrorized the countryside and killed rival abbots and kings with equal vigor. There is evidence that twenty-seven kings of Cashel ruled "under a crozier," although this may mean only that they were in holy orders and not necessarily that they were bishops. The Church, then, transformed Ireland and at the same time Ireland transformed the Church. As Professor Hughes notes:

> The church had been founded as a religious force, and such it remained; but by the seventh century it had become an institution accommodated to secular law, and by the end of the eighth century certain churches were beginning to play a more direct and decisive part in secular politics. As we have seen, most of the so-called "abuses" in the church which are usually ascribed to the evil effects of the Viking settlements were present before the Vikings arrived. Yet they did not exclude the beneficial uses of power. An ambitious monastic community, willing to fight for its own advantage, could also use its wealth to encourage learning and art; abbots who succeeded their fathers in office made efforts to maintain peace and order in society; they saw to it that the sacraments were performed, that Christianity was preached and hospitality provided. During the eighth century ascetic discipline had become increasingly (though not universally) relaxed, but the church still respected ascetic practice and was still conscious of her spiritual mission.[6]

The Irish Church was not merely different in structure from the rest of the Western church; it had developed practices and customs which were bound to be offensive to Roman authorities and their advance agents in Britain and France. Married clergy, lay abbots,

---

6. Hughes, *op. cit.*, p. 172.

sons succeeding their fathers as abbots and bishops, offices held in plurality, constant and frequently bloody strife among monastic confederations—all these seemed to cry out for reform; and there were ambitious political leaders who were only too ready to use ecclesiastical reform as a pretext for aggression.

Irish monasticism and Irish liturgy had much in common with what we now call the Eastern Church. By our standards, and even by the relatively gentle standards of the Benedictines, monasticism was fiercely ascetic, and the liturgy was much more elaborate than the simple, reserved Roman rite. Scholars suggest that both the monasticism and the liturgy of Ireland came from Gaul of the third, fourth, and fifth centuries and that those traditions, effectively wiped out in Europe by barbarian invasions, survived in Ireland and in some places in the British Isles and Spain remote enough to evade the barbarian invasion and later papal reform.

The Irish liturgy, for example, as contained in the *Stowe Missal*, prays for the "most pious emperors," which indicates a time when there were two Roman Emperors; and the prayer for the living in the *Stowe Missal* reminds one of the prayers of petition of the Eastern Church (which have now found their way back into the Western Church in the liturgical reform of the Vatican Council).

> *the body of their elders*
> *and of all ministers,*
> *virgins and widows,*
> *tempering of the air,*
> *fertility of the fruit of the earth,*
> *return of peace and the end of strife,*
> *kings, and the peace of the people,*
> *return of captives,*
> *forgiveness of our sins,*
> *repose of the dead,*
> *prosperity of our journey,*
> *the hierarchy,*
> *the Roman Empire,*
> *the Christian kings,*
> *erring and the sick*[7]

---

7. John Hennig, "Old Ireland and Her Liturgy," *Old Ireland*, edited by Robert McNally, S.J. (New York: Fordham University Press, 1965), pp. 78–79.

Irish spirituality was fierce; the body was not to be trusted, and penances and punishments were imposed. Fasting, confinement to the cell, and blows with the scourge are examples of penalties in St. Columbanus' *Rule*. Some monastic imperfections were punished with 200 blows of the scourge, twenty-five at a time. The monk who showed up at Mass unshaven was to receive six blows.

The highest form of penance was self-exile or pilgrimage, and the most noble act of Irish monasticism was the vow of pilgrimage. The great Irish missionaries such as Columbanus and Columcille were in fact not missionaries in the modern sense of the word. They took the vow of pilgrimage and left Ireland as a form of penance. Their work with the pagans in France and Germany was a secondary impact of the primarily penitential nature of their wandering. St. Brendan the Navigator was not an explorer like his successors from the north who looked for new lands. He was a pilgrim venturing forth because of a vow of self-exile.[8]

While there is no doubt that those pilgrim monks brought Christianity and civilization to many parts of Europe, it is also true that they did not fare well with the local citizenry. Anglo-Saxon St. Boniface, for example, complained about the nonconformism and individualism of the Irish clergy who worked side by side with him in the east Frankish kingdom.[9] O'Sullivan describes the stormy career of St. Columbanus in Gaul:

> St. Columbanus's stay in Gaul was stormy, to say the least. His *Letters* and *Sermons* give evidence of a sharp denunciatory tongue that whip-lashed the local episcopate, exposing their sins for all to see. His tone toward Pope Gregory, while respectful and conscious of the papal primacy, was at times equally sharp. The local bishops retaliated by criticizing his

---

8. We will leave to others the debate as to whether Brendan or any of his followers reached North America. Samuel Eliot Morison tells us that the Irish monks certainly reached Iceland, probably Greenland, and that it is at least possible that some of them washed up on the shores of North America. Morison thinks it plausible that the legendary account of Brendan's trip contains the germ of a story of a voyage that actually happened, but even interpreting his story at face value does not, according to Morison, give us any reason to think that he got beyond the Azores.

9. McNally, *Old Ireland*, p. x (Introduction).

peculiar Irish tonsure which called for the front of the head being shaved. . . . But nowhere did St. Columbanus shine more than in his stand on the bad morality of the royal court, so much so that Queen Brunhilda ordered him to be expelled from the land in 610.[10]

I have often wondered whether the ease with which the Irish missionaries still depart for the farthest points of the world may have some connection with the ancient tradition of the *peregrinatio pro Christo.*[11]

Irish monasticism, with its hundreds of blows from the scourge, its long hours of prayers, strict fasts, and hundreds of genuflections, strikes us as a bit bizarre and nonhuman. Yet, because its forms are different from those with which we are familiar and its style is difficult for us to comprehend, it does not follow that there was not much goodness and insight in the monasticism of the Irish. One of the ancient prayers indicates that the montastic spirituality was not without power and beauty.

> *May thou be my vision,*
> *O God of my heart;*
> *no one else in anything,*
> *but the king of the seven heavens.*
>
> *May thou be my meditation*
> *by day and by night;*
> *may it be thou I see*
> *ever in my sleep.*
>
> *May thou be my speech,*
> *may thou be my understanding,*
> *may thou be to me,*
> *may I be to thee.*
>
> *May thou be my father,*
> *may I be thy son;*

10. Jeremiah O'Sullivan, "Old Ireland and Her Monasticism," in McNally, p. 107.

11. Father Conor Ward points out to me that there are as many Irish-born priests serving outside the country as in it—some 6,500. Some 1,200 of these are in Great Britain and another 1,500 in the United States and Canada. The rest are scattered all over the world.

may thou be mine,
may I be thine.

May thou be my battle-shield,
may thou be my sword,
may thou be my honour,
may thou be my joy.

May thou be my protection,
may thou be my fortress;
may it be thou who will raise me
to the assembly of angels.

May thou be every good
to my body, to my soul;
may thou be my kingdom
in heaven and on earth.

May thou alone
be the special love of my heart;
may it be no one else
but the High King of heaven.[12]

Whether the peculiar forms of Irish monasticism were an importation of early Christianity (before the much more gentle style of Benedictine monasticism became common in Western Europe) or a reflection of Celtic culture is a question which, so far as I have been able to learn from scholars, has not yet been answered in any sort of satisfactory way. Part of the difficulty, of course, is that both the monastic culture with its high-quality scholarship and art and the pre-Christian culture, which the monasteries to some extent preserved and transformed, were practically obliterated by the Viking invasions of the ninth century. All that seems to have survived are a few ruined old churches, some Celtic crosses, names and runes of monastaries such as Clonmacnois and Glendalough, and, of course, the names and memories of the Saints immortalized in parish churches in all the large cities of America—Columcille, Columbanus, Killian, Brendan, Brigid, Mel, Finbar, Kevin, and that well-known immigrant, Patrick.

It is difficult to assess how much ancient Irish religious influences persist into the present time. Irish Catholicism (Irish or American)

---

12. Hennig, in McNally, pp. 44–45.

is largely a counter-Reformation phenomenon. The Irish hierarchy, for example, was not particularly opposed to the early efforts of Henry VIII to achieve national ecclestiastical supremacy, and the success of the counter-Reformation in Ireland owes something at least to the identification of Catholicism with the freedom of the Irish nation, an identification forced on the Irish by their British oppressors.

We know very little about the religion of the ordinary Irish people between the Danish invasion of the ninth century and the counter-Reformation seven centuries later. Christians they surely were, but their Christianity, in all likelihood, was no more free of pre-Christian superstition than that of other peasant peoples in Europe. The survival of the ancient folklore leads one to assume that the medieval Irish must have had their share of banshees, leprechauns, pookies, and other bizarre creatures, which, however much fun they may be to the American Irish, were taken rather more seriously by the people in the west of Ireland who had to live with them.[13]

"The little people," the "good people," the "gentry," or simply "they" are in all probability Celtic deities which have survived in a transmuted form alongside official Christianity.[14] While it is rare to find the fairies in Dublin, Cork, or Galway, they were present in County Clare at the time of Kimball's study in the 1930s and in the Aran Islands during Messenger's research in the late 1950s.

There are trooping and solitary fairies. The former are relatively benign and spend most of their time feasting, singing, dancing,

---

13. What respectable banshee, leprechaun, or pookie would show up on the South Side of Chicago?

14. Whether they are good or evil spirits is a matter for discussion. They are not diabolic in the strict sense of the word, though surely the behavior of some of them is evil. One school of thought holds that they are the souls of unbaptized children. Another suggests that they are a group of unfortunates who must work out their purgatory on earth. Still another explanation is that they are the angels who sat on the fence during the War in Heaven between Lucifer and Michael. Since they had kept clear of the former they couldn't be sent to hell; and since they had not rallied to the cause of the latter they couldn't stay in heaven. They were therefore informed that they were being exiled to earth, and as a special favor they could choose where they wanted to go. They opted for Ireland on the grounds that it was the place on earth most like heaven. Indeed!

fighting with each other, playing spirited games, and making love. They generally leave humans alone, unless humans offend them, in which case the fairies respond either with pranks or vicious punishment. Occasionally a fairy will fall in love with a human and carry her (or occasionally him—there are female fairies, too) off. Also they may courteously prepare a coffin when they know someone in a village is going to die; hence the sound of the fairies making a coffin is a sure sign of death.

The solitary fairies include the banshee—a withered, wailing hag whose presence indicates that death is at hand but only for families to whom she has traditionally attached herself; and the pookah—an animal spirit with crude rough manners. But the most famous of the solitary fairies is the leprechaun. There are really three different spirits who constitute this fascinating creature—or maybe it is only three different manifestations of the same spirit:

1. The leprechaun is the fairy cobbler, an uncivil and unpleasant character who has either a pot of gold or at least a coin in his purse which he must give you if you catch him. He cannot trick you into letting go.

2. The cluricaun is a bit of a sot and spends most of his time stealing drink from people's liquor stores.

3. The red man is a poltergeist, a practical joker who wears pointed cap and delights in pranks, from which he is driven only by holy water.

Obviously no such creatures exist. Yet in the midst of his sober, scholarly study of the Aran Islands, John Messenger makes the startling claim that a red man attached himself to Messenger and his wife while they were on Inis Beag and then followed them home to such a very non-Celtic place as East Lansing, Michigan.[15]

This particular red man, appropriately named Brendan, has achieved enough notoriety to be immortalized in the studious pages of the *American Anthropologist*.[16]

15. John C. Messenger, *Inis Beag, Isle of Ireland* (New York: Holt, Rinehart, and Winston, 1969), p. 99.
16. ———, "A Critical Re-examination of the Concept of Spirits," *American Anthropologist*, April 1962, pp. 367–373.

We named him "Brendan" for a literary figure who occasionally visits Inis Beag and is renowned among the islanders for his love of "spirits" and his practical jokes. Our friends thought it strange for us to name a *leipreachán,* since it is not an Irish custom to do so. The folk peoples of the west country avoid the fairies, seldom talk about them publicly, and refer to them respectfully as the "gentry" or the "good people" if the need arises. But during our stay on the island, we came to feel the immaterial presence of this creature so intensely and to anticipate his pranks with such enthusiasm that we eventually came to view him as a third member of our family, well deserving an affectionate and suitable name.

Initially, Brendan's particular mode of expression was to open our door or one of our windows during the night when we were asleep, a practice that continued intermittently month after month, no matter how carefully we checked bolted door and locked windows before retiring. At first we suspected an actual or potential thief, but nothing was ever stolen; besides, crime of any nature is virtually unknown on the island. Then we considered a practical joker, but no one ever admitted "codding" us in this manner, and local pranksters eventually call attention to their deeds. Finally, after examining and discarding in turn other possible explanations, we were forced to conclude that a leipreachán had taken up residence in our apartment and was calling attention to his presence in this way.

Our neighbor, an elderly, unmarried nurse who lived in the adjoining apartment of our ancient building, complained of hearing violin music emanating from beneath the eaves outside her bedroom window late at night. Her door and windows were never opened, and we never heard violin music, but Brendan may have been responsible for both. We don't know if the music continues, but we suspect not, for it has become obvious that Brendan returned home with us.[17]

When he came to East Lansing, Brendan really began to raise hell.

Brendan has always shown a predilection for opening doors and windows, but after settling down here he soon took to switching on the basement lights and manipulating the thermostat. When the weather first became uncomfortably

17. *Ibid.,* p. 367.

cold in late October, we turned on the furnace and kept the thermostat at 68 degrees during the day and six degrees cooler at night. The outdoor temperature suddenly rose one night, and we were awakened by the discomfort of being bathed in perspiration. Our warm room was being fed even warmer air from the vent. I hurried downstairs to find the thermostat set at 74 degrees. My immediate reaction was to sit down then and there in the living room and check through in my memory my final movements before retiring; they most certainly did not include pushing *up* the thermostat control! Conversely, a week later, when the thermometer plunged to the lower regions for the first time, we were once again aroused from sleep, but rather from the discomfort of an icy bed. The cause of this condition was an upper window opened wide in the front bedroom, which had been locked since late August. Brendan's great strength was attested by the fact that locking and relocking the window almost proved too much of an effort for me.[18]

There was more in Brendan's bag of tricks than just opening windows.

As well as possessing heroic thews for one so diminutive, Brendan is telepathic. One evening I went to bed suffering from a severe headache and, once comfortably settled under the covers, recalled that I had neglected to take an aspirin. So I swung out of bed muffling curses, but as my feet touched the floor I heard the sound of running water from the bathroom. Both my wife and I were startled into a quick exchange of baffled exclamations, following which I stumbled into the bathroom to find the cold water faucet fully opened. Brendan had anticipated my desire. It took us more than an hour to recover from this experience and compose ourselves for sleep. Had the aspirin bottle with cover removed been standing on the ledge above the cooperative tap, we would never have slept that night. However, Brendan is seldom too obvious. Another example of his psychic powers is his ability to awaken one of us a few minutes before the alarm clock is due to sound, so that we can discover that he has depressed the alarm button sometime during the night. Pulling out the button marks the final stage of an almost compulsive retirement ritual we follow.[19]

18. *Ibid.*, p. 369.
19. *Ibid.*, p. 370.

Brendan began to get his hosts into trouble. How would you like to be a landlady who discovered that an unruly Celtic spirit had settled into your house?

> Early on election day, while standing in a cold schoolroom at the end of a long, slow moving line that led to two polling booths, my wife and I had occasion to chat for several minutes with our landlady. She introduced the subject of cold weather and storm windows, which gave rise to a train of thoughts in my mind leading, as you might guess, to Brendan. I very cautiously broached the subject of self-opening doors and windows in her half of the duplex, but found that her doors and windows opened only at her own bidding. Soon her curiosity was aroused by my further, rather clumsy probing into the allied matter of self-regulating basement light switches and thermostat controls, and I was at last put into the position of revealing all. Rather than describing the uncommon happenings either in a light manner, punctuating my conversation with gay laughter, or in a serious mode consonant with my genuine sentiments, I unfortunately tried to do both. This left her bewildered, to say the least, not knowing whether or not to believe me and possibly a little uncertain as to the wisdom of renting to us. I have not mentioned the matter again in her presence, nor has she in mine. This is an unfortunate state of affairs, for I forgot to ask her about hearing violin music. The Inis Beag nurse refuses to answer our questions concerning her island virtuoso, and we are curious to know if Brendan has a penchant for entertaining elderly widows and spinsters with lively jigs.[20]

The Messengers had assumed that their leprechaun was in fact a red man—a west of Ireland prankster. But soon there was evidence of other proclivities.

> In Eire we could never induce Brendan to drink our whiskey; thus we were forced to conclude that he was either a deviant or a member of the Pioneer Total Abstinence Society. Early in December, surprisingly, he began to imbibe. I became aware of it when twice the cork was pushed only part way into the neck of the bottle, a practice that my wife and I assiduously try to avoid. So we began to mark the

20. *Ibid.*

liquid level by pencilling a line on the label each time that we put the bottle away. Frequent inspections of the fifth revealed that at least once each week the level dropped an eighth of an inch. Does such pilfering reflect Brendan's size, or is he an inexperienced drinker, polite, or of the opinion that he is outwitting us? More important, however, is the question: why did he choose to reveal his clúracán tendencies here rather than on Inis Beag? Possibly he disliked the Tullamore Dew that we ordered monthly from a shop on the mainland, as did some of the islanders, but finds the Powers that we brought back with us (duty free) more to his taste. On the other hand, he may be reading our magazines and has been taken in by those clever Whiskey Distillers of Ireland advertisements.

None of Brendan's doings are malicious, you must understand. The fairies most often harm those who have maltreated them, and many fairy pranks are gestures of amicability. A careful examination of the circumstances surrounding Brendan's many deeds reveals that each is committed shortly before our attention is drawn to it, as in the case of the impotent alarm clock. The purloined whiskey is, of course, another story, but Brendan knows that we can well afford a thimbleful of Irish each week. We do wish, however, that he would switch his allegiance to the cheap Scotch or bourbon we keep on hand to serve guests who insist upon mixed drinks. Irish whiskey is never cheap in this state.[21]

As is the fate of most academics, the Messengers have been in many places since East Lansing. Whether Brendan has accompanied them, I know not. Could he live in Bloomington or Columbus? There are places which would be too much even for a leprechaun. But if the Messengers ever come to Chicago, Brendan would make an excellent precinct captain.

Everyone, of course, knows there are no such creatures.

A good deal more scholarly work must be done to separate the various components of Irish Catholicism. To what extent, for example, is the sexual puritanism of the Irish a result of the Jansenist influence on the Irish clergy who were trained during Penal times in French seminaries? To what extent the much more ancient roots

---

21. *Ibid.*, p. 371.

of early monasticism and pre-Christian culture have influenced modern Ireland is a fascinating and as yet unanswered question.

But whatever the rigidities, the austerities, and, by our standards, the incredible self-mutilation of Irish monasticism, it did keep alive one ancient practice that seems anything but Jansenistic, and would profoundly shock most modern Irishmen. Not very many Irish Catholics have ever heard of agapetism.

It would be good if they did. In the early Church there was a tendency for religious life to be "coeducational." Arguing that conversion in Christ Jesus had enabled them to conquer the flesh and, in the words of St. Paul, they were neither male nor female but one in Christ Jesus, men and women lived lives of religious community together, not only in separate religious monasteries but sometimes in the same dormitories and even in the same beds. The practice, it hardly needs to be said, was viewed with great suspicion by many of the Church, and that splendid old curmudgeon St. Jerome railed against it: no matter what anyone else said he *knew* what went on in those places. Most historians, however, are not quite so suspicious. They are willing to concede that, incredible as it may sound, most of the agapeti communities were indeed platonic —in more than one sense of the word. Agapetism died out in most places of the Church well before the sixth century, but it continued to flourish in Ireland. Apparently there were even monasteries in sixth-century Ireland that were presided over by abbesses who were presumably selected by their colleagues.[22]

The chroniclers tell us the story of the sainted Brendan the sailor and his colleague, the monk Scuthian. Brendan remonstrated with his colleague because the latter had developed the pious practice of sleeping at night between two beautiful virgins. Brendan apparently hinted to Scuthian that the two young women were probably no better than they ought to be, but Scuthian said that he engaged in this practice merely to prove how virtuous he was and what discipline he had over his flesh. Then he challenged the sainted

---

22. If the truth be told, there are Catholic parishes in the United States which are presided over by mothers superior, or housekeepers, or presidents of the women's sodality—or at least there were such parishes before the Vatican Council.

sailor to prove his virtue the same way. Like many other Irishmen since then, the holy navigator was not one to turn away from a challenge, so he recruited two young women—how, the chroniclers do not tell us—and began to emulate the piety of his colleague. However, we are informed that he shortly abandoned the effort, for though he did not lose his virtue, he found the experience most distracting and was unable to sleep at night.

Only in Ireland . . .

Whatever is to be said of the practices of Brendan, Scuthian, and their colleagues, and however interesting and even insightful the experience may have been, it did not represent a tradition that would survive to shape the future forms of Irish Catholicism. More's the pity, perhaps.

It was not only agapetism that was destroyed by the Danish invasion. Dr. Brian O Cuiv[23] describes the religious state of the country in the eleventh century:

> We might suppose that with numerous religious houses throughout Ireland and the missionary movement under way again, the moral well-being of the people was assured. Unfortunately this was not so, for after the long centuries of the Viking wars and consequent upheavals, there was spiritual and moral laxity. Deeds of violence were frequent, even against priests and nuns and against church property. The Sacraments were neglected, there was a reluctance to pay tithes, and the marriage laws of the Church were disregarded. The laxity about marriage, it is true, may have been due to the brehon which differed from the rules of the Church in this regard. However, there was clearly a need for spiritual renewal, and with it reform of the Church itself, for part of the trouble lay in the organisation of the Church which was monastic rather than diocesan, a feature which resulted in a lack of priests engaged in pastoral work. Another characteristic of the Irish church was that there was hereditary succession to certain Church benefices and that these were frequently held by laymen. Of course, to a people accustomed to the principle of hereditary succession in other walks of life, including poetry, this would not have seemed strange.[24]

23. An Irish way of saying O'Keefe.
24. Richard Roche, *The Norman Invasion of Ireland* (Tralee, County Kerry: Anvil Books, 1970, paperback), p. 46.

Hence when the only English pope, Adrian IV Breakspeare, decided to give Ireland to Henry II of England, there was perhaps some legitimate purpose in his action. His Bull declares Henry's responsibility:

> . . . to extend the bounds of the Church, to proclaim to a rude and untaught people the truth of the Christian faith, and to root out nurseries of vice from the field of the Lord. . . . So we . . . are pleased and willing . . . that you shall enter that island and do therein what tends to the honour of God and the salvation of the people.[25]

Pope Breakspeare's plan worked, of course, but hardly in the way he intended, for the combination of the English invasion of Ireland and a later Henry's departure from the Roman church guaranteed that as far as the Irish Catholic was concerned, to be Irish and Catholic meant exactly the same thing.

The contemporary image of fervent and pious Irish orthodoxy leads many to suppose that the Irish were always that way. However, sober accounts of medieval and pre-Reformation Irish behavior present a very different picture.

Divorce, concubinage, and incest (in the sense of marrying within the forbidden degrees of kinship) were widespread, particularly among the aristocracy. The "brehon" (ancient Celtic) law approved of divorce for a wife on the grounds of childlessness, ill treatment, the absence of the husband from the country, criminal conduct, accession to the clerical state, insanity, and incurable disease. For a husband, divorce was justified also on the grounds of childlessness, constant stealing, abortion, child murder, and "general mischief-making." Divorce by mutual consent was lawful, and polygamy was not only tolerated but subject to complex regulation, which dictated the compensation to be paid to a man for the violation of his secondary wives and also the duties and responsibilities of the various degrees of wives. Whether a man was permitted to marry his sister or his daughter is debatable, but he certainly was permitted to marry his stepmother and to take as concubine his brother's wife

---

25. *Ibid.,* p. 43.

while the brother was still alive. It was also possible for a man to live in concubinage with two sisters simultaneously. Such practices persisted even into the fifteenth and sixteenth centuries. The famous reform synod of Cashel in 1101, while it denounced clerical concubinage, did not mention lay marriage customs, probably because so many of the laymen who were delegates to the synod were living according to the provisions of the brehon law.[26]

There were many married priests and bishops, the sacrament of Holy Orders was sold, confirmation was administered without charism (which led St. Bernard in France to conclude that the sacrament was not known in Ireland). "Corabs" and "erenagh"—quasiclerical lay abbots—appropriated Church lands and passed them on to their offspring. Illegitimacy was widespread (one contemporary observer guessed that only one-fifth of the births were legitimate). Church services were irregular, slovenly, or often omitted. Communion was received only once a year; the Sunday Mass regulation was not honored; clandestine marriage was common. In some areas, children were not baptized. By the time of the Reformation, vocations had sadly declined and abbots had become little more than civil princes who exploited the people as much as did their lay counterparts. Religious education and even training for the clergy were almost nonexistent. Gambling, banditry, perjury, violation of contracts, tribal murder were widespread.[27]

Hence the worries of Pope Adrian that caused him to "give" Ireland to the English king were not altogether unjustified. Unfortunately, the English efforts at reform—which included attempts to impose both canon and common law as a substitute for the brehon law—were doomed to be failures, since the Norman invasion created two societies in Ireland and added to the confusion instead of reducing disorder. From many points of view, Irish Catholicism ought to have been ripe for the Reformation.

In truth, many of the nobility and the hierarchy (including Arch-

---

26. See Aubrey Gwynn, "The Twelfth-Century Reform," in Corish, *op. cit.*, Vol. II, No. 1, pp. 4–18.

27. See Canice Mooney, "The First Impact of the Reformation," in Corish, *op. cit.*, Vol. III, No. 2, for details of the Irish religious situation just before the Reformation.

bishop Browne of Dublin) either went along with Henry VIII or at least tried to walk a tightrope between Henry and the Pope. It was only in the time of Elizabeth I that the mass of the Irish people rejected the Reformation just as surely as the mass of the English people accepted it.

There were a number of reasons for the difference. Ireland had no intellectual dissidents such as Wycliffe; the "old Irish" developed a special loyalty to the Pope because it was to him they turned for some kind of equity in the unfair competition with the Anglo-Norman clerics. The main reason why the Irish identified firmly with Rome, however, was the Cromwellian genocide. As Corish puts it:

> The Cromwellian settlement made the "Irish" and "Catholic" synonymous: to be the one was automatically to be the other. It was of course the logical development of previous policy— the union of Catholics in Ireland was, from first to last, a Protestant achievement, not a Catholic one. The decision to which Irish history had been feeling its way for over a hundred years was now finally imposed by the sword of the Lord Protector. It was imposed effectively.[28]

During the Cromwell years when the Papists were being driven to "hell or Connaught," most of the bishops were dead or in exile, and every priest was a hunted man with a price (five pounds) on his head. Concentration camps were set up for priests on the desolate Aran Islands. A large number were deported to the Barbadoes. Priests lived in caves on the mountains and kept on the move to avoid spies and informers. They traveled at night or in disguise, said Mass by moonlight on "Mass rocks" or for small congregations in private homes. The sick were also visited at night, and communion was distributed furtively by priests wandering about disguised as peddlers or farmers.[29]

The worst of the terror came to an end with the restoration of Charles II, but by then the issue was decided: Ireland was irrevo-

---

28. Patrick J. Corish, "The Origins of Catholic Nationalism," in Corish, *op. cit.,* Vol. III, No. 8, p. 57.

29. See Benignus Millet, "Survival and Reorganization, 1650–1695," in Corish, *op. cit.,* Vol. III, No. 7, pp. 1–12.

cably Catholic, and its priests, the only successful resisters of the Cromwellian tyranny, were the acknowledged leaders of their hungry, miserable, persecuted people.

If the Irish are so unquestionably loyal to their church, the reason is not hard to find: they were made loyal by English barbarism.

What did it mean to be Catholic? Again, one must surmise, because there is not much scholarship on the subject. To be Catholic, of course, was to go to church, to receive the Sacraments, and pass on the symbols of faith to one's children; to rally around the parish priest, not only religiously but frequently politically, and to define oneself "Catholic!" against the hated English Protestant; to go on pilgrimages, say the rosary, to fast, make vows, and to feel guilty about one's sinfulness.

But I think it also meant to have a confidence in life. Despite the Jansenism, the self-hatred, the sexual puritanism, that confidence in life gave Irish Catholicism its greatest strength and also its most peculiar institution, the Irish wake.

The official Church was ambiguous about the wake.[30] There were strains of paganism, much drunkenness, and frequently dancing, and the Church was *very* suspicious of dancing. Still, the Church could hardly oppose the idea that death was not the end. Even in contemporary Irish-American Catholicism the wake is an extraordinary phenomenon, both heartless and reassuring, melancholy and rejoicing, unbearably painful and stubbornly hopeful.

It would be easy to write off the wake as merely the symbolic hope for a better hereafter of an oppressed and miserable people who had precious little in this world, a kind of Celtic "pie in the sky." While there is unquestionably some element of that in the wake tradition, there is also, I think, a stubborn refusal to believe that death is the end, a refusal on which, of course, the Irish have

---

30. And even more so about the custom of the "American wake," a ceremony held for someone migrating to America which assumed that he was already dead for all practical purposes, that his "death" must be commemorated and celebrated by his family and friends just as though he were about to be physically buried.

no monopoly, but few people have ever asserted this conviction with so much stubbornness.

I am not sure whether the Irish response to death is healthy or not. When I consider my own reaction to the death of my parents, I frequently think that there was a good deal of grieving that should have occurred and has not, and probably cannot. Whatever can be said about repression of grief (and repression seems to be a characteristically Irish response), I have no doubt that refusal to accept death as the end is at the very core of the Irish religious commitment.

Professor Emmet Larkin of the University of Chicago has made a very persuasive case that the intense level of religious devotion characteristic of the Irish on both sides of the Atlantic is a rather recent phenomenon, dating to the time after the Great Famine of 1847–1849. Part of the problem in the previous half-century was a shortage of priests, with one priest for every 2,100 of the faithful in 1800, and one for every 3,000 four decades later. The Church, badly disorganized from the persecution years, was inundated by a population increase of almost 100 per cent in a few decades. In addition, the clergy were often avaricious, contentious, and un-disciplined, not infrequently given to heavy drinking and on occasion even to adultery. There were not nearly enough churches or chapels, and perhaps no more than 40 per cent of the population went to church each week. Finally, many of the clergy were still working in the casual, free-wheeling style of the persecution days. The hierarchy found it difficult to bring them into line, and its members were not infrequently dragged into court when they tried to exercise discipline.

According to Larkin, the effort of such reformers as the remark-able Cardinal Paul Cullen to modify the ecclesiastical style of a persecution clergy to that of a much more effectively organized and disciplined clergy was aided considerably by the horrors of the Famine, which drove both priests and people back to religion. He suggests that the Famine was a final blow to the old Irish sense of identity. Despite the relative prosperity of the potato economy in the first four decades of the century and the relative success of the O'Connell political movement, the Irish were gradually being

"Britonized" as they lost their culture, their language, and their way of life. In addition to striking terror into their hearts, the Famine gave the final death blow to the old Irish heritage. The "devotional revolution" of the years after the Famine, according to Larkin, provided the Irish (and their American cousins) with a new symbolic language and a new cultural heritage around which a new Irish identity could focus.[31]

There is also some evidence that sexual puritanism may be to some extent a post-Famine phenomenon.

The Irish came to the United States with a stubborn, dogged, counter-Reformation form of Irish Catholicism, about the only explicit cultural form left them by their tragic history. There was no reason why they should have interpreted anything in the Protestant response to their entering the United States as a sign that the Protestant churches were going to be any more friendly to them in the New World than they were in the Old. If religion was all they had in Ireland, it was practically all they had in the United States, too.

The nativist myth insists that the Irish are priest-ridden, a myth that is, incidentally, not completely absent from American society even today. The fact that John Kennedy was able to restrain the exhibition of his piety and had no close priest friends was reckoned a point in his favor; and the columnist Joseph Kraft has recently written admiringly that Senator Muskie does not go to church all that often.

The Irish had immense respect for their clergy. That their respect was not unmixed with fear, particularly in the old country, can scarcely be denied. The nativist mistake, however, is to assume that the respect meant that the Irish took their cleric all that seriously. What they miss completely is that the almost servile respect of Irish behavior toward their priests was in fact a devious Irish way of keeping the cleric in his place. Like most other sacred personages, the parish priest was and is a source of a good deal of ambivalence on the part of his people. Respect was a marvelous way of ex-

---

31. Emmet Larkin, "The Devotional Revolution in Ireland, 1850–1875."

pressing that ambivalence. The priest is praised, honored, fawned upon, and not allowed for a second to step out of his priestly role. In the United States there seems to be more willingness on the part of the Irish to acknowledge the humanity of their priests and to give them some latitude in self-expression and personal relations. A number of times in Ireland I have been surprised to note that interpersonal cues that would have been met with a warm response on the South Side of Chicago are neither liked nor understood by people who have very similar faces in Dublin, Galway, or Mayo. Their response to these cues was not just reverence, it was a warning, total and effective, that I was stepping out of my proper role. The banter between a cleric and teen-agers—particularly teen-age girls —which is not only acceptable but expected on the South Side of Chicago is quickly rejected in Ireland.

Unquestionably, the parish priest is a man of great, but limited, power. He may denounce sin, close down the tavern, suppress the dances at the crossroads, chide the lazy and admonish the unfaithful, but when he enters politics he does so at his own risk—unless he happens to choose the side that his people are already on. The nativist myth says that the people vote the way their clergy tell them to—a myth which the clergy and hierarchy have on occasion tried to sustain for their own purposes. In fact, however, an open endorsement from a parish priest is more likely to be harmful to a candidate. Those priests in the old country who denounced revolutionary activity were not taken seriously by large numbers of their congregations. The priest personifies the religious tradition, and as such he is an extraordinarily important person, especially to those who have little education and no other leaders. The loyalty to the priest and the parish, whether in Ireland or America, is a symbol of the fact that one is Irish and Catholic. It is also an important component of the cement that holds one's community together. But it neither blinds one to the personal failings of the priest, nor compels one to take him seriously as a political or social leader. The nativist may think that when the Irishman says, "Ah, poor Father doesn't feel well this morning," he is blinding himself to the fact that Father is on the bottle again, but no such deception is going on. On the contrary, the Irish may be tolerant about the many alcoholics among the clergy, but they don't deny the fact of alcoholism, and no Irishman is ignorant of the code expression "poor Father doesn't feel well." That Father is an alcoholic is to be lamented, that he may be completely incompetent is to be regretted, but the distinction between his personal characteristics and his priestly role is one that most Irishmen, on either side of the Atlantic, find no difficulty in making.

Some of the younger Irish-American clergy deeply resent the prison of respect (and the resulting clerical culture) that shapes the relationship between priest and people. Some of the younger laity also demand a different style of relationship with their priests. For the young priest especially, the burden of the role of being a sacred personage is far too heavy. They want to be loved for who they are rather than for what they represent. They understand that respect is a way of keeping a priest in his place. What they understand less clearly, perhaps, are the social, historical, and psychological reasons behind the respect.

Man is ambivalent about the sacred, and when it is about the only thing he has in his life, he is likely to be even more ambivalent. As the personification of religion, the priest was inevitably an extremely important and sacred person; that they should admire him, deeply need him, and still fear him was perfectly natural. The younger clergy are quite correct when they say there is a need in a different era for a different relationship, but they are, it seems to me, quite wrong in assuming that the Irish (or indeed anybody in the race) can do without the sacred and without sacred persons. They are also wrong, I think, in writing off the respect of the past as something that had little religious merit; as an act of faith and devotion, it was extremely important to the people. In a way, I suspect, it is still important to many Irish-Americans, even the younger ones.

I am not arguing that the parish priest on either side of the Atlantic was without power in his community. Obviously he had immense power, but he 'had to be very careful how he used it. Frequently he deluded himself as to how effective his exercise of power really was. It is amusing to see how some of the anti-clericals among the Irish-American intelligentsia think that they are the first of the Irish to dare criticize the clergy or the hierarchy. One need only read the works of the nineteenth-century radicals, both in Ireland and the United States, to realize that Irish anticlericalism did not begin with the founding of *Commonweal*. The parish priest, of course, determined how many collections there were to be on a Sunday, which textbooks were to be used in the school, what time the Masses were to be said, when the young people could use the gymnasium, and how the parish books were to be kept. This was part of his role, and few of the Irish laity in the past, or the present either for that matter, wanted to be bothered with such things. (One excepts those perennial parish busybodies who thought they could do a better job than the priest—busybodies who more recently lump their activities under the slogans of "Catholic Action" and "Lay Participation.") But if the pastor was sovereign in parish affairs, and if he laid down the general moral norms by which the community felt obliged to live, his political, social, and economic influence was severely circumscribed. His ventures into party politics either amused the local precinct captain or offended him mightily, but did not seriously threaten his power.

The importance of the priest in the parish in immigrant Catholicism in the United States had little or nothing to do with delivering the Catholic vote, censoring magazine racks, condemning the neighborhood theater for showing dirty movies, urging one's parishioners to have large families, or any of the other mythical hobgoblin activities that the nativists (and more recently their Jewish allies) have depicted as the function of the parish priest. The parish was, on the contrary, a symbol of loyalty around which the immigrants and their children and grandchildren could rally in a society that was at first hostile and then not especially friendly. For many of us, it is no exaggeration to say that the parish was the center of our lives; it provided us with education, recreation, entertainment, friendships, and potential spouses. It was a place to belong. When asked where we came from, we named the parish rather than street or neighborhood. A simpleminded analysis might argue that it was something the clergy forced upon us, particularly through the parochial school system. In fact, however, I suspect that the opposite was the case: the parochial school system was the result of Irish parochial loyalty rather than the cause. Far from forcing the structure of the comprehensive immigrant parish, the clergy were given little choice but to provide such parochial services for their people. Indeed, even in the post-Vatican Church, when many of the clergy tried to break out of the structure of the comprehensive parish, they found that substantial majorities of their laity protested strongly. What the Irish suburbanites want is not the frequently authoritarian parish of the old neighborhood but rather a democratized version of that parish. The suggestion that they ought not to have any parish at all seems to them to be dangerously close to blasphemy.

Not all of us were deeply involved in the parish life. I suppose that even in the 1930s most of the people in the parish I lived in spoke with the parish priest rarely. I can think of only a couple of times in my life, in fact, that the priest was in our house. Neither my father nor my mother were active in parochial societies, and we rarely attended parish social functions. Yet we thought of ourselves as very much part of the parish, admired and respected the priests, and would proudly say "St. Angela" when asked where we were from. The importance of the parish, I suspect, was not that we were actively involved in it, but that it was there. The possibility for active involvement when we wanted it was a symbolic context for our lives.

The parish was a name; in other words, a symbolic expression of an ideology around which an Irish Catholic community rallied during the years of the Great Depression and the Second World War. Our friendship patterns were largely with people in the parish, even though there was no necessary connection between these patterns and our religious devotion or involvement in parish activities.[32]

Despite the Vatican Council, despite the emergence of a younger

---

32. In my research on Irish Catholics at a country club I found that (a) Catholics play golf most of the time with other Catholics, particularly with other Catholics from their own parishes, and (b) there was no relationship between religious devotion and the choice of fellow parishioners as golf companions; indeed, on the contrary, the few ecumenical golfers were also the most devout parishioners.

clergy looking for "relevance" through radical political and social action, I very much doubt that this attitude toward the parish and priest has been substantially modified in recent years. The well-to-do and the well-educated Irish parishes I know may be more democratic, more flexible, more free-wheeling than their immigrant predecessors, but they are still parishes, and, *mutatis mutandis,* are still expected to play very similar roles in the lives of their people. The priest may be called by his first name and he may not wear a Roman collar, but he is still expected to be a religious symbol, a community leader, a man to turn to in time of trouble, and a source of reassurance in time of conflict. The Irish intelligentsia may write very learned articles for the *National Catholic Reporter* or *Commonweal* about the demise of the immigrant parish, the need for part-time clergy, small-group communities, married priests and deacons, and a wide variety of other reforms which would make Irish Catholicism quite indistinguishable from Methodism. They may even be correct, for in the post-Vatican Church, some parochial structures will take these new forms, and there will be much greater pluralism in many parishes; but most of these intelligentsia (or would-be intelligentsia) and their admirers in the clergy are quite mistaken if they think that is what the majority—even the majority of well-educated, post-Conciliar Irish Catholics—want or will settle for. The parish was too important to too many of us in our early lives for us to imagine that it will not be part of the lives of our children.

Herein, I think, lies the most serious conflict that will face the Irish-American Church in years to come. The myth says that a successful, educated, Americanized laity want new parochial forms while the conservative clergy want to preserve the old. In fact, however, the opposite is more likely to be the case. The clergy, no longer sure of their own identity and in some instances of their own faith, are desperately seeking "relevance" by seeking "revolutionary" structures. The laity, who scarcely doubt the relevance of either the clergy or religion, are willing and indeed eager to accept more democratic forms but are unwilling to tolerate the abolition of the parish. As the Catholic clergy are increasingly educated in divinity schools instead of seminaries, it is to be feared that they will become increasingly like many of their Protestant counterparts: pale, cliché-mouthing imitations of the academic intellectual, with little insight into the problems of their parishioners; men who think they have discharged their obligations by preaching radical social reform and denouncing their parishioners as immoral racists or war criminals.

While I am opposed to both racism and war and have strongly supported social reform for all my life, I would argue that such forms of religious leadership are bound to be ineffective, both because they display no grasp of the rhetoric required to persuade and no understanding of the complexities of the human and religious condition, of the profound human need for the religious community.

An earlier generation of Irish clergy may not have read many theology books or understood much of existential psychology, but they were in touch with their people and had an intuitive feel of the human need for belonging. At their best such clergy were able to lead their people very far indeed. Whether their successors will be able to do nearly so well in their efforts to isolate the religious (frequently defined in terms that have only the vaguest connection with religion) from the cultural and the communal remains to be seen. If they are successful, it will be the first time in human history that religion will have been effectively divorced from the cultural and communal context in which people find themselves.

All of which is a way of saying that both the anticlerical intellectuals and the anticlerical younger clergy ought, perhaps, to take a more sympathetic second look at the immigrant parish which they so enthusiastically decry. The current cliché suggests that the priests should "build a community engaged in service"; but the clergy and the immigrant parish did build community and did engage in service. Their communities and their service were limited, of course, and the limitations are especially obvious to us who have the advantage of hindsight, but all human service and all human community have limitations. It can be said of the Irish immigrant parish—even in its present democratized, suburbanized forms—that it was a strong community and rendered service to large numbers of people. It displayed a tenacity and vitality in the face of severe hardships and pressures. These qualities are found in very few religious communities throughout human history. That it was frequently parochial and almost always anti-intellectual is not to be denied. That it was static, inflexible, essentialist, and sometimes racist is also true, but given the historical and cultural context in which it worked, the amazing thing is not that the parish was parochial but that it was not infinitely more so.

Very early the parish and the priest elected to take the great risk of becoming American, confident that "the faith" would not be lost. Far from being a barrier to Americanization, the parish and its school rigorously insisted that the Irish immigrants, their children and grandchildren should become as American as possible. On the whole, the campaign was immensely successful, perhaps too successful. It is necessary and laudable that a new generation of clergy and laity should seek new parochial forms. I only wish they were not so quick to write off the older forms, especially without even trying to understand them.

If the parish chose to become American, it has become increasingly democratic American, particularly in its suburban forms. The same thing cannot be said of the structure of the church beyond the parish level. Even though John Carroll, the first American bishop, insisted, for example, that the only way to select bishops in the United States was by election, and his successors throughout the nineteenth century repeatedly tried to make the nomination of bishops something in which at least the clergy of the diocese could participate, in fact the selection of bishops now is done by an Italian apostolic delegate on the advice of a shadowy but very powerful ruling clique of bishops. The net result is that the American hierarchy is probably in poorer shape now than ever before. While there are many gifted men, the majority votes of the bishops are controlled by a handful of men whose incompetence is matched only by their lack of awareness of what is happening beyond their hierarchical circle. There are no giants today like the nineteenth-century liberals—Keene, Gibbons, Ireland, Spaulding, and England. The potential leaders, the thinkers, innovators, and dreamers in the American hierarchy, are presently without power and influence. Polarization between clergy and hierarchy, demonstrated conclusively by recent social research of the National Opinion Research Center, is likely to grow more and more serious until finally more democratic forms of election and governance are introduced into the American hierarchy. One of the great ironies of history is that the Vatican Council endorsed these attitudes for which the nineteenth-century American hierarchy battled, and the twentieth-century American hierarchy, while giving lip service to such values, does little to implement them. It has been argued repeatedly that men with such undeveloped political skills as the American bishops would not even make assistant precinct captains in Irish political organizations. This argument assumes that the power and influence of an American bishop depends on the support of his priests and people; while, in fact, many American bishops do care about what their priests and people think, this is a function of their personalities and not of the organization of the American Church. The typical American bishop can if he likes completely ignore the wishes of his clergy and people; he need have no fear for the progression of his ecclesiastical career, so long as his fences are mended with the apostolic delegation in Rome.

The Catholic Church, then, and the religious symbols which it embodies, created not only the religious but also the social context within which the Irish immigrants acculturated themselves to the American way of life. There is no reason to think that their loyalty to the symbols and parochial structure of their church has diminished as they move to the suburbs. The principal problems that Irish Catholicism faces in the United States are those of a hierarchy unable to grasp the facts of the social and religious changes of the last three decades and a younger intelligentsia, lay and clerical alike, which is not sufficiently mature to understand and learn from the accomplishments of the past. Whether the stubborn refusal to accept death that stands at the core of Irish Catholicism will continue to survive is a question that only the future can answer. My own impression is that even the American suburbs have not yet eliminated, at least not from all Irish-Americans, the fierceness and the stubbornness which foreign observers from Strabo to Alexis de Tocqueville have noted. The escapades of the Berrigan brothers and their allies suggest that Irish Catholicism still has the capacity to produce visionaries and mystics, though they may at times be hard to distinguish from kooks. Whether visionaries and prophets will appear with appeal beyond a limited clique of worshipers remains to be seen, but no one who knows anything of the history of Ireland would bet against it.

Worth noting, but beyond the scope of this book, is the question of the relation between the Irish Catholic hierarchy and the immigrant groups that came after the Irish or lacked the advantage of speaking English. There can be no doubt that there was considerable conflict between the Irish and the other immigrant groups. Seventeen per cent of the Catholic population, 35 per cent of the clergy, and 50 per cent of the hierarchy are Irish. The Irish hierarchical leadership has vigorously insisted on the need for Americanization, which is frequently seen by other ethnic groups to mean they should abandon their own Catholic customs. A number of Italian sociologists have suggested, for example, that as the Italians become more American their patterns of religious behavior become more Irish, precisely because the Irish have a stranglehold on the structure of the American Church.

It is undeniable that at one time many of the Irish hierarchy were quite insensitive to the needs and feelings of other immigrant groups, despite the existence of national parishes and other ethnic institutions. But since the Irish were here first and have been the most successful of the Catholic immigrant groups, there was probably no way for the Irish clergy and hierarchy to avoid the animosity of other ethnic groups. The whole history of this controversy needs to be written. Interestingly enough, some of the scholars who have most sympathetically presented the anti-Irish position have been Irishmen themselves, especially men like Coleman Barry and Philip Gleason. On one hand, the inability of those who just escaped from oppression to be sympathetic and understanding to those who escaped a few decades later is to be regretted. On the other hand, it may also be asserted that very little in the cultural experience of the Irish prepared them to be understanding, tolerant, or sympathetic. The only other group the Irish knew was the English, and while an occasional saintly Irishman might have been capable of sympathy for them, he was necessarily a rare man.

It is fashionable to denounce Irish Catholicism. Among the most outspoken is the "intellectual" alienated Irish Catholic (which usually means journalist and frequently means ex-seminarian). Such denunciations, however, are manifestations of a temporal ethnocentrism, a peculiar form of prejudice by which we evaluate the past in light of the insights of the present and attack our predecessors for not having or learning from our experiences. Temporal ethnocentrism is romantic and anti-historical and may be found frequently in authoritarian personalities. Perhaps the most effective response to those who are so pathetically eager, for whatever reasons of their own, to excoriate Irish Catholicism is to ask with Philip Gleason, "If not Irish, then what?" Which of the available forms of European Catholicism would the critic prefer to the Irish form? Viewed in that light, one can argue that the fact the Irish did indeed shape American Catholicism has probably been a good thing for all concerned.

Irish Catholicism, both from the Old Country and the New World, has, like all human religious forms, its limitations and inadequacies. Like all forms, the past is not what is needed in the present, but it does not follow therefore that for all its stubbornness, its narrowness, its Jansenism, its authoritarianism, immigrant Irish Catholicism did not respond rather well to the challenges it faced in the light of its own definitions. On the contrary, those various religious forms which are seeking to replace it would be fortunate to do as well.

5.

The Irish Family

Look at him Pat there laid out, it's all mighty sad
A better friend in life no man ever had

They've done it up right now with flowers and all
I seen one in the corner from old Marty McCall

It gives me a bit of a laugh—hope Martin's conscience is clear
'Twas the first communication between them in twenty-one years.

Oh yea, and didn't ya know about their famous brawl
Tho can't think now exactly what started it all

Don't know which one it was that opened the clatter
But them who knows says it was over a political matter

Oh look at her now, Pat's widow's coming through
A fine-looking female and holding up well too.

Well, I've always said she's a strong one—make no mistake
And with what she's had to suffer—'tis a wonder it's not her wake.

But sure a fine man Pat—him always just and fair
Even if he was given to puttin on airs.

Well, the Rosary's beginning—I'm going for a pint and a smoke
God Rest Him—

In the Name of the Father and Son and the Holy Ghost

Nancy McCready,
"The Passing of Pat"

The study of the family system of Ireland has received far less attention than the family system of Italy. The works of such social scientists as Edward Banfield, Leonard Covello, Constance Cronin, Talcott Parsons, Herbert Gans, Gerald Suttles, and, more recently, Thaddeus O'Brien provide a continuous story of the development of Italian family structure from Sicily to the Italian suburb of Melrose Park, Illinois. No such continuity exists in the study of the Irish family. The work of Conrad Arensberg, *The Irish Countryman,* and Arensburg and his colleague Solon Kimball, *Family and Community in Ireland,*[1] gives us a picture of rural Ireland (County Clare) in the 1930s. We know little of urban Ireland, and much less of the Irish in the urban and suburban United States. Once we get beyond the careful anthropology of Arensberg, Kimball, and John Messenger,[2] who describes the Aran Islands in the 1950s, we must rely on hearsay, impression, and a scattering of empirical data.

As Arensberg and Kimball point out, the family system of Ireland is essentially similar to the rest of Western Europe, patrilinear (the family lives in the house of the father and traces descent through him) and bilateral (the marriage brings a union of two families, not the absorption of one into the other). Like all family structures the Irish is concerned with land inheritance and enculturation. In County Clare the passing on of land was an extraordinary act in the life cycle, for when the eldest son married, the land became his. His new wife moved into the cottage and became its new mistress. The father and mother were moved into "the good room," reserved for them in their old age and for any of the "fairy people" who might be passing by. Naturally, the father was in no hurry to have "his boy" marry, and before the eldest married the others might not unless they left the land for the cities, England, or the United States. Many boys were needed to work on the farm, but there was little left for them once their elder brothers married, and the shortage of land meant both enforced celibacy

---

1. Conrad Arensberg and Solon Kimball, *Family and Community in Ireland* (New York: Harcourt, Brace & World, 1965).
2. John C. Messenger, *Inis Beag, Isle of Ireland* (New York: Holt, Rinehart and Winston, 1969).

(functional for containing the Irish population) and considerable strain and heartache when the eldest son finally married.

The father was the unquestioned master of the family, apparently making all the necessary decisions. He ruled, without challenge, in the field and in the home; but the mother was an important partner because of the work she performed in the kitchen and garden and because she was responsible for the administrative organization of family life.

There are some important differences between the Italian and Irish family structures. First, the daughter seems to be much more equal to the sons in the Irish family. Arensberg and Kimball state that in the Irish family the sons and daughters are equally subordinate. Second, there seems to be more solidarity among siblings in the Irish family. Third, the extended family in Ireland seems to have more actual importance than the Italian extended family ("la famiglia").

> . . . the term "friendly" is applied to the extended (and also immediate) relatives of "friends."
>
> When asked especially why they were cooperating, the farmers' answer was that they "had right to help." In general terms they would phrase it that "you have right to help friends," or again that "country people do be very friendly; they always help one another."
>
> Now the phrase "have right" is an expression in the brogue or English dialect spoken in Ireland (and in Clare) which, like "friendly," is a translation of a Gaelic idiom. It expresses an obligation, duty, or the traditional fitness of an act. The Gaelic word for which it is a substitute is *coir,* and a bilingual countryman translates the Gaelic phrase *coir orm* (the obligation is on me) into "I have right to." The countrymen of Clare, at least, do not ordinarily use or understand the phrase "I am right" to mean "what I have said is true." The countryman is explaining his economic acts in their traditional family setting.[3]

The obligations of an extended family exist in Italy, too, but both Banfield and Cronin stress that the Italian nuclear family does its best to avoid contact with the extended family which might impose obligations. The description of Arensberg and Kim-

---

3. Arensberg and Kimball, p. 75.

ball of County Clare in the 1930s shows that the actual manifestation of "friendliness" was more extensive than in Sicily.

Incidentally, this is not to suggest that the Irish family is less "amoral" (to use Banfield's unfortunate word) than the Sicilian family. Rather, it is likely that the history and structure of Irish life have kept the extended family serviceable longer.

Completely missing from the account of Arensberg and Kimball is the phenomenon of the Irish matriarch. That she exists in America is obvious to anyone with any experience of Irish-American life or novels. Irish social scientists with whom I have spoken claim that in Ireland, "herself" (the stereotypical Irish matriarch) appears far more often in the cities than in the countryside, which suggests that when the man is no longer able to work on the land he loses the fundamental basis of his dignity and authority. It may also be valid in the United States, and for any immigrant group. In the first and second generations the husband loses his role of provider and leader of the family; the wife, frequently better able to get employment, may become the sole provider and enhance her power and influence thereby.

Alexander Humphreys, in his study of the immigrants to Dublin, confirms the suspicion that the father's power wanes in the city and that the mother's role, already very important, becomes all powerful. Furthermore, the mother "spoils" the sons by waiting on them hand and foot, perhaps seeking affection from her sons that she does not find in her relationship with her husband.

> But her sons, as they grow into adolescence, cannot look to her as an adult model for the simple reason that she is a woman and they are going to be men. Within the normal New Dubliner household, where the husband comes home tired from an exhausting day, there is no adequate model of manhood for the sons to contemplate and to imitate and they must, often without complete success, look outside of the home for substitute guides as to what a man should be.
>
> Inevitably, in this situation the wife's authority over family affairs increases considerably and her relationship to her husband changes significantly. Where the rural wife is generally subordinate to her spouse, the New Dubliner wife has equal authority with her husband and, though technically he is still

the "head of the house," both husband and wife feel, act and speak of themselves as "partners." This very fact modifies the delicate set of affectional relationships between parents and children. Because he no longer exerts constant daily authority over his sons in the rural fashion, the New Dubliner father, while maintaining essentially the same relationship with his daughters, is much more companionable with his sons in their late adolescence and they in turn are much more relaxed, open and frank with him. But in regard to all of her children, and especially her sons, the New Dubliner wife is in an ambivalent position. By position and by cultural definition she, above all, is supposed to be the source of warmth, affection and intimate, friendly relations, and she strives to maintain this role especially, like the rural mother, with her sons. Yet force of circumstance puts her in the central position of authority and this tends to reduce intimacy between her and her children and to beget restraint and even, under certain conditions, resentment.

Humphreys notes that not only does the mother "slave" for her sons and force her daughters to do the same, but there is a considerable reluctance to see her sons marry:

> . . . especially in late adolescence and early manhood the mother "slaves for the boys" and, what is more, makes the girls do likewise. She not only lessens the sons' range of domestic responsibility, but conceives that it is part of her and her daughters' job to provide the sons with special service and comforts. This is so established that the daughters are resigned to it. An excellent description of the situation is the following passage which is notable, not only for its vividness, but also by reason of the fact that, made by a girl of twenty-six before her whole family, it met only with confirmation even from her mother and brothers:

> Mammy will serve the boys hand and foot. If Matt is upstairs and he yells down that he hasn't a shirt, Mammy will run into the room here to the hot-press and get a shirt and take it up to him. But if it were myself or Betty that needed something, we would have to come down and root it out for ourselves. If I am sitting in the easy chair there and Matt or Charley come home, I am expected to get up and give them the chair. They just say "Pardon me" and up I get. Well, I do not mind giving it to them, because I know that they work harder than I do, but that is the idea. There is no use fighting against it. I used to, but I soon

99

found out which way the wind blew—we have to wait on the boys from sole to crown. I do not mean that the boys do not do anything for us. Matt, for example, will always fix my bike. But Mammy is just a slave to them, a willing slave, and we are expected to be, too. And that is general. That's the common attitude.

Furthermore, all the artisan mothers interviewed not only admitted that this "spoiling" of the boys is quite common but acknowledged that commonly mothers are reluctant to have a son marry, even when loss of his income would not have severe economic consequences for her or the rest of the family. Often, indeed, they hardly conceal their sorrow at a son's marriage, although, as one husband said: "It is not as bad as it was in the old days when sometimes you'd think the wedding was a wake the way a boy's mother would be crying and carrying on."

Most artisan mothers interviewed were, understandably enough, very adroit in avoiding a direct statement as to how they themselves felt on this matter. But it may be significant that only one mother openly stated that she would be quite happy to see her sons marry in their early twenties and openly condemned the opposite attitude of many mothers. On the other hand, two mothers admitted that even the remote prospects of a son marrying filled them with sadness. Thus a relatively young mother of two girls and one boy, who was four years old and named Seumas, said: "The mothers always love the sons and always prefer them to the daughters. And, sure, they shower them with affection and spoil them altogether. . . . I feel the same way about Seumas. I think the world of him, and indeed I can't see anything further than him. I hate the thought of his ever getting married and I simply shudder at it."[4]

No one who has had any experience with the families of the American Irish can question the persistence among many of the "slaving" (by mother and sister, whether the latter likes it or not) and the fear of losing the son to another woman in marriage.

In the brilliant research of Herbert Gutman and his students, there is also some evidence that the number of father-absent families among Irish immigrants in the nineteenth century was higher than for other immigrant groups, suggesting that the

4. Alexander Humphreys, *The New Dubliners* (New York: Fordham University Press, 1966).

matriarchy, or at least the mother-supported family, was especially prevalent among the Irish. Where the missing Irish fathers were is something we do not know; they may have been dead, they may have been off working on the canals or railroads, they may have deserted the families, or been in jails or hospitals for drunkenness. We have no data to determine the present rate of father-absent families. I will therefore crawl out on a limb and offer my impressions of the west of Ireland and the United States.

In the west, even in the country, it appears that the role of the woman is far more important than at the time of Arensberg and Kimball. In conversations with strangers or distant relatives, she does most of the talking. She is praised by her neighbors, not just for the management of the house, but for her shrewd real estate transactions and for the education of children. Frequently she is also credited with the decision to move to the city in order to provide better education for the children. It may be that even in the countryside the changing nature of the Irish economy gives more importance and control in the family to the one whose task is administration rather than physical labor. In any event, I was struck by the similarity between the very powerful and autocratic Irish matron I encountered in the west of Ireland and the Irish matriarch, mythical and real, of the United States.[5]

Mother-dominated or not, the Irish family as studied by Messenger is cold, anxiety-ridden, repressive, and one of the most sexually naive of the world's societies.

> Sex never is discussed in the home when children are about; only three mothers admitted giving advice, briefly and incompletely, to their daughters. We were told that boys are better advised than girls, but that the former learn about sex informally from older boys and men and from observing animals. Most respondents who were questioned about sexual instructions given to youths expressed the belief that "after marriage nature takes its course," thus negating the need for anxiety-creating and embarrassing personal confrontation of parents

5. Professor Edmund Doogan of University College, Galway, tells me that it is his impression that in the rural districts of Western Ireland at the present time the mother of the family has virtually complete responsibility for raising the children.

and offspring. We were unable to discover any cases of child-lessness based on sexual ignorance of spouses, as reported from other regions of peasant Ireland. Also, we were unable to discover knowledge of the sexual categories utilized by researchers in sex: insertion of tongue while kissing, male mouth on female breast, female hand on penis, cunnilingus, fellatio, femoral coitus, anal coitus, extramarital coitus, manifest homosexuality, sexual contact with animals, fetishism, and sadomasochistic behavior. Some of these activities may be practiced by particular individuals and couples; however, without a doubt they are deviant forms in Inis Beag, about which information is difficult to come by. . . .[6]

As in many primitive societies, sex is considered dangerous; indeed it can even cause insanity.

And it is commonly believed that the menopause can induce "madness"; in order to ward off this condition, some women have retired from life in their mid-forties and, in a few cases, have confined themselves to bed until death, years later. Others have so retired as a result of depressive and masochistic states. Yet the harbingers of "insanity" are simply the physical symptoms announcing the onset of menopause. In Inis Beag, these include severe headaches, hot flashes, faintness in crowds and enclosed places, and severe anxiety. Mental illness is also held to be inherited or caused by inbreeding (or by the Devil, by God punishing a sinner, or by malignant pagan beings) and stigmatizes the family of the afflicted. One old man came close to revealing what is probably the major cause of neuroses and psychoses in Ireland, when he explained the incarceration of an Inis Beag curate in a mental institution for clerics as caused by his constant association with a pretty housekeeper, who "drove him mad from frustration."[7]

It is assumed that women are virtually sexless—at least as far as sexual pleasure is concerned.

Asked to compare the sexual proclivities of Inis Beag men and women, one mother of nine said, "Men can wait a long time before wanting 'it,' but we can wait a lot longer." There is

6. John C. Messenger, "Sex and Repression in an Irish Folk Community," in Donald S. Marshall and Robert C. Suggs (eds.), *Human Sexual Behavior* (New York: Basic Books, 1970), p. 15.

7. *Ibid.*, p. 16.

much evidence to indicate that the female orgasm is unknown —or at least doubted, or considered a deviant response. One middle-aged bachelor, who considers himself wise in the ways of the outside world and has a reputation for making love to willing tourists, described one girl's violent bodily reactions to his fondling and asked for an explanation; when told the "facts of life" of what obviously was an orgasm, he admitted not realizing that women also could achieve a climax, although he was aware that some of them apparently enjoyed kissing and being handled.[8]

Under such circumstances, drinking and fighting are outlets for sexual frustrations.

It is often asserted that the major "escape valve" of sexual frustration among single persons in Ireland is masturbation; frustration-aggression theorists, however, would stress the ubiquity of drinking, alcoholism, disputes, and pugnacity as alternative outlets. Pugnacity can also be linked to the widespread problem of male identity. Our study revealed that male masturbation in Inis Beag seems to be common, premarital coitus unknown, and marital copulation limited as to foreplay and the manner of consummation. My wife and I never witnessed courting—"walking out"—in the island. Elders proudly insist that it does not occur, but male youths admit to it in rumor. The claims of young men focus on "petting" with tourists and a few local girls, whom the "bolder" of them kiss and fondle outside of their clothing. Island girls, it is held by their "lovers," do not confess these sins because they fail to experience pleasure from the contact. The male perpetrators also shun the confessional because of their fear of the priest.

We were unable to determine the frequency of marital coitus. A considerable amount of evidence indicates that privacy in the act is stressed and that foreplay is limited to kissing and rough fondling of the lower body, especially the buttocks. Sexual activity invariably is initiated by the husband. Only the male superior position is employed; intercourse takes place with underclothes not removed; and orgasm, for the man, is achieved quickly, almost immediately after which he falls asleep. (I must stress the provisional nature of these data, for they are based on a limited sample of respondents and relate to that area of sexual behavior least freely discussed.)[9]

8. *Ibid.*
9. *Ibid.*, p. 17.

The rigid taboos that surround sex on the Aran Islands apply to other phenomena which might be related to sex.

> Many kinds of behavior disassociated from sex in other societies, such as nudity and physiological evacuation, are considered sexual in Inis Beag. Nudity is abhorred by the islanders, and the consequences of this attitude are numerous and significant for health and survival. Only infants have their entire bodies sponged once a week, on Saturday night; children, adolescents, and adults, on the same night, wash only their faces, necks, lower arms, hands, lower legs, and feet. Several times my wife and I created intense embarrassment by entering a room in which a man had just finished his weekly ablutions and was barefooted; once when this occurred, the man hurriedly pulled on his stockings and said with obvious relief, "Sure, it's good to get your clothes on again." Clothing always is changed in private, sometimes within the secrecy of the bedcovers, and it is usual for the islanders to sleep in their underclothes. . . .
>
> Despite the fact that Inis Beag men spend much of their time at sea in their canoes, as far as we could determine none of them can swim. Four rationales are given for this deficiency: the men are confident that nothing will happen to them, because they are excellent seamen and weather forecasters; a man who cannot swim will be more careful; it is best to drown immediately when a canoe capsizes far out in the ocean rather than swim futilely for minutes or even hours, thus prolonging the agony; and, finally, "When death is on a man, he can't be saved." The truth of the matter is that they have never dared to bare their bodies in order to learn the skill. Some women claim to have "bathed" at the back of the island during the heat of summer, but this means wading in small pools with skirts held knee-high, in complete privacy. Even the nudity of household pets can arouse anxiety, particularly when they are sexually aroused during time of heat. In some homes, dogs are whipped for licking their genitals and soon learn to indulge in this practice outdoors.[10]

It is not a warm or attractive picture. The Irish are a cold, frustrated, sexless, repressed people with little emotional flexibility, and practically no capacity to give themselves in intimate relations.

10. *Ibid.*, pp. 17–18.

Emotions are kept under control by internal guilt feelings and external ridicule. Not only is the person who "gives himself airs" cut down to size, so too is the one who attempts tenderness.

Irish Catholicism is an obvious explanation for such behavior; Messenger quotes with approval the comments of Humphreys:

> The specific doctrinal tradition to which Ireland and the Irish countryman in particular has fallen heir is the Augustinian. . . . [It] lays relatively greater emphasis on the weakness and evil to which human nature is prone as the result of original sin. By the same token, it attributes relatively less efficacy to natural knowledge and human action and relatively more validity to God's revelation and more power to the action of God's grace. . . . [The] Irish countryman has acquired a more than average distrust of native human reason. As a Catholic he cannot and does not deny the validity of rational thought, but he tends to be quite suspicious of the pride of the mind and so wary of ultimate rationalism that he shies away from reasoned discussions of high truths. . . . The tradition he inherits tends toward a certain historical and theological positivism in regard to the major truths and values of life, and, together with other historical factors, has led him to an intensified reliance upon the teaching power of the Church as voiced by the clergy. At the same time, while appreciating the need for positive good works, he is inclined to place relatively greater emphasis on those which are directly concerned with obtaining grace and relatively lesser store by simple ethical behaviour. And finally, although he is certain that man's bodily nature with its emotions is at root good, he is rather more suspicious of it and deals with it somewhat more severely. As a result he inclines to a jaundiced view of sex and a generally ascetic outlook which places a high premium upon continence, penance and, in most spheres of life, on abstemiousness.[11]

The editors of *Psychology Today* introduce Messenger's article with a comment about "narrow-minded priests," and Messenger himself—normally a fair and kindly man—closes with a quote from Paul Blanshard, of all people.

---

11. Humphreys, pp. 25–26.

By far the most important reason why Inis Beag has long had a faltering population is the total cultural impact of sexual puritanism and the secular "excesses" of the clergy. Paul Blanshard writes in *The Irish and Catholic Power:* "When all the reasons for a flight from Ireland have been mentioned, there still remains a suspicion that Irish young people are leaving their nation largely because it is a poor place in which to be happy and free. Have the priests created a civilization in which the chief values of youth and love are subordinate to Catholic discipline?" What "remains a suspicion" to Blanshard is fully confirmed by a wealth of data from Inis Beag.[12]

One wonders why those who are so eager to blame the Church fail to wonder why Catholicism takes very different forms in other countries. Might it not be that the Irish Church is as much shaped by the culture of the island as it shapes that culture? Nor does it seem fair to blame the Church for the misery generated by a thousand years of foreign oppression. It takes only the relatively modest prosperity of recent years to lead to a rapid decline of emigration. The Irish Church surely cannot be accused of libertarianism, heaven knows, but it is hardly the only factor which has shaped Irish culture and perhaps not even the most important.

Besides Inis Beag is not all of Ireland, nor is it Irish America— as Mr. Blanshard's quote might like to imply. Despite this, there are few Irish-Americans who can read Messenger's account of Inis Beag without feeling that he has discovered behavior which is still very much with us.

I had the same feeling when I read an article by an Irish psychiatrist named David Dunne from Castlebar, County Mayo. In describing the problems of his patients, Dr. Dunne observed:

Emotions which seem to me, and indeed to others, to cause particular problems to many persons presenting themselves as patients in this region are greed, envy, bitterness, frustration, sexual and otherwise, guilt, hatred, anger, a general feeling of a lack of love, often associated with a fear of love, a fear of loss, indeed a very high expectancy of and apparent resignation to loss, with consequent fear and avoidance of tenderness and

---

12. John C. Messenger, "The Lack of the Irish," *Psychology Today,* February 1971.

intimacy. The results of these latter feelings can be found in the very high numbers of unmarried individuals who are to be found living all over the County and who as they grow older help fill St. Mary's Hospital here at Castlebar.[13]

Castlebar is only twenty miles down the road from that part of County Mayo (God help us!)[14] whence came my ancestors. I had the uncanny feeling in reading Dunne's article that he knew my family all too well.

He portrays one of the most effective and psychologically deadly means of social control used in County Mayo—ridicule or "taking the mickey."

> Next I shall discuss ridicule. Ridicule or taking the mickey, or having a crack is a method of cutting others down to size, especially those who try to shake off the local apathy and get ahead, or show feeling for others. In other words it is a form of psychological castration or mutilation, and is probably the most damaging single factor in Mayo life, acting as it often does as a social cloak for envy, bitterness, hatred and fear, thereby reducing the humanity of both the ridiculer and the ridiculed.
>
> I have heard for instance of men who were afraid to buy flowers and carry them openly to their wives on occasions such as the birth of a baby for fear of ridicule by other men.
>
> Some individuals in fact, practice a particularly vicious form of ridicule, in which the victim is never sure whether the ridiculer is serious or not. If the victim treats matters as a joke he or she is insulting the ridiculer who is serious; if the victim takes matters seriously he or she is too serious and lacking in humor. This form of ridicule, only too common in this County, apart from being a sign of deep unhappiness and envy in the ridiculer, may have tragic consequences for some American psychiatrists believe it can cause schizophrenia in its victims, who if subjected to it as children grow up without a properly developed sense of who they are in relationship to other people, and hence at times in their lives when this becomes important, such as the onset of adult life, marriage,

13. David Dunne, M.D., "Psychiatric Problems in County Mayo," *Corridor Echo: The Journal of St. Mary's Hospital,* February 1970.
14. This phrase is supposed to be uttered after mention of Mayo—for reasons that are obvious when one has seen that barren, rocky, inhospitable, but strangely lovely slice of land.

childbirth, middle or old age, death of a close relative, etc.,
break down into the state of perplexity which we call schizophrenia.[15]

Ridicule is the matrix for many presumably intimate relationships in Irish-American families. Husband and wife, parents and
children, brothers and sisters, use it constantly to keep each other
at bay. Obviously it is more frequent in some families than in
others and completely absent in many. But it is still extremely
common among the American Irish I know. It is also quite different
from the black forms of ridicule such as the "dozens." Black
ridicule is an exercise in verbal skill, designed to display virtuosity
in the ability to be outrageous. Irish ridicule is intended to hurt,
to give as much pain as is necessary to keep the other at a distance. It is almost entirely unconscious and oblivious to how it
might embarrass onlookers. It is as much part of life as breathing
the air and one does not stop ridiculing in the presence of outsiders
any more than one stops breathing.

It is constant and incredibly nasty. Some Irish-Americans begin
it when they encounter those they "love" and keep at it mercilessly
as long as they are in each other's presence. It is as though the most
cruel verbal viciousness is absolutely essential for survival in intimate relations. Father Humphreys quotes a Dublin woman describing a situation in her family which will sound familiar to not
a few Irish-Americans:

> If you started to express any ideas of your own, or take on any
> projects, my father would put a stop to it. He would tell you
> not to be ridiculous, and he would put you in your place. I am
> not sure it wasn't a good thing. Perhaps we would have made
> ourselves ridiculous . . . but sometimes I think we Irish carry
> it a little far.[16]

And watch an Irishman respond to a present! He dare not express too much pleasure with a gift because that will leave him
open to the one who has given it to him. And nothing could be
worse!

---

15. Dunne, p. 25.
16. Humphreys, p. 146.

This harshness and narrowness of Irish familial relationships has been noted in the United States by psychiatrists, students of alcoholism, and those scholars who study human response to sickness and pain. The Irish of course respond to pain by pretending it isn't there. Pain is a punishment for guilt. Mark Zborowski describes the Irish reaction:

> The most striking aspect of Irish response to pain is lack of communication during the pain experience. The patient does not share his feelings with anyone; neither does he expect any help in his struggle with pain. The anxieties associated with the physical effects of pain and the fear of losing his working capacities suggest that the patient is extremely concerned with what will become of him in the case of a permanent crippling. As long as he works, he has a place in his family, he has status, and he is respected. The strength of his body is his only tool in forming his social position. The loss of physical strength is equated with loss of work and consequently with loss of status. There is nobody he can rely on in case the physical strength is impaired by pain. He knows that, even among the closest members of his family, he will not find a supportive action or word.
>
> It is in the Irish family structure and its emotional atmosphere that these attitudes are shaped, and it is there that one can hope to find the clues for understanding the patterns of lonely suffering.
>
> A number of authors have commented on the tendency among Irish males to remain bachelors or to marry late. The information offered by the Irish patients about their marital life not only confirms these observations, but also points toward another phenomenon that seems to be characteristic of Irish intrafamily, interpersonal relationships: the centrifugal tendency of the Irish family. It seems that even after marriage the ties between husband and wife remain rather weak, as are the ties between parents and children and among siblings. At one point or another in the family life, its members tend to drift away from one another. The separation between members of the family might be temporary or permanent. Although divorces are infrequent because of religious interdiction, separations between husband and wife occur rather often. The ease and calm—indeed, almost indifference—with which these separations are accepted by husband and wife, regardless of who initiates the move, suggest that neither views the event as a traumatic experience. The same lack of emotion is expressed

by children when they speak about leaving home or about their parents' separation. Members of the family leave one another; they stay away permanently, or they may come back after years of absence; all this occurs without causing too much upset, worry, or distress. . . .[17]

Thus there is at least some evidence in American research to lead us to believe that the Irish inability to give oneself in intimacy has migrated across the Atlantic. We may well be the same sort of cold, harsh, repressed people in the New World as we were in the Old.

Most American observers—particularly the students of alcoholism—stress the importance of the grim Irish mother. And well they might. Before I get into any worse trouble with Irish mothers, let me insist that I am talking about a tendency; I do not assert that all Irish mothers are dictators or, in their American suburban form, nagging neurotics. Nor do I assert that the Irish have any monopoly on the maternal domination of families. My argument is much more modest: it is my impression that there is a tendency for Irish women to have far more power in the family life than do women in some other ethnic cultures; and in some instances this produces a situation in which a strong and domineering mother rules either by sheer force of will or by the much more subtle manipulation of constantly appealing to the sympathies and the guilts of her husband and children.

One of the notable examples of the Irish matriarch is "The Woman of Property," a person I have never seen depicted in fiction, which is a pity because she is a fascinating character. She does not necessarily have a lot of property, she rather "deals in property." It is never altogether clear exactly what her husband does for a living, though he does have a job and dutifully goes off to it every day; but then he is a shadowy figure, sitting in the background saying practically nothing. So far as anyone knows, he agrees completely with his wife's elaborate schemes in the buying, selling, and renting of property.

Her basic strategy seems to be to buy a house, preferably a two-flat or one with an adjoining apartment somewhere, and then

17. Mark Zborowski, *People in Pain* (San Francisco: Jossey-Bass, 1969).

to sell it after a couple of years at a profit, which she will promptly invest in a larger building to be sold again in a couple of years. In a twenty-five-year period she and her family may live in five different buildings. There is never any resistance from the rest of her family to the move and no disagreement with her in her endless conversations about property values, and this is to say that there is practically never any disagreement with her at all because property values is the only subject she discusses. She may appear unrefined and uncouth, and she is absolutely ruthless in her real estate dealings, but no one tries to cheat her, at least not twice, because she is an acute operator who can be counted on to squeeze every last penny out of a deal.

She must squeeze that last penny; her profit margins are small. If she makes $1,000 or $1,500 on each sale, it is an accomplishment. Of course, there is always the possibility of a setback. Blacks, for example, might move into the neighborhood and property values might fall, at least in the short run, and then all those years of planning and scrimping and saving are in vain. "The Woman of Property" is not especially attractive; she is loud, compulsive, and in desperate quest of economic security. One assumes that she and her family are not very happy, though one would never know from the family because they say so little. Her husband is not ambitious or acquisitive, which may be why she married him. She has more than enough of that quality for five men.

Much more common is "The Pious Woman," who generally is "in very bad health" and whose combination of religious devotion and noble persistence in facing her ordeal wins the admiration of all who know her. Her devotions are multitudinous and unending, and while she frequently says, "I really can't complain," she does in fact complain almost as much as she prays, though in a style that frees her from the charge of being a complainer. Needless to say, she works tirelessly for her husband and children. The house is always clean, the laundry is always done, the meals are always cooked—no matter how sick she is or how many prayers she must say. She is very close to the parish priests (closer, if the truth be told, than most of them would like to have her), and is enthusiastically committed to the good of the parish (which is, of course, good as *she* sees it). Despite her devotions and her illness, she manages to find a great deal of time to spend on the telephone. She has been accused, uncharitably, of telling tales. Her family responds to her devotion with devotion of its own, both to her and to the Church. Although she insists she never forces the religious life on her children, indeed, that she never even suggests it, there are likely to be many "vocations" in her family, and her other sons and daughters marry late, if at all. She often says that her sons simply don't seem to be interested in the "girls" yet, and, of course, they are not; and if the truth be told, after they are married they don't seem all that interested either. When marriages do occur in her family, she can count on the unquestioned loyalty of her daughters and on all the advantages in the struggle with her daughters-in-law, most of whom breathe a sigh of relief when she goes forth for whatever reward the Almighty has in store for her. To tell the truth, sometimes one has the impression that the husbands of the daughters-in-law also breathe a sigh of relief, however moving their grief at the wake.

A third type of Irish matriarch and easily the most frequent of the three is "The Respectable Woman," whose whole life is governed by the categorical imperative "What will people say?" She is acutely conscious of the niceties of social class and knows her position in society very well. While she is not as close to the parish clergy as "The Pious Woman," she nonetheless takes it to be very important that they dine at her house at least once a year; this guarantees that she can be counted as someone in the parish, perhaps not of the parish elite but equal or superior to the middle range of parishioners and obviously above the "shanty Irish" whom she sees at the lowest reaches of the parish status scale. Just as the mother of Studs Lonigan could cheerfully contemplate the abortion of Studs's unborn child and at the same time claim to be a paragon of respectability, so her real-life counterpart is more concerned about the appearances of righteousness than about righteousness itself. Her daughter's clothes and hairdo, the times she comes in at night, the sort of car her boy friend drives—all of these are to be judged by what people will say about them. Similarly, if her son is caught breaking a window or drinking beer in the schoolyard or "borrowing" a neighbor's car, the principal response of this good woman is horror over the reaction of her friends and neighbors. She has good reason to be suspicious of their reaction, because while she may not throw the first stone, if somebody is guilty of violating a canon of respectability, her stone does get thrown pretty early in the game. The struggle for respectability is an arduous and challenging one. There is only a limited amount of it around, and someone else's gain in community esteem is a potential loss for her. Someone else's fall from respectability is a potential gain for her. The account books, therefore, must be kept carefully, and she must be ready to do to others what they would do to her if they were given a chance.

When respectability is transferred to the suburban environment it finds itself a congenial companion to the American norms of conspicuous consumption, with a special Irish twist. One must live well, of course; one must have the clothes, the home, the landscaping that are necessary to assert the success that the good Lord has seen fit to bestow upon one's family, but in order to be respectable in the suburban environment, one must underplay the nature of his success. One's husband *could* drive a Cadillac, of course, but because of his eminently sound taste and his desire to avoid ostentation, he will settle for an Oldsmobile 98.

It is from the family of "The Respectable Woman" that the most hardworking, ambitious, and achievement-oriented of the American Irish come. There is so much emphasis on respectability in their childhood years that they soon decide that they must have more of it if only to protect themselves from what people might say. College, profession, career, and marriage are all means to the end of earning respectability.

What is the sex life of the Irish-American family? One is almost tempted to say, on the basis of anthropological literature and external evidence, that there isn't any, save for the fact that children are conceived. Ireland controlled its population problems for almost a century by the simple expedient of delaying or avoiding marriage. People who can accomplish such remarkable feats of self-denial certainly can be said to have their sexual instincts well in hand. Furthermore, the obsession with sexual morality of the

113

Irish clergy reinforces the suspicion and disdain which many Irish-Americans seem to have for sex. Even some of the more liberated "sexologists" who write for the progressive Catholic journals usually succeed only in making sex sound dull.

One has the impression—obviously from the secure but biased perspective of the celibate—that many, if not most, Irish-Americans get rather little enjoyment out of sex and are not very skillful in the art of lovemaking. This may stem from the fact that the Irish are generally not very good at demonstrating tenderness or affection for those whom they love. The Irish male, particularly in his cups, may spin out romantic poetry extolling the beauty of his true love, but he becomes awkward and tongue-tied in her presence and clumsy, if not rough, in his attempts at intimacy. She, on the other hand, finds it hard to resist the temptation to become stiff, if not frigid, in the face of his advances, however much warmth she may feel. For her especially, sexual relationships are a matter of duty, and if she fails in her "duty" to her husband she will have to report it the next time she goes to confession. Some Irish women, with obvious pride, will boast that they have never once refused the "duty" to their husbands, even though in twenty years of marriage they have not got one single bit of pleasure out of it. A sexual encounter between a twosome like that is not likely to be pleasurable.

Children who grow up in an atmosphere of sexual tension, where it is never mentioned or, for all they see, never practiced, are not likely to have too strong a grasp on their own sexual identity, or to be very well equipped for heterosexual relationships of their own. Even though the more sophisticated of the clergy have long since passed beyond preaching sermons in which it is suggested that the really virtuous people become priests and nuns and have nothing to do with sex, the atmosphere of Irish Catholicism is still pervasively anti-sexual—even among those more liberated suburban intellectual and would-be intellectual types. The principal difference between this latter group and their predecessors in the old neighborhood is that one talks compulsively about sex and the other is compulsively silent about it. Neither group seems very much at ease with this troubling subject. Most of the wives of such marriages are faithful, largely, one suspects, because they have vigorously repressed almost all traces of sexual passion. But the Irish male may occasionally "play around," especially when he finds himself far from home. When he does so, he is likely to be overwhelmed with the most intense kinds of guilt feelings, which of course drive him to the escape and solace he finds much more rewarding than a woman's body—the bottle.

There is some evidence in the sketchy data available on American ethnic groups that the Irish have a much higher level of sibling loyalty than other American populations, with the possible exception of the Italians. My own impression is that this sibling loyalty is both powerful and ambiguous. The well-publicized relationships of the Kennedy clan demonstrate very clearly both intense loyalty and fierce competitiveness, which is frequently seen among the rest of the American Irish. We cannot be indifferent or apathetic on the matter of our siblings; we fight with them, quarrel with them, sometimes don't speak to them for years, but when they are in trouble, we rally fiercely around them. We may have spent a lifetime in conflict with them, yet we are nonetheless overwhelmed with sorrow when they die. I suspect that this loyalty may be part of this "friendliness" recorded by Arensburg and Kimball. It may also be traced to a reaction to the British Penal rule when siblings had to stand by one another for survival, since the whole non-familial structure of society was explicitly directed against them. In many second- and third-generation Irish-American families, it seems clear that the siblings are not friends (in the American sense of the word); that is to say, often they do not have common interests, they are not especially eager to spend time with one another. Yet on the various ritual feast days, Thanksgiving, Christmas, Easter, Mother's Day, birthdays, confirmations, first communions, they dutifully, if unenthusiastically, discharge the obligations of family, and in times of trouble and conflict, rally around one another with all the old fierceness of the past. Many of the younger Irish I know feel guilty that they don't spend more time with their siblings and that they do not enjoy it when they do. I

115

observe that the relationships they are describing have long since lost any interpersonal authenticity, and they shrug their shoulders in agreement, but add, "What can I do? They're my family."

Sibling relationships may often persist even when they are not marked by much friendship, but the Irish-American—even suburbanite—is intensely loyal to his friends. Indeed, a close friend can become for all practical purposes a surrogate sibling. The Irish political adage "You stand by your own kind" is but a specification of a large principle of friendship loyalty. "My friends," the Irishman says in effect, "right or wrong, they are still my friends."

Unfortunately, we have very little in the way of the empirical data that delights the heart of the social scientist to substantiate any of these hunches, impressions, and stereotypes. If my assumptions are correct, these subtle differences in role expectations are passed on in early childhood and then reinforced by later role behavior in adolescence and adult life. The relationship between husband and wife, parent and child, sibling and sibling, friend and friend correspond for most of us more or less precisely as templates built into our personalities in such a way that we are rarely if ever explicitly conscious of them. Of course you stand by a friend, no matter what he does, and the Irishman is astonished when other ethnic groups seem to disagree. Of course you don't let the children know that there is any passion between the mother and the father; who ever heard of things being any different? Of course you spend the official holidays with your siblings even if you don't like them; it's the way things are supposed to be. And of course you keep a marriage going for a quarter century even though there is no affection in it and it was clear after the first year that it was a mistake; everyone knows marriage should be preserved for the good of the children.

And so it goes. It may well be that many of the norms of intimate behavior about which we have speculated in this chapter will be eroded as the Irish become more and more assimilated into American life.

But don't bet on it!

6.

Arrival in America

*Is there one [thoughtful Irishman] who is not grieved by the general
result of Irish immigration to America? . . . It is not to be denied
that the Irish immigration has been one of the most perplexing and
menacing elements in American development. It has been the sure
reliance of the demagogue and the traitor. There have been noble
and generous and admirable Irish citizens in the country, but not one
of the great steps of human progress which it has taken was due to
the inspiration or received the support of the Irish element of the
population. Yet no other class has been so flattered. . . .*

*These are not pleasant things to say. But it is not by faintly echoing
lies, but by telling the truth, that the unquestionable evils of the Irish
immigration are to be corrected. And that correction is a work in
which all honorable Irishmen should make common cause with all
honorable Americans. So long as the more intelligent Irish citizens in
America identify themselves with the perilous and un-American political designs of the priesthood—so long as they do not sternly frown
upon the pandering of demagogues to the ignorance and passions of
their countrymen—so long as they refuse their sympathy to the spirit
of justice which has emancipated the slave and which seeks an honorable equality of all citizens—so long will they be untrue to the cardinal principle of the government, and the political society which they
have chosen. . . .*

*When intelligent Irishmen permit priests and demagogues to form
political combinations for the overthrow of the fundamental guarantee
of liberty of every kind, they must not be surprised if they forfeit the
respect and confidence of all good citizens. And in exposing such a
conspiracy with all the resources of pictorial satire, it is not the Roman
Church as such, it is political ambition hiding itself under the mitre
and the chasuble which is denounced. If . . . ecclesiastical Rome has*

117

conquered Ireland, she will not be suffered, even with the aid of her captive, to conquer America.

Harper's Weekly, October 21, 1871

It is no secret that the Irish were not particularly welcomed when they entered the United States. One can understand this reaction. Most prior immigrants had been if not wealthy at least reasonably skilled workers or artisans. They were the most ambitious and vigorous of the Europeans seeking to carve new lives for themselves in a more prosperous country; but the famine Irish were from the very lowest rungs of society. They were poor, uneducated, confused, fleeing not to a better life but from almost certain death. They were dirty, undernourished, disease-ridden, and incapable of anything but the most unskilled labor. That they arrived in hords and filled up whole sections of cities almost overnight did not go unnoticed by the natives who saw that when the Irish moved in, the neighborhood went to pieces. They were a slovenly, crude people; they did not have sense enough to take care of property, and foolishly permitted tremendous overcrowding of their dwellings. Nor did they understand how important it was to keep clean, especially when there was almost no provision made for sewage disposal. They failed to understand the importance of health and seemed satisfied to live in crowded, dark, dank basements.

If the Irish were to be accepted into American society they must be sober, industrious, and ambitious, like the Protestant immigrants who had come before them. There, of course, was the kernel of the problem; not only were they poor, sick, dirty, and uneducated, they were also Catholic.

The Irish Catholics, with their strange celibate clergy, had an equally strange propensity not to want to send their children to schools where every effort would be made to convert them to good Americans, which meant, of course, good Protestant-Americans. From the nativist point of view, it was small wonder that converts and churches were burned and that Catholics were occasionally murdered in riots. Fundamentally inferior, the only way they could

118

gain acceptance was by abandoning drink, religion, and the life styles they had brought to this country.

The nativist was fond of comparing the Irish with the black, and if he was a Northern Protestant abolitionist, he was especially fond of such a pastime. The comparison was always favorable to the blacks, most likely because the freed black "knew his place" and the Irishman did not; the black was properly grateful for what the abolitionists had done for him, and the Irishman seemed not at all grateful for his second-class citizenship. On the contrary, hardly had he been permitted to become a citizen when he promptly joined with others of his kind in political organizations which threatened native American control of the cities. The Irish, then, were not only bigoted, slovenly, Catholics; they were also organizers of political "machines" with potentials for control that were a direct challenge to the established powers. The political mood of the ilk of the Know-Nothings, the Nativists, the Ku Klux Klan, and the American Protective Association gained a considerable amount if not all of their support from their strong appeals to anti-Catholic sentiment.

Professor Appel of the University of Michigan has collected a series of nineteenth-century cartoons showing how the image of the Irishman has evolved over 120 years of American cartoons. In the early nineteenth century Paddy was a rough and uncivilized looking creature, but still distinctly human. By mid-century he was a gorilla, stovepipe hat on his head, a shamrock in his lapel, a vast jug of liquor in one hand and a large club in the other. His face was a mask of simian brutality and stupidity. It was only in the late nineteenth and early twentieth centuries that Paddy began to evolve from an ape to a leprechaun, a figure of gentle fun instead of the crude, rude, filthy monster.

Practically every accusation that has been made against the American blacks was also made against the Irish: their family life was inferior, they had no ambition, they did not keep up their homes, they drank too much, they were not responsible, they had no morals, it was not safe to walk through their neighborhoods at night, they voted the way crooked politicians told them to vote,

119

they were not willing to pull themselves up by their bootstraps, they were not capable of education, they could not think for themselves, and they would always remain social problems for the rest of the country.

Just as it is hard for us to imagine the horrors of the Famine, so it is extremely difficult for us to comprehend what life in the early immigrant ghettos must have been, both physically and psychologically. There are practically no Americans today who live in anything equal or even remotely resembling the squalor of the immigrant ghettos in Boston and New York. While the psychological degradation of the Irish was certainly no worse than that to which blacks have been subjected, it must also be said that from 1850 to 1950 there were no dissenting voices being raised on the subject of the American Irish; no one praised any aspect of their culture, no one suggested that Irish might be beautiful, no one argued that their treatment was both unjust and bigoted. The Irish managed to crawl out of the mud huts and wooden hovels in which they lived, and to leave behind the day labor and domestic service by which they eked out a living, not because American society was especially open (as the native Americans would like to believe), nor because of a superior merit which enabled them to overcome obstacles (as the Irish would like to believe). The Irish "made it" because the American economy was expanding at a fantastic rate, and the Irish were a large pool of laborers with knowledge of the language. The expanding economy, plus the almost unlimited number of jobs, and the relatively small amount of prosperity made available to some Irishmen by the political machines, accounted for the opportunity of the American Irishman to move first into the respectable working class, then into the lower middle class, and more recently into the upper middle class. An occasional well-to-do Irish family like the Kennedys shows that even the Irish can become aristocrats. From canal workers and railroad builders they became policemen, streetcar conductors, schoolteachers, and clerks. From the coal mines, stockyards, and steel mills they moved into offices, classrooms, and political headquarters. Then some began to go to law school, medical school, and dental school. Their heroes were political leaders, entertainers, singers, comedians, and athletic virtuosos. John L. Sullivan, Ralph Smith, James Cagney, Pat O'Brien, and the Fighting Irish of Notre Dame were folk heroes of which to be proud.

And of course they flocked to the seminaries and the convents just as they had in the Old Country. They founded grammar schools, high schools, colleges, and even universities. These institutions became strongholds of the faith where the religion of the Irish Catholic young would not be subjected to attack by pagan materialists—an attack not altogether absent in fact but existing more in dream.

These changes took generations. The rate of social improvement accelerated as the economy waxed and slowed down as the economy waned. The Irish were probably on the verge of making it when the Great Depression rolled the nation into a decade of economic stagnation. It took the prosperity of World War II and the postwar economic boom, plus the G.I. Bill, to enable the Irish to make it definitively into the ranks of the upper middle class. In other words, the worst of the immigrant experience was over about a century after the Famine; and when John Kennedy was elected President, 110 years after the Famine, the immigrant period of American history came to an end. Whether the Irish were in fact accepted into American society even then seems dubious. The Kennedy brothers became folk heroes only after their deaths. Before that, in the pages of the liberal journals, John Kennedy was an unscrupulous Boston politician and his brother was a ruthless, vindictive hater. Even now, only a few years after their deaths, the liberal elite is engaging in the exercise of "revisionism" on the subject of the Kennedys. We are told, for example, that John Kennedy was responsible for getting us into Vietnam, and that the spirit of world responsibility enunciated in his first inaugural address is the cause of many of our present problems. Robert Kennedy has not been dead long enough for writers of the *New York Review of Books* to begin to recall his associations with Senator Joseph McCarthy. One suspects that in the not too distant future those aspects of his past will be unearthed once again for public discussion. The liberal elite simply cannot resist the temptation to impose judgments on the dead, not in the name of the wisdom of their own time, but in the name of the hindsight wisdom of our time. I think this hindsight judgment of the Kennedys has an especially sharp twist to it because the intelligentsia has not yet forgiven them for being Irish—any more than it is willing to forgive such Irish figures as Richard Daley or Daniel Moynihan.

There has of course been no research on the subject of late anti-Irish sentiments in the American population, partly because there is no Irish equivalent of the Anti-Defamation League to fund such research, yet anyone who operates in the world of upper academia or the national media is naive indeed if he is not aware that there is still considerable suspicion and stereotyping of the Irish. It is, I suppose, a relatively harmless type of bigotry which certainly causes no Irish political leader to lose an election and perhaps only occasionally prevents an Irish academic from achieving tenure. Maybe the anti-Irish bigotry of the nineteenth century has died a slow and natural death; it has been a long time since anyone has seen a sign that says "No Irish Need Apply." The remnants of anti-Irish feeling are probably not very important and may have been reduced to the residue that is the absolute minimum in any pluralistic society.

Maybe, and then again, maybe not.

One of the myths that remains about the Irish is that they have not been economically successful in the United States. The Irish, it is suggested, are still lower middle class and because of their political and religious interests have missed the opportunity of achieving the influence, power, and wealth that were available in the American republic.

Such a suggestion is patent nonsense. On a wide variety of measures the Irish are at least as successful as any other American group except the Jews, but the norm for comparison, even in such a distinguished book as *Beyond the Melting Pot*,[1] is the Jews. The Irish clearly have not done as well, occupationally, socially, or educationally, nor do they wield similar influence in the mass media and governmental agencies. The Irish have become upper-

---

1. Nathan Glazer and Daniel Patrick Moynihan, *Beyond the Melting Pot,* 2nd ed. (Cambridge, Mass.: MIT Press, 1970, paperback).

middle-class business and professional men. The Jews have become wealthy entrepreneurs and intellectuals. The different channels of upward mobility and the relatively greater financial success of the Jews can easily be explained by the different backgrounds and heritages they brought to this country, but why the economic and educational achievements of the Irish must be always compared to that of the Jews by the native Americans escapes me completely—unless anti-Irish prejudice and Irish self-hatred make this comparison the most convenient and useful.

The truth of the matter is that National Opinion Research Center data show that the American Irish are as economically and educationally successful as white Protestants from the same cities and areas of the country. The younger generation of Irish are even more likely to go to college than their white Protestant counterparts. Furthermore, the Irish are the most successful of the Gentile immigrant groups, even when the generational advantage of the Irish is held constant. These findings ought not to be surprising. The Irish came knowing both the language and the political system. What is surprising is the curious myth that the Irish failed. A lot of people— some of them Irish—seem to have a considerable investment in believing that the Irish haven't made it.

Further research by the National Opinion Research Center indicates that Irish college graduates are more likely than average Americans to choose careers in law and government service; in the arts and sciences they are more likely to choose social sciences and the humanities than the biological sciences (though no less likely to choose physical sciences and mathematics). Within the social sciences, political science is more popular than sociology, political psychology more popular than experimental psychology, and history more popular than economics. In none of these fields is there any evidence that the Irish do less well in graduate work than other Americans, and, at least in the 1960s, they were considerably more likely to retain their religious faith than were either Jewish or Protestant graduate students. How many of these Irish-American scholars of the 1960s will become eminent in their fields, how many will even seek appointments at major universities remains to be seen.

One other phenomenon that emerged in our occupational research in the 1960s was that one-quarter of those who took the foreign service examination were Irish Catholic, and one-fifth of those who took the Peace Corps exam were Irish Catholic (even though the Irish are, at most, 7 or 8 per cent of the American population). This suggests that the Irish may be leaving behind the precinct for the embassy or the jungle classroom.

It is not hard to elaborate an explanation for this particular pattern of career choices; law, government, and political science represent careers the Irish have traditionally pursued. History and the humanities have been strongly emphasized in the Catholic educational system; experimental psychology is much safer than Freudian-oriented clinical psychology, with which Catholicism has only recently made its peace, and sociology has always been viewed with suspicion by the Irish, who have been convinced that most sociologists are either communists or atheists, or both.

Many of the brightest of the Irish became priests, and while the enrollment of young Irish-Americans in seminaries is presently declining, the Irish are still dramatically overrepresented in the American Catholic priesthood. It may be argued that if these bright young men had not gone to the seminary they would have become the kinds of scholars that would have given Irish Catholics in the United States more impressive scholarly credentials than they possess even today. I am inclined to doubt this, however; if they had not gone to the seminary, the Irish priests probably would have been policemen, lawyers, or politicians. There was little in the thousand years that went before the Great Famine that would have predisposed most young Irish-Americans to pursue either the arts or the sciences. The only art in fact for which there was some traditional support was the art of storytelling. No one can deny that the American Irish produced more than their share of storytellers—F. Scott Fitzgerald, Eugene O'Neill, John O'Hara, Flannery O'Connor, Edwin O'Connor, J. F. Powers, Elizabeth Cullinan, and, most recently, Tom McHale. Most of these storytellers wandered away from the mainstream of the Irish community and were in open conflict with it, particularly its ecclesiastical manifestations. In the narrow, provincial, rigid, achievement-oriented community of the

Irish parish, scholarship, art, and even storytelling were luxuries. To move beyond the parish ghetto to the world outside where art and scholarship were valued was to run the risk of "losing the faith" and cutting oneself off. The prophecy tended to be self-fulfilling; if you predict that someone will be a renegade, it is likely he will indeed become one. A more recent generation of Irish scholars and storytellers has not left the Church because the boundaries of the Church are now both more extensive and more permeable than they used to be, but even the youngest of the Irish novelists, Tom Mc-Hale, is still obviously trying to work out his conflict with the immigrant parish—and the Catholic Church as presented in *Farragan's Retreat*[2] is, despite some superficial resemblance to the post-Conciliar Church, really Irish Catholicism of the 1920s and 1930s, not out of the sixties or seventies at all.

Despite the predictions of non-Catholic social scientists and the fears of the Catholic clergy, upward mobility did not mean for most Irish-Americans departure from the Church. Just as they brought their Church with them, and modified it to meet the needs of the American situation, so they took it from the old neighborhoods to the new suburbs, modifying, changing, adapting it as they went. On the basis of a decade of experience in one of these new suburban parishes, I would be prepared to assert that, if anything, there is more intense loyalty to the new parish than to the old. The younger generation, people in their late twenties and early thirties, move back into the parish in which they were raised in order to give their children "all the advantages" they had when they were growing up. Some of the scholars and some of the artists were lost in the upward push; yet one hears that today James T. Farrell lectures at Catholic colleges and feels very benign about the Church in which Studs Lonigan lived and died, and more recent scholars and artists have not been under any constraint to leave. The mainstream of the American Irish may not yet fully understand what art and scholarship are about; it nonetheless respects the expert and is even willing to respect the artist providing he is "successful." Nor is the Church prepared to write off someone who attended Harvard

---

2. Tom McHale, *Farragan's Retreat* (New York: Viking Press, 1971).

or Yale or the University of Chicago; on the contrary, it is more likely to try to hire this person, either to teach at one of its own schools or, short of that, at least to "do a study." Nevertheless, upward mobility has exacted a heavy price.

The story of the American Irish has been a success story, I suppose. In one century the destitute Famine immigrants have become successful, upward-middle-class Americans with an elaborate ecclesiastical structure and the beginnings of a reputable scholarly and literary tradition. Many of them who are able to go back to visit the land of their ancestors are shocked by, from their viewpoint, its lack of economic development. The casual and sometimes unambitious style of its people and the quiet almost primitive life of the countryside may charm if baffle them somewhat. The Irish-American is astonished that his ancestors could have ever lived on this soggy and impoverished island. If the truth be told, he also finds the island just a little bit dull, for despite the economic growth of the last decade, the Old Country is a place where the action is not.

Who could criticize the immigrants for taking advantage of the economic movement of America to claw their way out of the hovels toward respectability and affluence? It ill behooves those of us who stand tall over the social and economic achievements of our ancestors to question whether other goals besides economic success and social respectability were more worthy. How could the Irish immigrant parish have been different from what it was? The members were incapable of making it something else, and if they had tried, it is unlikely that the larger society would have tolerated it. From the Famine down to John Kennedy, the American Irish had no other choice but to strive to "make it." And they did. The only problem, then, is, what next? It is a particularly sticky question when in the process of "making it" one loses the sense of who he is, where he comes from, and why he has to make it.

The American Irish made it by forgetting their past and trying to be like everyone else; they successfully imitated much of the achievement and style of big-city Protestants. During the process, much of the poetry, the laughter, the mysticism, and the style of the Irish past was lost. These qualities may be exaggerated. Not all Irishmen were mystics or poets or dramatists or storytellers or brawlers or lovers or comedians. Not all the "great gaels of Ireland" were "merry warriors and sad singers," as G. K. Chesterton's famous line asserts. The point is that practically none of the American Irish are. It is as though, in the desperate quest for respectability, the American Irish overreacted and eliminated not only the unfavorable components of the stereotype but those that gave them a positive distinction. It is as though we said, "We will show you that we are not slovenly, lazy, improvident drunkards, and at the same time we will also show you we are not poets, mystics, dreamers, or saints."

Well, we have succeeded. We have become so much like everyone else that there is practically nothing unique about us save our Church, and even that seems well on its way to becoming indistinguishable from any American Protestant denomination. We have not merely forgotten the tragic and glorious history of our past, we have also seemed to do everything possible to lose those characteristics of the past which might make us different from anyone else. Respectability we finally gained; now what do we have left to enjoy it with?

More than that should be said. One need not live very long in an Irish-American neighborhood to realize the fantastic price in human suffering that had to be paid for economic success. It is not so much that the Irish new rich are ostentatious or vulgar; indeed, on the contrary, they are rarely either of these. It is rather that they are frighteningly insecure and very conscious that everything they have might be taken away from them. I suppose that in the minds of many of us, at least in our unconscious minds, the memories of the Great Depression still linger. We and our parents were particularly vulnerable at that time; we were just at the point of making it, only to have the Great Depression shatter our dreams and postpone our entry into the upper middle class for fifteen years. For some of our parents, of course, it was postponed forever.[3] The ordinary insecurities, then, of the new rich plus the experience of the Great Depression make suburban Irish communities terribly insecure and threatened places. The young people growing up there

---

3. One presumes there are no class distinctions in heaven.

are caught in a network of rigid emotional constraints which seriously impedes anything even remotely resembling the development of their full potential.

Again, I must write from impression rather than hard statistical data. Economic prosperity has not meant either peace or security for young Irish-Americans. They must work at least as vigorously, worry at least as much, strive at least as hard as their parents with much less of a clear and explicit understanding of the reasons for their effort. Their parents worked in order to achieve respectability; the younger generation must strive so as not to lose it.

I am astonished at how paralyzing the neurotic defenses that young people develop under such circumstances can be. I don't know whether other groups in American society are so skilled at developing mechanisms of self-defeat and self-destruction, but the young Irish are very good at it, indeed. Oh, not so good that they will literally kill themselves (though some do) and not even so good that we can expect massive downward mobility among the Irish. They are self-destructive enough to make their lives and their marriages exceedingly miserable and their professional careers much less successful than they might have been. Of course, there is absolutely no room for creativity, imagination, spontaneity, playfulness—the necessary prerequisites, I take it, for poetry, philosophy, politics, and sanctity.

We've made it all right. We're in much better shape than we were in the mud huts of the west of Ireland or the wooden hovels in Boston or Canaryville. Physically and economically we are much better off; whether we are happier or whether we have improved as human beings is another question. Personally, I do not want to return to Ballendrehid, Ballyhaunis, County Mayo, Ireland. I rather doubt that I would be fond of mud floors, peat fires, or thatched roofs. Nor am I eager to return to Western Avenue and Roosevelt Road; I much prefer Lake Michigan as seen from the shores of Grand Beach. We've made it all right, but we have lost something in the process, and it may be too late to get it back.

7.

"The Creature"

In a misguided moment during a vacation in pagan Italy, after the first thirty-five years of my life, I developed a certain moderate fondness for the fruit of the vine, a fondness which never exceeds a second glass. My mother and father did not drink, and my sisters are almost as abstemious as I. I know many other Irishmen whose drinking habits are equally moderate, if not more so; therefore, when I assert that alcohol is an extremely serious problem for the American Irish, I am not saying that all the American Irish are drunks.

I will admit that there are times when it seems that way, or, as one Irish-American matron put it, "The Irish are only half sober when they start to drink."

This close relationship with "The Creature" seems to be part of the history of the Irish. Travelers' accounts of the sixteenth, seventeenth, and eighteenth centuries abound in reference to the drunkenness of the Irish.[1] Things have not changed much, as witness this excerpt from the *Irish Times,* December 12, 1970:

> The 11% of personal income spent on alcohol in Ireland was the highest of any European country, and appropriate action should be initiated to deal with this public problem, said Mr. Richard Perceval, executive director of the Irish National Council on Alcoholism, when he addressed the inaugural meet-

---

1. See, for example, Edward MacLysaght, *Irish Life in the Seventeenth Century* (County Cork: Cork University Press, 1950), for a discussion of Irish drinking habits in the seventeenth century.

ing of the South-East Regional Council of I.N.C.A., at Belmont Park Hospital, Waterford, last night.

Warning that alcoholism in Ireland was likely to increase rapidly with the rising levels of income, Mr. Perceval said that in the south-east area of Ireland it was probable that there were some 90,000 drinkers. Every indication showed that about 5% of all drinkers, or 4,500 in this case, were likely to become dependent upon ethyl alcohol. Some were partially addicted alcoholics, and probably half of these were still working. Each working alcoholic cost his employer £100 a year in absenteeism, inefficiency, and accident proneness. Each alcoholic affected the lives of four to five other persons.

Mr. Perceval said that with the increased leisure, increased spending power, increased materialism and increased pressures of all kinds, allied with decreasing discipline, there was inevitably a tendency for some people to seek escape or relief by chemical means, or to conform with an attitude which invested alcohol with a special mystique of virility and social significance.

Either way he said, an increasing number of people were going to become psychologically dependant upon alcohol, and many also would become physically dependant [sic]. This in turn would mean considerable social and economic damage which would adversely affect not only the individual concerned, but also families, employers, and the whole community.

"In our present state of scientific knowledge," said Mr. Perceval, "we cannot prevent alcoholism or other forms of addiction except by education, and the changing of attitudes. Even then, it is to some extent, secondary, rather than primary prevention. Yet, prevention should be one of our goals, and a national success in eradicating tuberculosis was surely proof of our ability to take effective preventive action."

Nor was the problem limited to the laity. Archbishop Brennan of Cashel, in the seventeenth century, urged his clergy to make sure that there was no excessive drinking at the wakes, and Blessed Oliver Plunkett observed, "Give me an Irish priest without this vice, and he is assuredly a saint."

Father Mathew's famous Abstinence League apparently had some success against "The Creature" in Ireland, and even today one can see the "pioneer" pin on the lapels of many young men and women there. Some statistics would indicate that presently the alcoholism rate in Ireland is lower than it is in England and the United States. Yet one need only visit the pubs in the west of Ireland or some of the lonely rectories in the rural countryside to realize that both clergy and laity still have a considerable problem. Just before the Famine an Irish priest wrote:

> . . . In truth, not only were our countrymen remarkable for the intemperate use of intoxicating liquors, but intemperance had already entered into, and formed a part of the national character. An Irishman and a drunkard had become synonymous terms. Whenever he was to be introduced in character, either in the theatre or on the pages of the novelist, he should be represented habited in rags, bleeding at the nose, and waving a shillelagh. Whiskey was everywhere regarded as our idol.[2]

And it was certainly a problem they brought with them to the United States. Oscar Handlin describes the situation in Boston in the 1840s:

> Nothing the Irish found in Boston altered their tradition of alcoholic indulgence. Instead, crowded conditions drove men out of their homes into bars where they could meet friends, relax, and forget their anguish in the promised land. In 1846 there were 850 liquor dealers in the city, but by 1849 fully 1,200 groggeries were open for the flourishing trade. A survey by the city marshal in November, 1851, showed the great majority of these to be Irish, and almost half to be concentrated in the North End and Fort Hill. In addition, numerous Irish families sold gin as a sideline, without license, to cater to the demands of their countrymen. Frequently drunk and often jailed for inebriety, the Irish "arrested and turned back" the short-lived temperance movement which had made promising progress up to their arrival. Other nationalities, particularly the Germans, were also fond of the glass, but neither their habits nor environment encouraged or even tolerated excessive drinking.[3]

2. Robert Freed Bales, "Cultural Difference in Rates of Alcoholism," *Quarterly Journal of Studies on Alcohol,* Vol. 6 (1945–1946), 484.

3. Oscar Handlin, *Boston's Immigrants* (New York: Atheneum, 1970, revised and enlarged edition, paperback), p. 121.

Considerable research was done on the subject of alcoholism in the 1940s, and one of its impressive findings disclosed that the problem of drink was not something the Irish left behind in the slums of Boston. In a lengthy article, Donald Davison Glad[4] presents various data on the subject.

Of those men rejected for military service in 1941 and 1942 for neuropsychiatric causes, the percentages of rejections for chronic alcoholism for various ethnic groups were: Irish, 3 per cent; Negro, 2.2; Italian, 1.2; Portuguese, 0.6; Jewish, 0.2. Similarly, in the First World War, of those draftees and volunteers diagnosed as neuropsychiatric cases, the following percentages were classified as alcoholic: Irish, 10.1; Hebrew, 0.5; Italian, 0.4; mixed, 0.3.

In the study of first admissions for alcoholic psychoses in New York hospitals, the rate per hundred thousand of population was: Irish, 25.6; Scandinavian, 7.8; Italian, 4.8; English, 4.3; German, 3.8; Jewish, 0.5. The veterans hospitals between 1936 and 1939 show the rate of alcoholism for Irish at 28.9 and for Jews at 0.9. In San Francisco, rates of arrest for drunkenness standardized per hundred thousand population were 7.876 for the Irish and for Jews 2.27. Three per cent of the Irish in the Boston area in 1941 and 1942 were rejected by Selective Service for reasons of chronic alcoholism. Glad administered a complex (by 1940 standards) questionnaire to a considerable number of Irish and Jewish respondents. He concluded:

> It was found that Jews tend to regard the functions of drinking as (a) socially practical and (b) religiously symbolic and communicative. The common element in these two uses lies in their instrumentality to the attainment of goals remote from the effects of alcohol per se. The Irish tend to regard the functions of drinking as (a) promotion of fun and pleasure and (b) conviviality. Both of these define the purposes of drinking in terms of affective consequences, in which the physiological and psychological changes produced in the individual by alcohol per se are of primary importance.[5]

4. Donald Davison Glad, "Attitudes and Experiences of American-Jewish and American-Irish Male Youth as Related to Differences in Adult Rates of Inebriety," *Quarterly Journal of Studies on Alcohol*, Vol. 8, No. 3 (December 1947).

5. *Ibid.*, p. 461.

In other words, Jews do not drink to escape, and the Irish do. The distinguished psychologist Robert Freed Bales in his early years was also a serious student of alcoholism. Noting that the Irish rate of admission to hospitals for alcoholism was three times higher than that of any other ethnic group, Bales suggested that alcoholism was a way of coping with repressed conflict, particularly in a mother-dominated family. Summarizing the evidence available to him, Bales comments:

> [In Ireland] even social contacts between the two sexes were at a minimum. It was apparently not considered a good idea to encourage love affairs when the land would not support more families. When the "boys" were not working as laborers for their father, they were expected to spend their time with the other boys. Small male groups of every age met at various farmhouses or taverns to pass the time. Drinking and aggressive "horseplay" were major activities. The "tee-totaler," as a matter of fact, was regarded as a suspicious character, since this implied he was not likely to be with the other boys and might be wandering around with the idea of molesting innocent girls. In short, the culture was such as to create and maintain an immense amount of suppressed aggression and sexuality. Both of these suppressed tensions found their outlet in drinking.
>
> It is not entirely clear just what happened to this family system in urban America, but it seems to have broken down in various ways and created still other conflicts. The males came in at the bottom of our occupational ladder, and no longer had the ownership of a farm as the mainstay of their self-respect and prestige. The tenement was not a place where aged parents could easily be kept after their working days were over. It was not easy to provide the money for their support out of small day-wages. There was uncertainty and inner conflict as to whether one was obligated to keep them at all. There was usually nothing a father could pass on to his son, or if he died and left a little property there was likely to be conflict over how it should be divided, since equal inheritance was not the rule in Ireland as it is here. The father in many cases seems to have dropped into a role of impotence and insignificance, and the mother became the dominant member of the family. She tended to bind her sons to her in the way which was usual and natural in Ireland. In this country, however, a strong attachment between a son and

133

his mother made it very difficult, and in some cases impossible, for the son to make a successful transition to independent adult status. In a survey of some 80 cases of alcoholic patients of Irish descent I found this mother-son dependence and conflict in some 60 per cent. Whether this is a higher percentage than would be found in other ethnic groups it is impossible to say at present, but the mother-son dependent pattern was certainly a prominent factor causing maladjustment in these Irish cases.[6]

Nor can we write off the findings of Glad and Bales as pertaining to a situation which was vanishing in the 1940s for, in the middle 1960s, NORC collected attitudes toward drinking that demonstrated that the Irish are still fond of "the jar."

Of all American groups, the Irish are least likely to be non-abstainers (Table 1), the most likely to report drinking twice a week or more (Table 2), and the most likely to consume three or more drinks of hard liquor at a sitting (Table 3)—33 per cent for the Irish as opposed to 24 per cent for Anglo-Saxon Protestants and 11 per cent for Jews.

Among those who drink, the Irish are second only to the Slavs in thinking that drink makes a social gathering more enjoyable (Table 4), but they lag behind American Protestants in having serious drink problems and are only slightly ahead of Slavs and German Catholics on this scale (Table 5), though they are considerably ahead of Jews and Italians. Finally, on a scale which measures incipient alcoholism (Table 6), the Irish drinkers are behind both the WASPs and the Slavs, though ahead of other American ethnics.

Thus the Irish drink more than and more frequently than any other ethnic group but, at least according to their own description, are no more likely to be "problem drinkers" than are Slavs or native Americans. Whether their descriptions are accurate or a result of self-deception remains to be seen. In terms of absolute proportions, more Irishmen are problem drinkers than are WASPs since Tables 4, 5, and 6 deal only with those who drink. If WASPs drink, their problems are as bad as the problems of the Irish; but

---

6. Bales, *op. cit.,* pp. 485–86.

WASPs are much less likely to drink (some 30 percentage points), so in absolute terms they have fewer problems.[7]

Particularly important, I think, is the suggestion of Bales that for many Irishmen drinking may be a means of asserting their masculinity. One short, aggressive Irish trial lawyer I know said to me once, with a can of beer in his hand, "The best trial lawyers in town are short, aggressive, insecure Irishmen who need a stage on which to perform and as much drink as they can get in order to re-assure themselves that they are indeed succesful males." In my own experience, many, if not most, of the alcoholic Irishmen I know come from families where the mother rules the roost and have married women who are very much like their mothers. "The Crea-ture" is at first a help in the struggle for success, then an excuse for not making it, and finally a solace for failure. Interestingly enough, in a number of cases, when the husband finally does lick the alcohol problem, his poor, long-suffering wife takes up the bottle herself.

The theory, then, is that the Irish drink for reassurance and escape because both the cultural history of the past and the family structure in which they are reared impose an intolerable psychologi-cal burden and a special need to repress aggressiveness and sexual-ity. It is an eminently plausible theory, and having known a con-siderable number of young American Irish who were well on their way to becoming alcoholics before their twentieth birthdays, I would be prepared to argue vigorously that however much they may have become Americanized in other respects, the Irish are still very Irish when it comes to John Barleycorn. They may have lost a consciousness of their cultural heritage, and many behavior traits may have become permanently submerged in the Americanization experience; but whatever the tradition which leads to alcoholism, it is alive and well today.

Nor is Archbishop Plunkett's prayer about the Irish clergy any less relevant now. Anyone who has had much contact with the clerical culture of the American Irish knows that many priests have an immense capacity to consume alcohol, and not a few of

---

7. Tables reprinted from Andrew M. Greeley, *Why Can't They Be Like Us?* (New York: E. P. Dutton, 1971), p. 205.

TABLE 1

RANK ORDER OF AMERICAN WHITE ETHNIC GROUPS
ON PROPORTION OF "NONABSTAINERS"

"Do you ever have occasion to use alcoholic beverages such as liquor, wine, or beer, or are you a total abstainer?"

	Percentage of "nonabstainers"
Irish	92
Jewish	90
German Catholic	89
Slavic	88
Italian	88
Scandinavian	77
German Protestant	70
WASP	63

TABLE 2

RANK ORDER OF AMERICAN WHITE ETHNIC GROUPS
ON PROPORTION OF DRINKING TWICE A WEEK
OR MORE (OF THOSE WHO DRINK)

"How often during the last year did you have one or more drinks?"

	Percentage drinking twice a week or more
Irish	42
Slavic	29
German Catholic	28
WASP	24
Scandinavian	22
German Protestant	21
Italian	15
Jewish	15

136

TABLE 3

RANK ORDER OF AMERICAN WHITE ETHNIC GROUPS
ON PROPORTION OF CONSUMING THREE OR MORE
DRINKS OF HARD LIQUOR AT A SITTING

"How many drinks of liquor (whiskey, gin, vodka, etc.) do you consume at a sitting?"

	Percentage of three or more
Irish	33
German Catholic	26
WASP	24
German Protestant	21
Slavic	20
Scandinavian	18
Italian	16
Jewish	11

TABLE 4

RANK ORDER AMONG AMERICAN WHITE ETHNIC GROUPS
ON THE USE OF DRINK AS AN ENJOYMENT
(RANGE = 0 - 4)

"Alcoholic beverages
   make a social gathering more enjoyable
   are customary on special occasions
   help me enjoy a party
   make me more carefree"

Slavic	2.22
Irish	2.15
German Catholic	1.96
Jewish	1.94
Italian	1.75
German Protestant	1.39
Scandinavian	1.33
WASP	1.26

137

TABLE 5

RANK ORDER OF AMERICAN WHITE ETHNIC GROUPS
ON SERIOUS DRINK PROBLEM*
(RANGE = 0 - 21)†

Items:
I neglect my regular meals when I am drinking.
Liquor has less effect on me than it used to.
I awaken next day not being able to remember some of
  the things I had done while I was drinking.
I don't nurse my drinks; I toss them down pretty fast.
I stay intoxicated for several days at a time.
Once I start drinking it is difficult for me to stop
  before I become completely intoxicated.
Without realizing what I am doing, I end up drinking
  more than I had planned to.

WASP	1.56
Irish	1.37
German Catholic	1.36
Slavic	1.32
German Protestant	1.25
Scandinavian	1.16
Jewish	.68
Italian	.55

*In this and subsequent tables both male and female respondents are included and
there is no standardization for social class.

†A response of "Frequently" was scored 3.

them manage to exceed that. In one major American see, which
will remain nameless, in the not too distant past the three bishops—
the ordinary and his two auxiliaries—were all alcoholics, and
when the third auxiliary was appointed, the prediction was that if
he was not alcoholic already, he shortly would be. While the records
and biographies are notably reticent on the subject, it would appear
that at least one other archbishop of a very large see died of chronic
alcoholism in this century.

One seventeenth-century traveler laments the fact that the vice
was not limited to the male sex, and while there is little data avail-

TABLE 6

RANK ORDER AMONG AMERICAN WHITE ETHNIC GROUPS
ON HAVING MAJOR TROUBLE WITH DRINKING
(RANGE = 0 - 5)

Items:

Has an employer ever fired you or threatened to fire
you if you did not cut down or quit drinking?

Has your spouse ever left you or threatened to leave
you if you didn't do something about your drinking?

Has your spouse ever complained that you spend too
much money on alcoholic beverages?

Have you ever been picked up or arrested by the police
for intoxication or other charges involving alcoholic
beverages?

Has a physician ever told you that drinking was injuring
your health?

Slavic	.750
WASP	.295
Irish	.294
German Catholic	.277
Scandinavian	.217
Italian	.214
Jewish	.183
German Protestant	.175

able about Irish women in the United States, I don't believe there
are many parish priests, particularly in suburban Irish communities, who would say that "herself" is more immune from problems
with "The Creature" than is "himself." The suburban matron
quietly sipping martinis alone in her parlor or with her cronies on
the country club veranda is becoming a frequent figure on the Irish
suburban scene. Her husband and children do their best to pretend,
frequently to themselves, that the good woman is just "nervous,"
but it doesn't take long for everyone in the community to learn that
she is a lush.

One of the interesting aspects of suburban Irish alcoholism—
male or female—is that it seems to be considered no longer a
religious problem, or at least not a problem to be shared with the

Church. In days of yore, the good Irish housewife would drag her husband by the ear over to the rectory where, shamefacedly, he would sign the pledge. In the suburbs there is much less inclination to mobilize the resources of the Church against "The Creature." In ten years in a suburban Irish parish, I was never once called upon to administer the pledge, or indeed to remonstrate with an alcoholic. I gathered that alcoholism was more of a social disgrace in the suburb than in the old neighborhood, and it was necessary to pretend even to the parish priest that the "old man's" frequent trips to the hospital were for "tests" and not for "drying out." The alcoholic in the family is a secret that is impossible to keep, but among the suburban Irish with their desperate need for respectability, it was a secret that everyone pretended to keep, and no one discussed it except behind the backs of the poor victim's family. Alcoholism, I suspect, is in substantial part the result of guilt feelings, but it also leads to even more serious guilt feelings in a cultural environment where it is seen as sinful and as a cause of failure. The Irish alcoholics I know, clerical as well as lay, are profoundly guilt-ridden men. Most of them, if the truth be told, in their sober moments were more gentle and likable than their more aggressive, successful friends and neighbors who managed to stop short of alcoholism. One young priest in Chicago once remarked, "The only decent pastors I know in this archdiocese are the drunks, and maybe the reason they're so nice to their clerics is that they feel so guilty."

Curiously enough, the preliminary indications are that this weakness for alcohol does not extend to other addictive drugs. While there is unquestionably pot smoking on many Catholic campuses, and some Irish Catholic young people are experimenting with hard drugs, most observers think that the Irish are less likely to become a part of the drug culture than other American population groups. One psychiatrist based on a Catholic university campus tells me that while there has been some increase in their use, drugs do not serve as a substitute for alcohol. This observer noted, "We still have the beer-drinking crowd we always had. The drug users are a new group we haven't seen before—the quiet, timid, diffident type." My only reservation would be to say that the loud, swaggering beer drinkers probably were pretty diffident too.

As one who moves in the social worlds of the university and of the middle-class Irish, I must say that the contrast in drinking habits is quite striking. At university parties one drinks beer; at Irish parties it is almost vulgar to ask for beer. At university parties a couple of drinks are enough; at Irish parties an evening is not a success unless a considerable number of the guests leave in advanced stages of intoxication. At a university party drinking is rarely an important part of the evening; at an Irish party it is one of the feature events.

It must be noted that the most recent (and as yet unpublished) research in Ireland calls into question the traditional explanation for Irish drinking. Seeking a sociological explanation—in the sense of a cultural and structural explanation instead of a psychoanalytic one—two young researchers, Richard Stivers of Southern Illinois University and Joyce Fitzpatrick of University College, Dublin, have emphasized the role of drinking as a focus for social life. Stivers points out that the pub serves as a center for "bachelor clubs" which are extremely important institutions for males in rural Ireland, and Miss Fitzpatrick observes that for both young men and young women in Dublin, drinking is an accepted part of social interaction, and that the overwhelming majority of Irish drinkers do not become alcoholics. Both scholars are extremely skeptical of the Bales analysis which addresses itself to why Irish are alcoholics and not why they drink. The NORC data cited previously gives some confirmation for their strictures. While the Irish are more likely to drink, the proportion of Irish drinkers who have serious problems may be no greater than the proportion of Anglo-Saxon drinkers who have serious problems. Miss Fitzpatrick, still in her early twenties, is now directing a major research project in England and Ireland on the sociology of drinking—a project which should shed considerable light on the question.[8]

---

8. In the conclusion of his study Professor Stivers comments:
"Certain changes in the structure of Irish society beginning in the early nineteenth century such as land reforms, single inheritance, few and late marriages, a weakening of father-son and husband-wife relationships, the segregation of the sexes, and an awesome emphasis on chastity led to the emergence of the Irish bachelor group, the new source of the avunculate.

It also would appear that the Irish are much less likely to have cirrhosis of the liver than the French—apparently because Irish drinking is concentrated at certain times while the French spread their drinking out over long periods of time.[9]

The drinking of the Irish is not a particularly amusing phenomenon, which may be why I am not enchanted with the Joe Flaherty, Jimmy Breslin, Pete Hamill style of Irish journalism. I am angry

---

'Negative' father-son relationships were offset by 'positive' avuncular relationships between bachelor group member and bachelor group initiate.

"The Irish bachelor group succeeded the occupational group as the source of an ethic of hard drinking and the role of the hard drinker. The bachelor group as institution was a means of controlling the large number of unmarried males in the interest of kinship and religion—single inheritance and chastity. The traditional roles of landowner, husband, and father, prior sources of male identity, were devalued at the expense of the roles of hard drinker, athlete, and conversationalist. Hard drinking was most intimately related to male identity in that the rite of passage from male adolescence to manhood centered about one's first drink in the local public house with adult males. Hard drinking was a means of establishing and sustaining one's status in the bachelor group; it was a prerequisite for membership. In Ireland the temperance ethic of nondrinking came off a poor second to the bachelor group ethic of hard drinking which had almost full community support (pp. 35-52)."

9. Professor R. Lynn points out that Ireland has the highest caloric intake of eighteen countries that he studied, the highest rate of psychosis, and the lowest rates of suicide and deaths from alcoholism. Assuming—with some justification—that psychosis correlates with low levels of anxiety, Lynn did a factor analysis of scores of the eighteen countries on eleven anxiety measures: mental illness, coronary deaths, vehicle deaths, caloric intake, suicides, alcoholism deaths, cigarette consumption, ulcer deaths, murders, celibacy, and hypertension deaths. A factor emerged with high loadings on the first seven items. Lynn then ranked the eighteen nations according to their scores on this factor. Austria, Japan, and Germany had the highest scores; Ireland had the lowest score. The United States was well down on the list (fifteen out of eighteen).

Lynn also found interesting correlations between his "anxiety factor" and certain climatic variables. There was a correlation of .46 between the anxiety factor and temperature in the hottest month and .40 between anxiety and the range of temperature from hottest to coldest during the year.

Lynn also sees a possible connection between anxiety and biological characteristics. There is of course a powerful prejudice in social science against explanations based on climatic and genetic factors, but Lynn's book deserves to be read very carefully. The possibility that Ireland's abominable climate may contribute to low levels of anxiety is startling to say the least. Perhaps even more startling from the point of view of Irish self-hatred is the thought that Ireland is number one on any variable. The United Kingdom is number two, which ought to establish another of Lynn's points: there is no relationship between anxiety and economic growth. (See R. Lynn, *Personality and National Character* (Oxford: Pergamon Press, 1971.)

with anyone who assumes that the Irish drunk is a happy and charming person. He is, on the contrary, a deeply unhappy and tragic human being. I am even more angry at the unfortunate truth that a weakness for "The Creature" seems to be one of the few residues of the Irish heritage that still survives. Finally, I am most angry of all at the thought that many of us can only be Irish when we have had too much to drink.

8.

The Men That God Made Mad[1]

> The great Gaels of Ireland
> Are the men that God made mad
> For all their wars are merry
> And all their songs are sad.
>
> G. K. CHESTERTON,
> The Ballad of the White Horse

> Hit 'em again . . . that's another one of them
> merry warriors.
>
> PADDY CLANCY,
> "The Clancy Brothers in Carnegie Hall"

Based on the anthropological work of Humphreys, Kimball, Arensberg, and Messenger, the alcoholic studies of Freed Bales, and others, and the psychiatric work of the various students of hospital behavior, as well as the impressions reported by the senior author of this chapter, the Irish emerge as a stern, aloof people, cold and rigid in their personal relationships, sexually repressed, prone to alcoholism in order to find emotional release, frustrated, unhappy, and maladjusted. From the various studies in Europe and the United States, the Irish do not look like a particularly fun-filled or attractive people. Imaginative, creative, mystical they may be, but neither very warm nor very affectionate.

---

1. Co-authored by William C. McCready.

None of the data on which the portrait presented in the previous paragraph is based represent national probability sample research. Fortunately, material was available which enabled us to test the image of the Irish against national survey data. Some time ago, the National Opinion Research Center collected data on a vast variety of social-psychological issues for Dr. Melvin Kohn of the National Institute of Mental Health. Dr. Kohn graciously agreed to make the data available and generously provided computer tabulations for us.[2]

Before we discuss the data, a number of technical observations must be made.

1. Using an analysis of variance model, the relationship between the ethnic factor and the attributes discussed in this chapter is statistically significant in every case. In addition, the relationship between ethnicity and the attributes in question within the Protestant and Catholic religious groups is also statistically significant. No statistically significant relationships from Kohn's data are omitted from this chapter.

2. Data presented in this chapter are based on the responses of a national probability sample of American males. Women were not included.

3. All the Irish, Italian, and Slavic respondents on whom data are presented are Catholic. All the Scandinavian respondents are Protestants.

4. The principal questionnaire items on which the factors constructed by Dr. Kohn and his associates are based (and they are all factor scores unless otherwise indicated) are included in each table. For a description of the construction of the factors, reference should be made to the Kohn monograph.

5. All the scores in this chapter are standardized for social class. Thus, the impact of social class is taken into account in all the tables. While obviously no claim can be made that one is dealing with a "pure" ethnic factor, one is at least dealing with the ethnic factor *not* of social class.

---

2. Readers who are interested in more details of Kohn's work are referred to his excellent monograph: Melvin L. Kohn, *Class and Conformity: A Study in Values* (Homewood, Ill.: Dorsey Press, 1969).

6. The scales were constructed by a factor analysis of fifty-seven items; in each table we give only the items which had a loading of over .200 on the scale.

7. The scores given are "standardized" or "Z" scores, that is, they measure the number of standard deviations from the mean score.

The first scale to be considered measures "authoritarianism." Two opposite cases can be made on *a priori* grounds about the Irish and "authoritarianism." It could be said that since the Irish are a rigid and sexually repressed group one could reasonably expect they would score high on "authoritarianism." On the other hand, following the argument presented earlier, it could be alleged that given their long fight against political oppression, the Irish might be less "authoritarian" than other ethnic groups.

The data in Table 7 do not confirm the view that the Irish are particularly "authoritarian." On the contrary, they are less "authoritarian" than all other American ethnic groups with the exception of the Jews and the Scandinavians, and they are rather substantially less "authoritarian" than white Anglo-Saxon Protestant Americans and all other Catholic ethnics. While this finding coincides with the data presented on the political liberalism of the Irish in another chapter of this bok, it nonetheless is quite surprising, and permits us to wonder why a group which apparently experiences so much emotional repression would not be more inclined to "authoritarian" attitudes.

But if they are low on "authoritarianism," it does not follow that the Irish are high on moral openness (Table 8). On the contrary, they have the lowest score on "moral liberalism" (which means the highest score on "moralism"). This is the first of a series of inconsistencies which we will discover in the Irish personality. The Jews are consistent—low on authoritarianism and high on moral liberalism—and have strong scores. The Irish have strong scores, too, but they do not run in a consistent direction as do the Jewish scores, but in the opposite direction.

One might expect from the portrait of the rigid, repressed Irishman that he would be inclined to be self-depreciating. But data in Table 9 indicate that this is not the case. While the Scandinavians

TABLE 7*

RANK ORDER OF AMERICAN WHITE ETHNIC GROUPS
ON PERSONALITY VALUES THAT INDICATE "AUTHORITARIANISM"†
(RANGE = —4 to +4)

Items:
Young people should not be allowed to read books that confuse them.
In this complicated world the only way to know what to do is to rely on leaders and experts.
People who question the old and accepted ways of doing things usually just end up causing trouble.
There are two kinds of people in the world, the weak and the strong.
Prison is too good for sex criminals; they should be publicly whipped or worse.
The most important thing to teach children is absolute obedience to their parents.
No decent man can respect a woman who has had sex relations before marriage.

Group	Rank Order	
Slavic Catholic	—1.535	(112)
Italian Catholic	—1.525	(130)
German Protestant	—0.205	(221)
German Catholic	—0.057	(122)
WASP	0.014	(1,290)
Irish Catholic	1.240	(102)
Scandinavian	1.590	(133)
Jewish	3.349	(86)

*In this and all subsequent tables, the means are *standardized for social class.* All respondents are males.

† The scores in these tables are based on scales derived from a factor analysis of fifty-seven items. Only the items with a factor loading of more than .200 are listed.

Note: A minus score indicates high "authoritarianism"; a plus score indicates low "authoritarianism."

seem to have a rather marked problem with self-depreciation, and the Jews and the Italians, and to some extent, the Slavs, have no problem of this sort, the Irish are right in the middle of American ethnic groups, neither very self-depreciating nor very "unself-depreciating."

It might also be argued that a group which has endured the rigid emotional controls of the Irish would be rather low on self-

TABLE 8

RANK ORDER OF AMERICAN WHITE ETHNIC GROUPS
ON "MORAL LIBERALISM" SCALE

Items:
When you get right down to it, no one cares much what happens to you.
If something works, it doesn't matter whether it's right or wrong.
It's all right to get around the law as long as you don't actually break it.
It's wrong to do things differently from the way our forefathers did.
Once I've made up my mind I seldom change it.
You should obey your superiors whether or not you think they are right.
It's all right to do anything you want if you stay out of trouble.
It generally works out best to keep doing things the way they have been done before.
Do you believe that it's all right to do whatever the law allows, or are there some things that are wrong even if they are legal?

Jewish	4.096
Italian Catholic	3.602
Slavic Catholic	3.189
German Catholic	− .413
Scandinavian Protestant	−1.450
WASP	−1.453
German Protestant	−1.660
Irish Catholic	−2.243

Note: A plus score indicates high "moral liberalism"; a minus score indicates high "moralism."

confidence. But the data presented in Table 10 indicate that as far as self-confidence is concerned, the Irish are neither at the top of the list nor the bottom. Jews, German Catholics, and Scandinavians are more self-confident than the Irish; and the Italians, white Anglo-Saxon Protestants, German Protestants, and Slavs are less self-confident.

Table 11 presents a scale that measures "fatalism." The Irish, it might be plausibly contended, ought to be a very fatalistic people. The history of that most distressful nation, particularly the Famine and the difficult years of the immigration experience, combined with the rather peculiar Irish attitude toward death, might very well produce a fatalistic people. In their political style, the Kennedy

TABLE 9

RANK ORDER OF AMERICAN WHITE ETHNIC GROUPS
ON PERSONALITY VALUES INDICATING "SELF-DEPRECIATION"
(RANGE = —4 to +4)

Items:
  I feel useless at times.
  I wish I could be as happy as others seem to be.
  At times I think I am no good at all.
  There are very few things about which I'm
    absolutely certain.
  If you don't watch out people will take advan-
    tage of you.
  How often do you feel that there isn't much
    purpose to being alive?

Group	Rank Order
Scandinavian	—2.360
WASP	—0.548
German Protestant	—0.375
German Catholic	0.451
Irish	0.508
Slavic	2.020
Italian	2.516
Jewish	3.519

Note: A minus score indicates high "self-depreciation"; a plus score indicates low "self-depreciation."

brothers displayed a considerable amount of "fatalism," and Daniel Patrick Moynihan, in his famous television comment at the time of John Kennedy's death, spoke for many Irishmen when he observed that the Irish know that they are going to get pushed around. The Irish are right up on top of the list of "fatalists"; indeed, no one else comes anywhere near them. Interestingly enough, all the Catholic ethnics are more "fatalistic" than Protestants; and Jews, while less "fatalistic" than the Irish or the Slavs, are more "fatalistic" than German Catholics or Italians.

There is scarcely any reason to expect that the Irish would be trusting. They have had a grim and bloody history. They have had

TABLE 10

RANK ORDER OF AMERICAN WHITE ETHNIC GROUPS
ON PERSONALITY VALUES WHICH INDICATE
A LOW LEVEL OF "SELF-CONFIDENCE"
(RANGE = −4 to +4)

Items:

I generally have confidence that when I make
plans I will be able to carry them out.

I take a positive attitude toward myself.

I feel that I'm a person of worth, at least on an
equal plane with others.

I am able to do most things as well as other
people can.

I become uneasy when things are not neat and
orderly.

Once I've made up my mind I seldom change it.

Group	Rank Order
Slavic	1.205
German Protestant	0.765
WASP	0.498
Italian	0.479
Irish	0.161
Scandinavian	−0.183
German Catholic	−0.759
Jewish	−0.901

Note: A plus score indicates low "self-confidence"; a minus score indicates high
"self-confidence."

to fight their way into American society. They are, if we are to
believe the standard social science image, a rather grim and inflexible people. In addition, we have discovered that they are the
most fatalistic of the American white ethnic groups. But the data
presented in Table 12 show quite surprisingly that the Irish are not
only the most "trusting" of the American ethnic groups but are,
indeed, a whole point higher on the "trust" scale than their closest
rivals, the Scandinavians. At this point it begins to become obvious
that the Irish are a great deal more complicated than their standard

TABLE 11

RANK ORDER OF AMERICAN WHITE ETHNIC GROUPS
ON PERSONALITY VALUES WHICH INDICATE "FATALISM"
(RANGE = —4 to +4)

Items:

To what extent would you say you are to blame for the problems you have—mostly, partly, hardly at all?

Do you feel that most of the things that happen to you are the results of your own decisions or of things over which you have no control?

When things go wrong for you, how often would you say it's your own fault?

How often do you feel that you are really enjoying yourself?

How often do you feel bored with everything?

How often do you feel guilty for having done something wrong?

Group	Rank Order
Irish	—1.971
Slavic	—1.378
Jewish	—1.240
German Catholic	—0.810
Italian	—0.540
German Protestant	0.013
Scandinavian	0.720
WASP	1.345

Note: A minus score indicates high "fatalism"; a plus score indicates low "fatalism."

social science image. A group that is at the same time "fatalistic" and "trusting" at least bears close watching.

To summarize the evidence presented in the first six tables, the Irish are high on "moralism," "trust," and "fatalism," in the middle on matters of "self-confidence" and "self-depreciation," and rather low on measures of "authoritarianism." A distressful people, unquestionably, but also a puzzling people.

In Table 13 we turn to a scale that measures occupational values. Dr. Kohn and his colleagues developed two different scales. One measures emphasis on the intrinsic worth of a job—whether it is interesting, provides freedom, offers the opportunity to use one's ability, and challenges one to help others. The second scale mea-

TABLE 12

RANK ORDER OF AMERICAN WHITE ETHNIC GROUPS
ON PERSONALITY VALUES WHICH INDICATE "TRUST"
(RANGE = −4 to +4)

Items:

It's all right to get around the law so long as you don't actually break it.

Human nature is really cooperative.

You should be able to obey your superiors whether or not you think they are right.

If you don't watch out, people will take advantage of you.

Do you think most people can be trusted?

How often do you feel that you can't tell what other people are likely to do, at times when it matters?

Group	Rank Order
Irish	2.506
Scandinavian	1.583
Slavic	1.481
German Protestant	0.767
German Catholic	0.757
Italian	0.502
WASP	0.242
Jewish	−3.106

Note: A plus score indicates high "trust"; a minus score indicates low "trust."

sures emphasis on the "extrinsic" aspect of the job—pay, fringe benefits, hours, security, and other such dimensions. The Irish were again in the middle. The intrinsic worth was less important to them than to the German Catholics, white Anglo-Saxon Americans, Italians, and Scandinavians, but somewhat more important than it was to Protestants, Slavs, and Jews. In other words, the Irish do not have particularly strong feelings on whether a job ought to have intrinsic worth or not. But (Table 14) they are the second least likely of all American ethnic groups to emphasize such aspects of work as pay, working hours, fringe benefits, and other conditions. They do not take a strong position on the importance of intrinsic qualities, but they do take a strong position against the importance of extrinsic qualities. The Irish may be success oriented but not so much as to make extrinsic concerns of critical importance.

TABLE 13

RANK ORDER OF AMERICAN WHITE ETHNIC GROUPS
ON VALUES FOR JOB INDICATING AN EMPHASIS
ON THE INTRINSIC ASPECTS OF WORK

Group	Rank Order
German Catholic	−0.778
WASP	−0.322
Italian	0.241
Scandinavian	0.309
Irish	0.426
German Protestant	0.739
Slavic	1.119
Jewish	1.567

Note: A high score indicates low emphasis on interesting work, amount of free-dom on job, ability to help people, and opportunity to use ability.

TABLE 14

RANK ORDER OF AMERICAN WHITE ETHNIC GROUPS
ON VALUES FOR JOB INDICATING AN EMPHASIS ON
THE EXTRINSIC ASPECTS OF WORK

Group	Rank Order
Scandinavian	−2.488
German Protestant	−1.613
Jewish	−1.002
WASP	−0.425
German Catholic	−0.299
Slavic	0.350
Irish	0.547
Italian	0.773

Note: A high score indicates low emphasis on pay, fringe benefits, hours of work, etc.

TABLE 15

RANK ORDER OF AMERICAN WHITE ETHNIC GROUPS
ON VALUES FOR SELF WHICH INDICATE EMPHASIS
ON SELF-RELIANCE (INNER-DIRECTION)

Group	Rank Order
Jewish	−1.594
Irish	−1.158
Slavic	−0.752
German Protestant	0.008
Scandinavian	0.039
German Catholic	0.191
WASP	0.498
Italian	0.642

Note: A high score indicates low emphasis on interest, responsibility, self-reliance, common sense, importance of facts, coping with pressure.

The next scale available for our consideration gets at what might be called (though Kohn does not use the term) "inner-direction." It measures emphasis on responsibility, self-reliance, common sense, and the importance of facing facts and of coping with pressure. On the basis of what we know about the Irish, it seems legitimate to presume that they would score relatively low on such a scale. Their religious otherworldliness, their troubled history, their inflexible personality, all would make it unlikely that the Irish would be inner-directed.

Nonetheless, as we observe in Table 15, the Irish are in second place on "inner-direction," behind the Jews and substantially ahead of their nearest rival, the Slavs. It ought to follow, therefore, that they would be low on "other-direction," and should have low scores on Kohn's scale which measures emphasis on people, helpfulness, truthfulness, doing well, being respected, and achieving success. Certainly the Jews, who were high on "inner-direction" are, as Table 15 indicates, low on "other-direction." The Irish, however, having achieved second place on "inner-direction," paradoxically, if not contradictorily, achieve first place on "other-direction." Not

TABLE 16

RANK ORDER OF AMERICAN WHITE ETHNIC GROUPS
ON VALUES FOR SELF INDICATING EMPHASIS
ON "PERFORMANCE" (OTHER-DIRECTION)

Group	Rank Order
Irish	−0.982
German Protestant	−0.880
German Catholic	−0.749
Slavic	−0.324
WASP	−0.252
Italian	0.323
Scandinavian	1.240
Jewish	1.338

Note: A high score indicates low emphasis on people, helpfulness, truthfulness, doing well, respect, and success.

only, then, do the Irish combine "trust" and "fatalism," apparently they also combine "inner-direction" and "other-direction." The strong Irish yearning for respectability is confirmed by the data in Table 15. But when Table 8 is combined with Table 16, one perceives that respectability is not something which is, for the Irish at least, to be purchased at the price of yielding self-reliance and responsibility.

We now turn to a series of tables which measure the attitude of Irish males towards child-rearing. Particularly here, one would expect the rigid, inflexible, and affectionless Irish family style to be confirmed. In Table 17 we present a rank ordering of American ethnic groups on the importance of good manners for children. Slavs and Italians are the most likely to think good manners are important, Jews and German Protestants the least likely, with the Irish standing between the WASPs and the Jews. Nor, in Table 18, is there any indication that Irish males are particularly obsessed with the importance of honesty as a value for a child. On the contrary, they are the least likely of any American ethnic group to be concerned about honesty, while the Jews are only slightly less un-

155

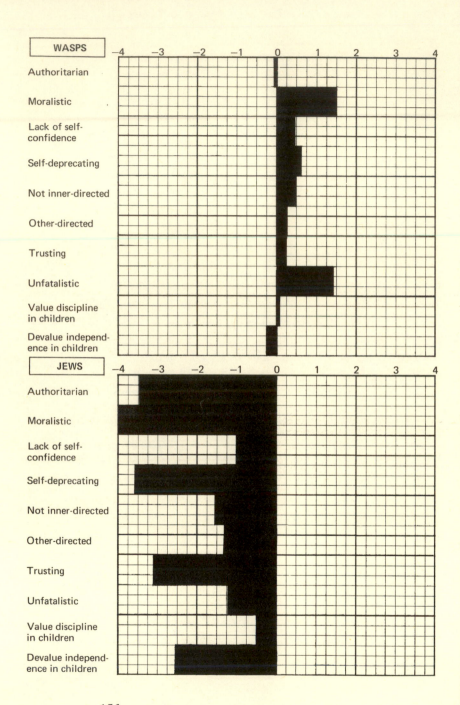

156

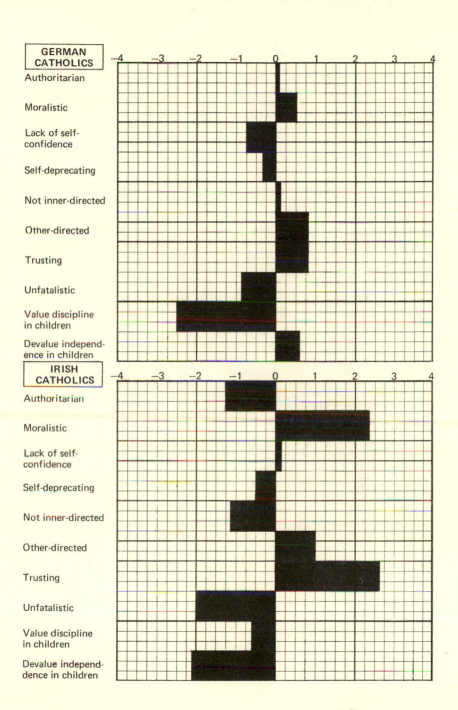

157

TABLE 17

RANK ORDER OF AMERICAN WHITE ETHNIC GROUPS
ON IMPORTANCE OF GOOD MANNERS FOR CHILDREN

Group	Rank Order
Slavic	1.591
Italian	1.686
Scandinavian	1.835
German Catholic	1.843
WASP	1.852
Irish	1.913
Jewish	1.991
German Protestant	2.009

Note: A high score indicates value is of less importance.

TABLE 18

RANK ORDER OF AMERICAN WHITE ETHNIC GROUPS
ON IMPORTANCE OF HONESTY FOR CHILDREN
(RANGE = 0 - 4)

Group	Rank Order
Slavic	1.091
Scandinavian	1.141
WASP	1.160
German Catholic	1.184
German Protestant	1.189
Italian	1.267
Jewish	1.465
Irish	1.473

Note: A high score indicates value is of less importance.

concerned. One might surmise that these two "victim-peoples" learned long ago how to use the spoken word to survive and, hence, are not nearly so concerned about literal honesty as other ethnic groups might be.

TABLE 19

RANK ORDER OF AMERICAN WHITE ETHNIC GROUPS
ON THE IMPORTANCE OF OBEDIENCE FOR CHILDREN
(RANGE = 0 - 4)

Group	Rank Order
German Catholic	1.137
German Protestant	1.254
Italian	1.271
Slavic	1.304
WASP	1.366
Irish	1.459
Jewish	1.493
Scandinavian	1.588

Note: A high score indicates value is of less importance.

TABLE 20

RANK ORDER OF AMERICAN WHITE ETHNIC GROUPS
ON PARENTAL VALUES INDICATING INDEPENDENCE
AND RELIANCE FOR CHILDREN

Group	Rank Order
Jewish	−2.542
Irish	−2.031
Scandinavian	−1.562
WASP	−0.403
German Protestant	−0.217
German Catholic	0.553
Slavic	1.408
Italian	2.816

Note: A high score indicates low emphasis on self-reliance and independence.

Finally (Table 19), the Irish are the third least likely to stress "obedience" as a desirable value in children. The Scandinavians are the least likely of all, followed by the Jews, then the Irish, then the WASPs. There is nothing, then, in Tables 17, 18, and 19 to give much credibility to the picture of the rigid, inflexible father. It is the Slavic Catholics, rather than the Irish Catholics, who place heavy emphasis on good manners, honesty, and obedience. The Irish are, on the contrary, the least emphatic on these attributes of any of the Catholic ethnic groups and share with the Jews the consistent low level of interest in such presumably admirable and praiseworthy American characteristics.

We are not, then, surprised by the data presented in Table 20. On the summary measure of the importance of independence and self-reliance for children, the Irish are in second place just after the Jews and substantially ahead of Scandinavians and WASPs. Despite the expectation that we might have from previous research, the presumed rigidity and inflexibility of Irish family life does not produce a high emphasis on conformity. On the contrary, it produces a high emphasis on initiative, independence, and self-reliance.

Furthermore (Table 21), the Irish are third from the bottom on a rank ordering of ethnic groups on the importance of conformity in children. Despite their reputation for rigidity, the Irish are slightly less likely than the Jews to emphasize the importance of conforming in children.

We can use a graph to summarize the personality profile of the Irish. In the graph the ten personality scales available to us are grouped in five pairs, each of which is related to its partner both logically and empirically. The pairs are:

"Authoritarianism"	"Moral liberalism"
"Self-confidence"	"Self-depreciation"
"Inner-directed"	"Other-directed"
"Trust"	"Fatalism"
"Discipline for children"	"Independence for children"

The graph is arranged in such a way that consistent scores (high on "self-confidence" and low on "self-depreciation," for example) within a panel will place the given ethnic group's bars on the same side of the center line. Thus the high Jewish score on "self-confidence" (0.9) and the low score on "self-depreciation" (3.5) puts the Jewish diagonal entirely on the left of the center line in the second panel. On the other hand, the WASP bars in the lowest panel cross from a positive score on the importance of "discipline

TABLE 21

RANK ORDER OF AMERICAN WHITE ETHNIC GROUPS
ON VALUES ABOUT CHILDREN INDICATING EMPHASIS
ON DISCIPLINE AND CONTROL

Group	Rank Order
Scandinavian	−1.932
German Protestant	−1.263
Slavic	−0.906
WASP	−0.047
Jewish	0.604
Irish	0.699
Italian	0.783
German Catholic	2.551

Note: A high score indicates low emphasis on importance of child being honest, considerate, having good manners, being obedient, getting along, etc.

for children" to a positive score on "independence"—indicating an inconsistent response, though the short length of the bars (a difference of .4 in the two scores) shows that the inconsistency is not large.

The following observations should be made about the Irish personality profile:

1. The previous research on the Irish would lead us to expect that the Irish profile would be to the right of the zero line in all panels but the fourth. The Irish ought to be high on "authoritarianism," low on "moral liberalism," low on "self-confidence," high on "self-depreciation," low on "inner-direction," high on "other-direction," low on "trust," high on "fatalism," high on "discipline for children," and low on "independence for children." In fact, the Irish are where they ought to be only four times—"moral liberalism," "self-confidence," "other-direction," and "fatalism."

2. The Jewish bars never cross the center line, hence there are no inconsistent scores for this group. The German Catholic bar crosses the line twice, though in one of these inconsistencies (that between trust and fatalism) the difference is quite small. The only

lengthy and inconsistent bars for the Germans are to be found in the last panel, indicating that the Germans value neither independence nor obedience in their children and that their devaluing of obedience is rather strong. (German Catholics were chosen because they came to the United States at the same time as the Irish and hence generation is held constant). The WASP bars cross the line only once, and the length of these bars, as we have already noted, is not great. The Irish bars cross the center line four out of five possible times, and in three of these the diagonal is 2.00 or longer. (Two are larger than 3.00, and one is larger than 4.00.) The inconsistency of the Irish personality is both extensive (it occurs on most pairs) and intensive (the differences within each pair are striking). The Irish are not only inconsistent often, but their inconsistencies are striking in size.

3. The only time the Irish are not inconsistent is in the last panel, where they are high on the need for "independence for children" and low on the need for "discipline." But this consistency is the opposite of that which previous research would have led us to expect. The Irish are *supposed* to be high on the need for discipline and low on the need for independence. In fact, their bar on child-rearing is in the same position and almost of the same length as the Jewish bar.

4. There are few variations in personality profiles for the WASPs and the German Catholics. Only one set of bars for either group is longer than 2.00. One merely has to inspect the lines on the table to see that the Jews and the Irish have long sets of bars. But the average length of the Irish set is over 2.00, while the average length of the Jewish set is a little under 1.50. Thus, the Irish are not only more inconsistent within each panel than the Jews (who never cross the center line) but the variation among pairs is greater for the Irish than it is for the Jews.

5. Finally, the four different ethnic groups seem to live in different personality space. The Jews inhabit the far left of the graph, having scores less than 1.00 only on the "self-confidence" (high) and "discipline for children" (low) scales (and even on these they are still to the left of anyone else). The WASPs and the German Catholics live in the center of the chart between .80 on either side

of the center line. The WASPs move out of this center zone twice, to the left on "moral liberalism" (high) and to the right on "fatalism" (low), and the Germans once. But the Irish wander all over the lot. They are in Jewish territory four times, in the central zone four times, and all by themselves on the right twice ("trust" and "moralism"—both, perhaps, the result of their religious convictions).

If the WASPs represent the mainstream of American life,[3] one can say that the Germans live in the same personality space as do "typical" Americans either because they were similar to begin with or because they acculturated. The Jews and the Irish have yet to move into this space. The Jews have carved out a personality space of their own on the "left" of the "typical" space and the Irish persist in being uniquely and bafflingly different.

No matter which way one looks at the graph, the Irish are a puzzle. They are not consistent in their personalities (with one exception, and that in a direction opposite from what one would have expected). Their inconsistencies are sharp and dramatic and very hard to explain. Finally, unlike the other three groups, they do not seem to have a "personality space" of their own but travel about like wandering gypsies.

Enough data has been presented thus far to justify our beginning to call into question previous anthropological and psychiatric generalizations about the Irish. Rigid, inflexible, harsh, cold family relationships may indeed exist, but they are, it would seem, only part of the picture. The other part of the picture is reinforced, and vigorously, by the data presented in Tables 22 and 23. The Irish report more time spent with their children per week than any other American ethnic group and are in third place behind the Italians and Slavs in the amount of time they claim to spend with their wives each week. One cannot, of course, equate the quality of a relationship with the quantity of it, but if the Irish are being harsh and unloving to their children, they are at least not doing it by

---

3. As a matter of statistical definition, the WASPs occupy the mainstream since they are the largest group in American society—between 35 and 40 per cent. Thus the clustering of their scores around the center line is statistically necessary since the scores measure deviation from the mean. A group which represents almost two-fifths of the population makes a substantial contribution to determining what the mean is.

TABLE 22

RANK ORDER AMONG AMERICAN WHITE ETHNIC GROUPS
ON TIME SPENT WITH CHILDREN

Group	Rank Order
Irish	14.069
Slavic	13.703
Italian	12.373
WASP	12.161
German Catholic	11.888
Jewish	11.168
German Protestant	11.059
Scandinavian	10.243

TABLE 23

RANK ORDER AMONG AMERICAN WHITE ETHNIC GROUPS
ON TIME SPENT WITH WIFE

Group	Rank Order
Italian	16.261
Slavic	14.324
Irish	13.971
German Catholic	13.760
Jewish	13.535
German Protestant	12.623
WASP	12.560
Scandinavian	10.246

withdrawing physically. And if the Irish husband and wife are cool to one another—and they may be—they are at least cool in one another's presence.

Can anything be said about the quality of the relationship? Obviously, it is extremely difficult to measure the quality of human affection, but Dr. Kohn and his colleagues asked their respondents how many times in a week an Irish male with small children hugged

TABLE 24

RANK ORDER AMONG AMERICAN WHITE ETHNIC GROUPS
ON AMOUNT OF HUGGING AND KISSING OF CHILDREN

Group	Rank Order
Irish	10.680
WASP	10.339
German Protestant	9.694
Italian	9.033
German Catholic	8.815
Slavic	8.547
Scandinavian	7.693
Jewish	7.687

TABLE 25

RANK ORDER AMONG AMERICAN WHITE ETHNIC GROUPS
ON AMOUNT OF CHILD SCOLDING

Group	Rank Order
Irish	4.819
German Catholic	4.600
WASP	4.306
Italian	4.227
German Protestant	3.992
Scandinavian	3.878
Jewish	3.756
Slavic	3.450

and kissed his offspring and how many times he scolded them. In an astonishing reversal of all previous expectations, the Irish were the most likely to report frequent hugging and kissing and also the most likely to report scolding. In other words, if the data in Tables 24 and 25 can be accepted as adequate though crude indicators of the quality of the Irish father's relationship with his children, then far from being a reserved, aloof, and distant relationship, it is an extraordinarily intense one, combining a high level of affection with a high level of disapproval. It is not so surprising that the Irish scold their children more than any other American group, but it is astonishing, indeed almost incredible, that they also shower more physical affection on them than any other ethnic group.

The picture of Irish family life which emerges from Tables 21 to 25 is completely at variance with our expectations. The Irish emphasize independence and self-reliance in their children, spend a good deal of time with them—and with their wives—and provide them with more physical affection than any other American white ethnic group. All of these phenomena can, of course, coexist with a family life that is cold, undemonstrative, repressed, and rigid, but it surely must be conceded that a group that can combine rigidity, coldness, and aloofness with the qualities indicated by Tables 21 to 25 is a very complicated collection of human beings.

And, indeed, this is the principal conclusion one must draw from the data made available to us by Dr. Kohn. The Irish are a very complicated crowd, combining fatalism with trust, inner-direction with other-direction, and a high level of affection for children with a high level of scolding. Of the sixteen tables based on Dr. Kohn's data, the Irish are at either the top or the bottom of the list in seven and in second place in three others. Only the Jews, who are at the top and bottom ten times and second from the top or the bottom four more times, display such affinity for positions.

A number of explanations are possible for these variations from our expectations:

1. Much of the previous research—Kimball and Arensberg, Humphreys, Messenger—occurred in Ireland. It may well be that the Irish have drastically changed in the United States, and have "overcompensated" by going to the opposite direction. However, the findings presented in this chapter are still at variance with psychiatric research, which has far more in common with the anthropological research done in Ireland than with the evidence presented in this chapter.

2. It may be that if data were available on Irish women, the picture would be substantially altered. The harshness, inflexibility, and repression reported in previous studies might be more character-

istic of women. There is at least impressionistic evidence, particularly in Humphreys' study in Dublin, to suggest that it is the woman who is more responsible than her husband for the "coldness" of Irish family life.

3. It may also be that many of those who have written previously on Irish family life have missed the subtleties and the complexities of Irish familial relationships. There is sufficient evidence in this chapter to justify the assertion that these relationships must be very complicated; relatively simple models of sexual repression, such as those adopted by previous literature on the subject of the Irish personality, may well be less than adequate to deal with the intricacies of the Irish personality and relationships.

The findings thus far reported also are counter to "common sense," and against the portrait of the Irishman to be found in most fiction and drama on the subject. A number of American Irish social scientists who have inspected the data presented in the present chapter simply refuse to believe it, and another American Irish sociologist, having reviewed the data, shook his head sadly and commented, "If we look that good, then everyone else is in much worse shape than I thought."

At the present rather primitive stage of research on American ethnic groups, it is difficult to know what to make of findings which are so much at odds with what previous research led us to expect— if indeed they do not flatly contradict it. The social scientist can only shrug his shoulders under such circumstances and politely suggest that further research is clearly indicated.

There were no items in Dr. Kohn's material which would enable us to test directly the assumption of repression of sexuality among the Irish. But in the same study in which NORC collected information on alcoholism, there were also questions asked about attitudes towards sexual permissiveness. The sample was relatively small and the questions might not be the best possible to test the hypothesis of repression of sexuality in the Irish as advanced by Messenger and others.

The first set of data (Table 26) would indicate that as far as permissiveness with regard to the sexual behavior of men, the Irish are in the middle range, more permissive than German and Italian

TABLE 26

RANK ORDER OF AMERICAN WHITE ETHNIC GROUPS
ON SEXUAL PERMISSIVENESS WITH REGARD
TO THE BEHAVIOR OF MEN*

(All Respondents)

Items:

I believe that kissing is acceptable for the male before marriage when he is engaged to be married.

I believe that kissing is acceptable for the male before marriage when he is in love.

I believe that kissing is acceptable for the male before marriage when he feels strong affection for his partner.

I believe that kissing is acceptable for the male before marriage even if he does not feel particularly affectionate toward his partner.

I believe that petting is acceptable for the male before marriage when he is engaged to be married.

I believe that petting is acceptable for the male before marriage when he is in love.

I believe that petting is acceptable for the male before marriage when he feels strong affection for his partner.

I believe that petting is acceptable for the male before marriage even if he does not feel particularly affectionate toward his partner.

I believe that full sexual relations are acceptable for the male before marriage when he is engaged to be married.

I believe that full sexual relations are acceptable for the male before marriage when he is in love.

I believe that full sexual relations are acceptable for the male before marriage when he feels strong affection for his partner.

I believe that full sexual relations are acceptable for the male before marriage even if he does not feel particularly affectionate toward his partner.

Group	Rank Order†
Jewish	3.30
Scandinavian	3.84
German Protestant	3.85
Slavic	3.85
WASP	3.92
Irish	3.95
German Catholic	3.97
Italian	4.78

*Low score indicates high permissiveness.

†In this and all subsequent tables score is mean number of *disapproving* responses.

168

Catholics but less permissive than Slavic Catholics and WASPs (though not by very much). Indeed, six of the eight ethnic groups cluster very close together, the Scandinavian score being 3.4 and the German Catholic score being 3.96. Only the Jews and the Italians fall outside this cluster, with Jewish respondents indicating a great deal more sexual permissiveness and Italians a great deal less.

The Irish also fall into the middle range in their attitudes towards sexual permissiveness for women (Table 27). The Irish are in third place behind the Scandinavians and the Jews and are part of the majority cluster that includes six of the eight ethnic groups. Once again, the Jews are the most permissive and the Italians the least. So it can be said on the basis of the admittedly less than perfect data available to us that there is no evidence of sexual repression on the part of the Irish.

But in Table 28 an extremely interesting phenomenon can be observed. If the respondents are divided into men and women, Irish men are the most permissive of all American ethnics in their attitudes towards sexual permissiveness for men, while Irish women (Table 29) are the least permissive in their attitude towards sexual permissiveness for men. Irish males, in other words, are more permissive even than the Jewish males and Irish females are even less permissive than Italian women.

Tables 30 and 31 disclose a similar phenomenon with regard to sexual permissiveness for women. Irish men are second only to Scandinavian men in permissive attitudes about female sexual behavior while Irish women are second only to Italian women in disapproving permissiveness in female sexual behavior.

If one combines permissiveness for males and permissiveness for females (Tables 32 and 33), one finds Irish men are the most permissive (though only slightly more so than Scandinavian men) while Irish women are resolutely and decisively the least permissive. As a result (Table 34), there is a greater difference between Irish men and women in their total sexual permissiveness than in any other American ethnic group.

Questionnaire items leave much to be desired, and the number of respondents is small, but to the extent that any judgment can be

TABLE 27

RANK ORDER OF AMERICAN WHITE ETHNIC GROUPS
ON SEXUAL PERMISSIVENESS WITH REGARD
TO THE BEHAVIOR OF WOMEN*
(All Respondents)

Items:

I believe that kissing is acceptable for the female before marriage when she is engaged to be married.

I believe that kissing is acceptable for the female before marriage when she is in love.

I believe that kissing is acceptable for the female before marriage when she feels strong affection for her partner.

I believe that kissing is acceptable for the female before marriage even if she does not feel particularly affectionate toward her partner.

I believe that petting is acceptable for the female before marriage when she is engaged to be married.

I believe that petting is acceptable for the female before marriage when she is in love.

I believe that petting is acceptable for the female before marriage when she feels strong affection for her partner.

I believe that petting is acceptable for the female before marriage even if she does not feel particularly affectionate toward her partner.

I believe that full sexual relations are acceptable for the female before marriage when she is engaged to be married.

I believe that full sexual relations are acceptable for the female before marriage when she is in love.

I believe that full sexual relations are acceptable for the female when she feels strong affection for her partner.

I believe that full sexual relations are acceptable for the female before marriage even if she does not feel particularly affectionate toward her partner.

Group	Rank Order
Jewish	3.21
Scandinavian	3.61
Irish	3.65
German Protestant	3.66
Slavic	3.71
WASP	3.72
German Catholic	3.88
Italian	4.17

*Low score indicates high permissiveness.

TABLE 28

RANK ORDER OF AMERICAN WHITE ETHNIC GROUPS
ON SEXUAL PERMISSIVENESS WITH REGARD
TO THE BEHAVIOR OF MEN*
(Male Respondents Only)

Group	Rank Order
Irish	3.35
Scandinavian	3.44
Jewish	3.45
Slavic	3.49
WASP	3.56
German Protestant	3.60
German Catholic	3.76
Italian	4.15

*Low score indicates high permissiveness.

TABLE 29

RANK ORDER OF AMERICAN WHITE ETHNIC GROUPS
ON SEXUAL PERMISSIVENESS WITH REGARD
TO THE BEHAVIOR OF MEN*
(Female Respondents Only)

Group	Rank Order
Jewish	3.72
German Protestant	4.20
Scandinavian	4.22
German Catholic	4.23
Slavic	4.24
WASP	4.29
Italian	4.35
Irish	4.55

*Low score indicates high permissiveness.

TABLE 30

RANK ORDER OF AMERICAN WHITE ETHNIC GROUPS
ON SEXUAL PERMISSIVENESS WITH REGARD
TO THE BEHAVIOR OF WOMEN*
(Male Respondents Only)

Group	Rank Order
Scandinavian	3.03
Irish	3.10
Jewish	3.25
Slavic	3.30
WASP	3.34
German Protestant	3.39
German Catholic	3.68
Italian	4.05

*Low score indicates high permissiveness.

TABLE 31

RANK ORDER OF AMERICAN WHITE ETHNIC GROUPS
ON SEXUAL PERMISSIVENESS WITH REGARD
TO THE BEHAVIOR OF WOMEN*
(Female Respondents Only)

Group	Rank Order
Jewish	3.29
German Protestant	4.02
Scandinavian	4.07
German Catholic	4.08
WASP	4.09
Slavic	4.12
Irish	4.21
Italian	4.23

*Low score indicates high permissiveness.

172

TABLE 32

RANK ORDER OF AMERICAN WHITE ETHNIC GROUPS
WITH REGARD TO TOTAL SEXUAL PERMISSIVENESS*†
(Male Respondents Only)

Group	Rank Order
Irish	6.44
Scandinavian	6.47
Jewish	6.70
Slavic	6.79
WASP	6.90
German Protestant	6.90
German Catholic	7.44
Italian	8.20

*Low score indicates high permissiveness.
†Total permissiveness indicates permissiveness with regard to sexual behavior of men plus permissiveness with regard to sexual behavior of women.

TABLE 33

RANK ORDER OF AMERICAN WHITE ETHNIC GROUPS
WITH REGARD TO TOTAL SEXUAL PERMISSIVENESS*†
(Female Respondents Only)

Group	Rank Order
Jewish	7.01
German Protestant	8.22
Scandinavian	8.29
German Catholic	8.31
Slavic	8.36
WASP	8.38
Italian	8.58
Irish	8.77

*Low score indicates high permissiveness.
†Total permissiveness indicates permissiveness with regard to sexual behavior of men plus permissiveness with regard to sexual behavior of women.

TABLE 34

RANK ORDER OF AMERICAN WHITE ETHNIC GROUPS
FOR DIFFERENCE BETWEEN SEXUAL PERMISSIVENESS
AS APPROVED BY MALE RESPONDENTS AND
AS APPROVED BY FEMALE RESPONDENTS*

Group	Rank Order
Irish	2.32
Scandinavian	1.82
Slavic	1.56
WASP	1.48
German Protestant	1.23
German Catholic	0.87
Italian	0.38
Jewish	0.31

*Figure given is total permissiveness of male respondents minus total permissiveness of female respondents for each ethnic group.

made on the basis of data presented in the last set of tables, one must say that there is evidence and support for the traditional image of the sexually repressed Irish woman. Furthermore, to the extent that Irish men and Irish women are married to one another, one can see a potential for considerable conflict over sexual attitudes and perhaps over sexual behavior. Finally, since the data made available to us by Dr. Kohn has only to do with men, it may well be that a one-sided picture of the Irish personality was presented.

Given the fact that the personality we described, based on Dr. Kohn's data, was complex enough, the possibility that Irish women may be strikingly different from Irish men would suggest that the personality of the Irish is even more complicated than the Kohn data would indicate.

The complexity of the Irish does not seem to have made them unhappy. Using a question devised by Professor Norman Bradburn to measure self-description as "happy" (Table 35), we can see that the Irish are the most likely of all American ethnic groups to describe themselves as very happy. Indeed, they are 12 percentage

TABLE 35

RANK ORDER OF AMERICAN WHITE ETHNIC GROUPS
ON SELF-DESCRIPTION AS "VERY HAPPY"

Group	Percentage of "Very Happy"
Irish	47
Jewish	35
Slavic	34
German Protestant	34
WASP	34
German Catholic	29
Scandinavian	27
Italian	27

points more likely to do so than their closest rivals, the Jews. Almost half of the American Irish describe themselves as "very happy." High in morality, low in authoritarianism, high in inner-direction, and also high in other-direction, high on fatalism, but also high on trust, most likely to scold their children, but also most likely to shower affection on them, and with the most sexually permissive men and the least sexually permissive women, the Irish appear to be a hopelessly confused group of human beings. On the other hand, their response to the happiness question indicates that, far from the confusion making them unhappy, they seem to thrive on it. G. K. Chesterton was right, the Irish are indeed the men that God made mad. There is absolutely no reason for people as badly mixed up as they to be so happy. But at least they are convinced that they are happy and are prepared to sit down and have a couple of drinks with you to persuade you how happy they are.

How can the contrariness, the contradiction, and the paradoxes of Irish personality and behavior be explained? There are no obvious and immediate answers. Perhaps their low score on authoritarianism and their political liberalism on the one hand and their high moralism on the other are the result of a history which combines a long struggle for national independence. The combination of fatalism and trust may be a manifestation of that peculiarly Irish variety of Catholicism which is symbolized by the Irish wake that is so frequently indistinguishable from a party. Perhaps the combination of inner-direction and other-direction is the result of a history of an ambitious people who had to learn to deal with the power of the military conqueror. Possibly the combination of self-confidence and self-depreciation reflects the same kind of history that explains why the Irish never stopped fighting England and why it took them so long to beat them.

Indeed, if one seeks for a historical explanation of the Irish personality, one might conclude that the paradoxes result from the fact that the Irish are half-Celt and half-Saxon, that they have managed to maintain some of their own cultural experience out of the past but have also been deeply affected by the culture of their British rulers. It may be that this cultural schizophrenia, symbolized by the language situation in Ireland in which the official language is Irish even though virtually everyone speaks English, is a cause of the peculiarities of the Irish personality. Another manifestation of the same mixed cultural background is the combination of a fundamentally Anglo-Saxon legal system—including unarmed police—with a very non-Anglo-Saxon religious system. If this explanation is correct, the battle in Ulster between Saxon and Celt is but an external manifestation of a battle that rages in the personality of every Irishman.

All these explanations deal with the Irish in their native land, but the American Irish are studied in this paper. If our explanation of cultural schizophrenia is correct, then it would seem that the American Irish have brought it with them from Ireland. Whether it has been attenuated by their century in the United States is a question that simply cannot be answered until national sample research is done in the social psychology of the Irish in their native land. Until such research is attempted and until much more detailed research is done on American ethnic groups, the idea that the wandering of the American Irish across "personality space" in our chart is a result of their inability to determine whether they are Saxon or Celt can remain only an intriguing possibility. Even more intriguing is the fact that the paradoxical nature of the Irish personality may have survived unaffected by the experience of a hundred years in the United States.

There is no reason, of course, why the Irish should be expected to give up their apparent psychological complexity. Consistency may not be necessarily a virtue. There is no reason in particular why the Irish personality should be limited to the narrow psychological space occupied by the Germans and the Anglo-Saxon Protestants. Nor is there any necessity for the Irish to carve out a space that is uniquely their own, as have the American Jews. It may very well be that the paradoxes and the inconsistencies of the Irish personality can be the source of many creative contributions to American life.

There are three concluding observations that we can make about the material presented in this chapter:

1. The assimilation processes have not eliminated differences among American ethnic groups. The Irish may have become paragons of suburban respectability, but beneath the outer veneer of upper-middle-class success there is still to be found a personality not unlike that which Strabo observed in his comment quoted at the beginning of this book.

2. While there is some confirmation for the standard portrait of a narrow, rigid, sexually repressed Irishman, the data in the chapter indicate that the picture is far more complicated for the American Irish. Rigidity there may be, particularly in the sexual attitudes in women, but the Irish personality pattern does not seem nearly as simple as the standard image would have made it. If our data are to be believed, the Irish are a very complicated people who seem to enjoy their complexity and, indeed, to flourish on it.

3. Psychologists, social psychologists, sociologists, and psychiatrists could have a field day studying the Irish. The strange combination of contradictions which makes up the Irish personality could easily be the subject of a score of doctoral dissertations.

Finally, this chapter might indicate that the title of the present volume is all wrong. It should not be *That Most Distressful Nation* but, rather, *That Most Happy People*. To be fair to the contradictions—or perhaps they are only paradoxes—we must say that neither title would be appropriate by itself. The Irish somehow or other manage to be both that most distressful nation and that most happy people.

9

Where Did the Past Go?

To be what these men are and have come from is, oh,
to feel the rushing push to own plush dreams of glory,
to see in the eyes the full, flamboyant joy inside,
Free—flying—spilling easily into victory,
overcoming the disease of underdog rickets
that split souls down the backbone,
shaking homes with trembling hands and private tears
that break over into life's plan for the damned!

To know who peoples this heritage,
is to render Adam's energy loose—escaped
seeking empty space to fill.
For the infaithful ones, it's killing—running,
but the faithful, new worlds create—
of passion clean and thorough,
of minds quick and clear,
Burrowing into men's cause with whole embrace,
and without pause
Chasing life down its myriad mounts and drops—
to catch all of breath by its flying hair,
Then turning it round and with laughing lips
bestow on life a brother's kiss.

NANCY MCCREADY,
"Heritage"

A young American-Irish mother told me recently that she had
purchased Webster's *History of the United States,* and beginning with 1896, the year of her father's birth, was carefully reading each year and fitting into it her own limited knowledge
of the events of her father's life.

I asked her why she had become so interested in American history. "I don't have a past. None of us does, and I don't think I can understand myself or my family unless I can rediscover our past."

Her point was well taken. As far as most of us American Irish know, we don't have a past. In the history books we can read about Ireland up to the time of the Famine and its subsequent struggle for freedom. We can find some account of what the early immigrant days were like in Boston, and we can read about famous Irishmen—entertainers, politicans, labor leaders, and athletic stars. There are also published accounts of the New York riots of 1863 and the Chicago of 1919. We learn very little about what has happened to most of the American Irish since they arrived on these shores. Using somewhat less than satisfactory statistics, one can say that in the last hundred years the Irish made it from the bottom of the occupational ladder almost to the top (although there are considerably more middle-class and working-class Irish). Statistics from 1900 through 1965 give only the barest outline of the social history of an immigrant group, and although some details may be added from novels like *Studs Lonigan,* it is still pathetically inadequate.

It is my impression that many of the other immigrant groups—Polish, Slovak, Greek, Italian—have been much more self-conscious about keeping detailed records of their experiences since immigration. In a conversation with the distinguished political scientist Matthew Holden, I was struck by how fully he could trace the history of the various branches of his family back to the slaves when James Monroe was President of the United States. I do not even know the first name of one of my grandfathers, or my grandmother on the other side. I know that one of the grandfathers died in the sewers in his early forties, and that his wife died only a few months later when my mother was fourteen years old. That was in 1908. I have no idea what my father's father's occupation was, where he was born, or when he died. Before my grandparents, there are only the names of two towns in Ireland. Who lived there, why they left, when and how they came to the United States, what happened to them after they arrived are complete blanks in our family history.

My conversation with Professor Holden was peculiar because he seemed just as surprised that I knew nothing about my past as I was that he knew so much about his. He pointed out to me that many American blacks consider it extremely important to keep the mostly oral records of their family history. I told him that until very recently most of the American Irish couldn't care less about their past. As I mentioned in the preceding chapter, it may be that we Irish did not want to remember the Famine, the migration, and the poverty of the early years in this country; hence we have repressed those memories. But isn't it curious that the blacks, whose history is considerably less pleasant than the Irish, remember so carefully?

Not only are the histories of individual families obscure, but so are the histories of communities. It is virtually impossible, for example, to trace the history of the Irish in the archdiocese of Chicago, in part because at least one archbishop took the precaution of having his housekeeper burn all his records shortly after he died. That there was a schism around the turn of the century, led by a priest named Crowley in conflict with an auxiliary bishop named Muldoon, which had something to do with the Fenians and the Irish Republican Brotherhood, constitutes a vague legend complete with the ghost of Bishop Muldoon haunting St. Charles Borromeo rectory, where he lived before going to Rockford, Illinois, as its first bishop.[1] The details of the Crowley schism, which was apparently a shocking and scandalous affair, have long since been forgotten, and all the witnesses who could have told the story are now dead.

Similarly, I am astonished at how few Irish politicians in Chicago know anything of the history of the Cook County organization. They vaguely remember the name of Anton Cermak, and they are aware that before the advent of Mayor Daley there were a number of different Irish factions in the organization. They might even be able to tell you who represented those repressed factions and where they are today, but they know practically nothing of the history of the factions. Only an occasional old-timer remembers the name

---

1. Urban renewal has since eliminated St. Charles Borromeo rectory, so if the good bishop's ghost was there, he has had to find a new place to haunt.

Roger Sullivan or acknowledges that there was once a mayor named Dever, a Democratic reform candidate who defeated the corrupt Capone machine and its mayor, William Hale Thompson. I can remember asking a group of young politicians, who were discussing the possibility of an Irish candidate for governor of Illinois, whether there had ever been an Irish governor in the state's history. They did not know.[2]

Only an occasional old-timer with a love for telling tales of the past can fill in some of the details. And one can never be sure that those details, fascinating as they are, have much relationship with what really happened in those days not so long ago.

In so far as there are any family histories, about the only details that can be found in family traditions are those that deal with the wars, the Great Depression, and moves from one parish to another. Most of us in Chicago, for example, know what our predecessors did during the First World War. We know, however vaguely, what the Great Depression did to our families. We know about when we left St. Gabriel's (Back of the Yards) and moved to Visitation on Garfield Boulevard or Holy Cross, south of the University of Chicago. From there the Irish moved to St. Leo's (Englewood) or St. Lawrence (where Studs Lonigan's family lived after leaving Fifty-seventh and Indiana); and finally to South Shore or Beverly Hills. But such factual information is more of a chronicle of the general movement from working class to upper middle class. Only the experiences of the Great Depression seem to have been bitter enough to stir up emotions: emotions of fear, insecurity, uncertainty, and heartbreak common to the whole American population. They tell us very little about what the Great Depression meant to the Irish. My own hunch is based on the fact that my father was well on his way to becoming a wealthy man before, as my mother used to put it, "the crash took everything away." The Depression must have been a severe blow to the Irish because the shopkeepers, the small businessmen, the emerging professionals, the upwardly mobile but still low-level corporation bureaucrats were on the verge of a major social and economic breakthrough as they rode the wave of

---

2. There was: one Edward Dunne.

prosperity in the 1920s. For them the Great Depression must have been a traumatic setback. Yet while the emotions engendered at that time remain strong, the specific historical details are still absent.

Even more odd, the defeat of Al Smith, which ought to have been a terribly heavy blow to the American Irish, might just as well have happened on another continent for the role it plays in collective American-Irish folklore. Even during the Kennedy campaign, although the mass media mentioned Al Smith frequently, the memories of that event, only three decades past, seemed quite extinct in the Irish community.

In the final analysis I can think of no good explanation why nothing happened in our past so far as most of us are concerned, but it must be said that those scholars who are now beginning to try to write the social history of the immigrant groups in the United States are going to have a very difficult time putting toegther all the pieces for, as of now, the Irish admit to having no history.

My own autobiography must await another and more appropriate day. However, it is not inappropriate to set down some details from my personal past, if only because they provide some hints of where the Irish have been.

My first consciousness of social reality was the parish of St. Angela in the Austin district of West Side Chicago in the 1930s. It was about as far as the Irish had managed to go, socially and geographically. St. Angela's would be considered a lower-middle-class neighborhood, but it still represented the upper limit for most American Irish. Up and down the street I lived on were policemen, firemen, city and state employees, an occasional newspaperman, an architect, doctor, or lawyer, shopkeepers, tavern owners, assistant department store managers (local stores, not the big ones downtown), assistant chief clerks in Loop businesses, and a rare impoverished stockbroker and corporation executive like my father. Most of the firemen were lieutenants or chiefs, and the policemen were sergeants or captains. (And judging by life style, our captain was surely one of the wealthiest men in the community. Where he got his money is a subject on which we did not speculate very much.) I do not think there was much unemployment among us in the 1930s—though several of my uncles and older cousins were out of jobs. We were, of course, Democrats and Roman Catholics. We were friendly enough with our non-Catholic neighbors although, as I remember it, we rarely visited each other's houses, but then there was not that much socializing in the 1930s. Very few of our young people went to college, at least not in the 1930s, though in the early 1940s considerable numbers of young men were in V 5, V 12, and other officers' training programs. By the middle '40s, many returning veterans swarmed into the colleges and universities. De Paul and Loyola, until then very tiny liberal arts colleges, suddenly became large universities with thousands of students.

My class graduated from grammar school in 1942, and I think only a few of us took it for granted that high school would be a preparation for college. I was one of those, and even if I hadn't gone to the seminary, it was a foregone conclusion that I would go to college. My father was aware that, while he had succeeded in the business world with only two years of college, the situation had changed radically. Even in 1946, in the midst of the immense expansion of college enrollments immediately after the end of the war, my grammar school classmates found it difficult to settle for the immediate security of a job or to take the risk of devoting four years to college. That seems like a strange attitude now, but in those days the memory of the Great Depression was still very much alive and going to college was viewed as a serious risk. Caution was the watchword even in 1946, and college graduates often had a harder time getting jobs than those willing to accept a safe civil service career. I think most of my classmates were urged by their parents to take the secure, if unrewarding, path; their advice would be bitterly resented by my contemporaries in the years that came after.

The majority, then, did not go to college. Many did go subsequently, either struggling through night school or taking advantage of the GI Bill after the Korean War. However, most of them were never graduated from college and they now find themselves permanently frozen in the lower middle class, though a lower middle class of moderate suburban comfort. Only a handful of girls went to college, mostly to become nurses or teachers. As far as I can tell, even those who did go to college became salesmen, middle management supervisors, or school principals, or ran a small business, their family's or their own. I don't think there is a doctor, lawyer, or college teacher in the whole group.

At the end of the Great Depression and during and immediately after the Second World War, the economic and social horizons of the American Irish were severely limited. Some have become successful without higher education, and most of the well-to-do Irish businessmen of the 1920s, '30s, and early '40s (and there were some, particularly in the construction business, who managed to flourish despite the Depression) had managed to achieve their success at a time when higher education was not required for upward mobility. Doctors, lawyers, schoolteachers, and nurses had to go to college, but no one else did. If you were ambitious, it was assumed you could make it by hard work and good luck. Surely that had been the case for my father, who was graduated from his two-year high school class as valedictorian, in the early 1900s. My mother's brothers were much less ambitious; they and their children were apparently quite content with their lower-middle-class respectability provided by the prosperity of the 1920s.

I have often felt that the seven years I spent at the major seminary, from 1947 to 1954, were the turning point for the American Irish. The GI Bill had made it possible for them to seek higher education, and the incredible expansion of the economy had created room for a vast number of technical and professional men and women and small business entrepreneurs. In 1947 it was not taken for granted that every young Irish-American who graduated from high school would go to college; seven years later, going to college was a matter of course, not only for the young man but for his sister, too. In the parish to which I was first assigned, peopled by American Irish much like those of St. Angela save that they had made a great deal of money in the last decade, it was taken for granted that young men and women would go to college. Christ the King was St. Angela, not merely fifteen years after the Great Depression was over; those years contained the greatest burst of economic prosperity the American Irish had ever experienced. If there is any point to these recollections of mine, it is that we were completely unprepared for prosperity. On the contrary, like most other Americans, we expected another depression after the war, and hedged our career bets to escape the worst effects. Instead of depression, however, we enjoyed continued prosperity. My own age peers made the wrong bets in 1946, mostly because we were unfortunate enough to be born at just the wrong time. Our younger brothers and sisters were much more fortunate; what was not obvious to us certainly was to them. The Irish were not ready for the revolution of rising expectations, but when the revolution came, we managed to take advantage of it in the space of a few years. In the 1950s, many of us made it big, and our full-fledged arrival in American society was sealed by the paper-thin triumph of John Kennedy in 1960. Since then, the problem for the American Irish has not been making it so much as knowing what in the world to do with it.

To stretch these personal impressions into a very tentative general theory, I would suggest that from the beginning of migration until the beginning of the present century, the Irish were essentially manual workers, with an occasional professional, small businessman, nurse, or schoolteacher. From 1900 through the 1920s they moved into the lower middle class; there were more small businessmen, professionals, skilled workers, government employees, supervisors in government agencies, and upwardly mobile, though not college-educated, corporation types like my father. On the eve of the Great Depression, about the time of the Al Smith campaign, it seems likely that if prosperity had continued, the weight of the Irish thrust would have carried many of us into the upper middle class. The Depression delayed this breakthrough for fifteen years, but the GI Bill and the economic expansion after the Second World War enabled us to recoup the losses of the 1930s. While all of us did not become upper middle class or well-to-do, we managed nonetheless to obtain an occupational distribution similar to that of the Northern urban Anglo-Saxon Protestants. We had few, if any, very poor, and only a tiny handful of very rich, but some of us were wealthy and practically all of us were comfortable. Even if John Kennedy had not been elected in 1960, the immigrant era for the American Irish would have been over.

We now had our nice suburban homes, our cars, our precious respectability, the responsibility of providing college educations for our children, the comfort of knowing we were successes in life, Florida vacations in the winter and an occasional trip to Europe in the summer, and the pride of having one of our own kind in the White House—however briefly.

We had made it, and many of us had made it big. We had little sense of our own history and could not describe exactly how the pilgrimage from impoverished peasant Ireland to well-to-do professional suburbia had been made, but we knew that we had overcome big obstacles on that pilgrimage and were ready to take credit for our own contributions to its success. We conveniently forgot that most of our achievement resulted from the good fortune of having been born at the right time. We certainly did work hard, but it was more the beneficent American economy than our efforts that made us successful. Nevertheless, we were successful, and no one could deny us our proper place in American society. In the early '50s, our fellow Irish-American, Senator Joseph McCarthy, confirmed our suspicions that not only were we as good Americans as anyone else, we were perhaps just a little better. And despite Pat Moynihan's unforgettable phrase, "Harvard men were to be investigated, and Fordham men were to do the investigating," in the Middle West we preferred to think of Notre Dame men as doing the investigating.

By 1960, the American Irish had everything they had ever dreamed of and a good deal more than their ancestors in pre-Famine Ireland could have imagined. But what happens to an immigrant group which for a hundred years has tried to prove itself to a skeptical and suspicious society? What happens to a group which, having invested all its resources and energies into making it, finally succeeds?

In other words, what do you do for an encore?

10.

The Next Generation

We are the music-makers,
  And we are the dreamers of dreams,
Wandering by lone sea-breakers,
  And sitting by desolate streams;—
World-losers and world-forsakers,
  On whom the pale moon gleams:
Yet we are the movers and shakers
  Of the world for ever, it seems.

We, in the ages lying
  In the buried past of the earth,
Built Nineveh with our sighing,
  And Babel itself with our mirth;
And o'erthrew them with prophesying
  To the old of the new world's worth;
For each age is a dream that is dying,
  Or one that is coming to birth.

ARTHUR O'SHAUGHNESSY
1844–1881

Recently, I spoke with a very distinguished American, part of whose professional responsibilities is to deal with very gifted young people who have just graduated from college.[1] I asked him about a young man I knew well who had been under his supervision for a period of time. My friend shook his head:

"Most of the young people I deal with are very bright Jewish kids. They have been adored all their lives. No one has ever said

---

1. For a number of reasons, I will leave his precise tasks "gray."

no to them on anything. They are unbelievably brilliant, but completely lacking in self-discipline and quite unused to disapproval of any sort. They may perform a task for me with extreme competence but less satisfactorily than their abilities warrant or less than what I need; then they are horrified when I tell them it is no good and has to be done over. Nobody has ever said anything like that to them before in their lives. Disapproval and rejection are traumatic at first, but once they get used to them they become much better organized individuals, and much more capable of focusing their energies and resources toward disciplined, high-quality performance."

He shook his head again. "But *your* young friend is another matter. He is at least as cocky and self-assertive in his manner as the Jewish kids, but I am afraid his ego is very fragile, and I am sure that if I leaned on him with the same technique I used on the Jewish kids he would dissolve. I wonder if this kid has ever experienced any real approval at all in his life. The Jewish kids have too much self-confidence, and he doesn't have any. They need self-discipline, and he needs . . . I don't know what he needs, but he certainly needs it."

I do not want to be trapped into a debate about whether the childhood experiences of the gifted Jewish boys described above is typical or not, but I must say my friend's generalizations certainly fit my own experience. There is little difference between the Jewish and Irish graduate students and young scholars who come to the National Opinion Research Center, but the Jewish young men are supremely self-confident and assertive and the Irish Catholics are quiet, timid, and diffident—sometimes almost paralyzed with the fear of making a mistake. If a Jewish graduate student does something wrong, he cheerfully admits his mistake, laughs it off, and goes charging merrily back into the fray. The Irish graduate student, on the other hand, is not likely to make a mistake because he is not likely to take any risks. One gets the impression that the young Jewish person considers an occasional mistake a minor event, while the young Irish person considers a single mistake to be a catastrophe.

188

Obviously, not all Jewish graduate students are as confident or self-assertive as my sketchy description might indicate, and they have emotional hangups of their own. But I shall leave, for the present, the problems of young Americans to scholars who are writing on that subject; I shall be content with the observation that, at least in the world of academia, the self-confidence of the young Jew is extremely helpful to his success, and the timidity and fear of making a mistake are disastrous for the young Irish Catholic.

I know little about the socialization experiences of upper-middle-class Jewish youth and have little feel for the neuroses which might be engendered by that socialization; but I know all too well what socialization is for the upper-middle-class Catholic, and I know far more than I like about what it does to them.

Let me be more precise. The sons and daughters of the well-to-do Irish are an extraordinarily gifted and creative group of human beings, in whom the literary, political, and creative skills, which historically have been attributed to the Irish, are as strong and powerful as they ever were. But these talents and skills are paralyzed by self-doubt and self-hatred. Unfortunately there are not very many Irish psychiatrists, and not very many young American Irish would be caught dead in a therapist's office. Therefore, we lack a clinical literature on the neurosis of the well-to-do Irish. It is a pity, because that particular neurosis, or set of neuroses, is one of the most destructive and wasteful forms of mental illness in our society.

I do not pretend even now, after seventeen years of fighting this neurosis, to understand its dynamics completely, but I do know where it is aimed. The socialization experience of the Irish-American child is geared to prevent him from doing anything that would cause him to lose the respectability that his family has worked so long and so hard to achieve. With few exceptions, the children of the Irish upper middle class are not so maimed that they cannot become reasonably successful in the business and professional world. But even following the career patterns of their parents, the young Irish are raised so that they display relatively little flair or brilliance; indeed, not even the amount of flair their parents needed to make it into the ranks of the "very respectable." Risk-taking was all right for your parents, the socialization experience seems to communicate, but you were born having "made it." Risks are no longer required, and, more than that, they are dangerous. If you take risks, you may lose that for which your parents worked so hard.

If brilliance and flair are counterproductive, then the slightest risk-taking beyond the limits of approved career and personal behavior is unthinkable. Art, music, literature, poetry, theater, to some extent even academia, politics of any variety other than the traditional, creative self-expression are all too risky to be considered. The two most devastating things that can be said to the young upper-middle-class Irishman who attempts to move beyond these rigid norms are, "Who do you think you are?" and "What will people say?"

With those words, many American-Irish parents systematically, if unintentionally, destroy the self-confidence and creative ingenuity of their children, precisely because they are afraid that the confident, creative young person might do something to embarrass the family or cause it to lose its hard-won respectability. Cutting him down to size, keeping him in his place, not letting him get a big head, forcing him to learn early how hard life is, warning him of the dangers of risk-taking, urging him to diligent and responsible work—all these are techniques well-calculated to prevent risk-taking of any sort, particularly those risks that are necessary to the creative process.

One way of visualizing the socialization experience of a young American Irishman is to observe how rarely he is praised by his parents. Failure is quickly pointed out and denounced, but success is noted without further comment. In my own life I cannot recall ever being praised by my parents for any achievement, and in my early years as a priest I remember waiting—in vain, as it turned out—for a word of approval from my pastor. (Seminary training being what it was at the time, the first pastor inevitably became a powerful father surrogate.) This experience is by no means unique to me.

Affection among the Irish is implicit. We assume that our

parents and spouses love us because they never say they don't and because their loyalty and fidelity can only be based on love, but explicit, conscious, articulated, and demonstrated affection seems denied us most of the time. Praise, I suppose, is merely another form of affection; it is affection which reinforces accomplishment. If the Irish don't know how to give affection, they can hardly be expected to know how to praise.

More than just the inability to express affection is involved. Praise is withheld as a matter of deliberate and conscious policy— partly, I think, because it is assumed that if the child doesn't know quite where he stands with his parents, his efforts to win approval will not cease. The withholding of praise and affection is not merely a strategy to prevent him from getting a big head and lording it over his siblings; it is not merely an attempt to prepare him for life in a world where he will receive little praise; it is also a means of control. Perhaps it is not fully conscious, but it is powerfully effective, nonetheless. If, as some Jewish writers would have us believe, Jewish mothers control their children by showering them with affection, Irish parents are inclined to control theirs by withholding affection and approval.

Interestingly enough, this technique of keeping the young person guessing where he really stands with his parents (or, to put the matter more specifically, whether his parents really love him or not) is a form of social control that is or was widely used in Catholic seminaries, convents, and novitiates. The "subject" was first reduced to a state of childlike dependence on the "superior," and then the "superior" would give or withhold affection in arbitrary and capricious fashion, thus reinforcing the dependency relationship. I sometimes think that the reason so many priests and nuns are leaving the religious life is that they are seeking a form of affection which is constant and predictable rather than uncertain and inconsistent.[2]

Brian Friel's play, *Philadelphia, Here I Come,* presents a classic

---

2. It should be carefully noted that most such practices have long since been abandoned in seminaries and novitiates. Now, instead of the superior becoming a surrogate matriarch or patriarch, he or she becomes a group therapist or T-group trainer. It is, on the whole, an improvement—I think.

example of an Irish father-son relationship, with the two men desperately trying to express their love for each other, and at the last moment just barely failing as the son goes off for Philadelphia. I do not think that most Irish parents are happy with the kinds of relationships that tradition demands they have with their children; yet they are terribly conscious of the danger of "spoiling" the young people with praise. For the folklore says that a praised child or an approved child is a spoiled child, and there is nothing worse.

In 1954, when I arrived in Beverly Hills (Chicago variety), the conventional wisdom maintained that the teen-agers of the parish had been "spoiled" because their parents had "given them everything" or "given them everything they wanted when they were children." More unspoiled children I cannot imagine; the young people of Beverly were intelligent, poised, serious, respectful—and, as it turned out later, desperately hungry for affection and respect. However, the mythology was powerful, and parents felt terribly guilty about not forcing their children to work their way through high school and college. They were wary of demonstrating approval or respect or showing confidence that their child would amount to anything. Obviously, there were some exceptions, but not very many. Most of the young people of Christ the King parish emerged from their childhood experience with the profound conviction that they were worthless and doomed to failure.

If one writes a book, or poem, or article, or if one ventures forth to announce the need for a new church or a new politics, or if one attempts a work of art, then one is exposing his whole self and runs the risk of "making a mistake." Every young Irish-American knows that to reveal the self is to reveal it as utterly worthless.

For some of the most gifted of the American Irish, success and creative behavior, whether in the traditional occupations or in new kinds of activity, can be even worse than failure, because if you succeed you mark yourself as different. For reasons not altogether clear to me, to be different is a horrifying possibility; it means that one must keep on being different, that one must get ever more deeply involved in behavior that will lead more and more people to say, "Who do you think you are?" The person who is different continues to take risks, and the more he pyramids risks, the farther he will fall when the inevitable disaster hits him. A venture into free-reined creativity will certainly bring disaster. Books, articles, songs, paintings, new organizations, and new ideas are undertaken without any intention of finishing them, at least not in an unmythological world.

Despite my experience with young people, I cannot comprehend this paralyzing neurosis. My whole tendency is toward the opposite: they refuse to take the slightest risk, and I tend to snatch at every risk. They won't gamble at all, and my life has been a series of gambles. They refuse to risk their fundamental selfhood on the printed page, and I have inundated my ego with thousands of printed pages. It took me a long, long time to understand anyone who could turn away not just from the possibility of publication, but from the absolute certainty of it. It is not, however, that my young friends do not believe intellectually that they are capable of publishing. On the contrary, they know very well that they are, but at the very core of their personalities they are so terrified of the consequences of revealing themselves in public that they do not want to be published. Better mediocre obscurity than the glaring light of publicity.

There are relatively few young Irish-Americans in the youth counterculture. The ones I know have little love for war and a strong dislike of racial injustice, but they also are contemptuous of what they consider to be the self-defeating political ineptitude of the counterculture. They insist that there is a middle ground between the Establishment and the counterculture, and it is in that middle ground that political and social action can occur. Unfortunately, when they are challenged to articulate their own political philosophies and goals, they become tongue-tied. Similarly, when they are challenged to articulate the religious convictions which they assert exist somewhere between the conservatism of their parents and the counterculture expressions of the young clergy, they also become vague and incoherent—or even worse, oracular and pontifical. They are great at criticizing both the left and the right; they are also great at coming up with excuses for not doing anything themselves. They yield nothing to their age peers in the counterculture—for example, in their dissatisfaction with the corporate structures of business, labor, government, church, education—though when one asks them for concrete programs of change, they reply in paragraphs where verbs are singularly absent.

Further, when one proposes to them that there is a vast literature on social problems which they should master if they are serious about reform, they will accept a reading list, but only rarely use it. Many of the young American Irish I know seem almost afraid to read for fear that the time spent on reading and thinking will be time taken from more critical activities, such as compulsive worry.

I do not know the origin of these paralyzing fears of self-disclosure, of risk-taking, of making a mistake, of being judged. They are filtered through a family situation where approval is infrequent and unconditioned love almost nonexistent. But why is the socialization process of the Irish family so destructive to the confidence, self-esteem, and creativity of its young people? Is it the memory of the Great Depression? Is it the pathetic desire for respectability of a despised immigrant group? Is it the horror of the Famine, the degradation and insecurity of the Penal years, the frustration of a thousand years of foreign oppression; or is it something that reaches back even to the pre-Christian Celtic twilight? I confess I do not know the answer. I do know that the tendency to cut others down to size is not a post–World War II Irish phenomenon. The organization of the agricultural economy and its accompanying family structure described by Arensberg and Kimball[3] certainly would have induced fierce competitiveness among siblings, as well as the parental inclination to prevent any one sibling from rising above the others. Furthermore, in the Penal years, any Irishman who had spectacular success would have achieved it by selling out to the English conquerors at the expense of his fellows.

We are, like most other groups of human beings, extremely ambivalent about our most successful colleagues. Some American Irish adore the Kennedy family, but others despise it: "Who do

---

3. Conrad Arensberg and Solon Kimball, *Family and Community in Ireland* (New York: Harcourt, Brace & World, 1965).

they think they are?" The most fierce hatred I ever heard expressed for the Kennedys came from Boston Irish clergymen ("Harvard bastards" is one of the few printable comments). The brilliant, successful child is, I think, much less prized by the Irish family than by the Jewish family, because if the child is too successful, others will try to cut him, and his family, down to size. Successful he must be, but not too successful, for then "What will people say?" At the risk of pushing the Jewish comparison too far, it seems to me that the Jewish-American culture has found much more effective ways of coping with competitiveness and the rivalry and envy it engenders than has the Irish-American culture. We teach our children to repress; Jews teach their children to express. On the whole, I am inclined to think that the Jewish adaptation—which is probably not without its weaknesses—is more healthy, for in the long run an excess of self-expression is probably not nearly so unhealthy as its total absence.

For all their problems the Irish youth are not doing that badly in American society. If one reads melancholy accounts of Irish failure of the sort presented by Glazer and Moynihan,[4] especially in the Introduction to the new edition of *Beyond the Melting Pot,* and if one goes through the Catholic liberal literature, which proclaims the mediocrity of Irish Catholicism, one would conclude that the Irish have limited their efforts to business, the professions, and politics, and have done well only in the last. And even in politics they are now being elbowed out by other groups as the Irish business and professional class settles down to conservative and anti-intellectual suburban comforts.

However, NORC's ongoing studies of young people suggest that things may not be quite so bleak.[5] Among young people who were graduated from college in 1961 and who were last interviewed by us in 1968 (Table 36), both the Irish and the Jews overchose

---

4. Nathan Glazer and Daniel Patrick Moynihan, *Beyond the Melting Pot,* 2nd ed. (Cambridge, Mass.: MIT Press, 1970, paperback).

5. In 1961 an Irish-American was a little less than twice as likely as a typical American to graduate from college. A Jew was a little more than twice as likely. All other major groups trailed far behind.

TABLE 36

RANK ORDER OF POPULARITY OF PROFESSIONS FOR AMERICAN
IRISH WHO GRADUATED FROM COLLEGE IN 1961
(AS RECORDED IN 1968), COMPARED WITH AMERICAN JEWS

	Ratio of actual choice to expected choice	
	Irish	Jews
Law	2.96	2.50
Medicine	1.88	3.21
Biological sciences	1.25	1.08
Physical sciences	1.02	.90
Education	1.02	.72
Humanities	1.01	.86
Social sciences	.99	1.25
Business	.95	1.41
Other professions	.80	.69
Engineering	.46	.75
	N = 355	N = 360

law and medicine—the latter being more likely to choose medicine and the former more likely to choose law.[6]

The Irish and the Jews differ greatly from the general population of graduates in their career choices but not very much from each other. The Irish are more likely than the Jews to be in the humanities, the physical and biological sciences, and education than are the Jews; the Jews are more likely to be in the social sciences and medicine than are the Irish.

The Irish are more likely to have Ph.D's or other advanced professional degrees than WASP Americans (19 per cent versus 12 per cent), and they have such degrees in about the same proportions as Jews (Table 36). The Jews, on the other hand, clearly make more money than the Irish and expect to in years to come.

---

6. If a profession was chosen by the same percentage of the Irish as of all other groups, the score would be 1.00. Thus a score of 2.96 says that the Irish are three times as likely to be lawyers as is the general population of 1961 graduates. A score of .46 means that the Irish are only half as likely to be engineers as the typical graduate.

TABLE 37

EDUCATIONAL BACKGROUND AND INCOME OF IRISH, WASP,
AND JEWISH YOUNG PEOPLE

(1961 college graduates interviewed in 1968)

	Percentages		
	Irish	**WASP**	**Jewish**
Ph.D. or professional degree	19	12	21
Income now more than $15,000	23	27	45
Expected income more than $25,000 in five years	21	22	43
Expected income more than $30,000 at age 45	41	40	65
	N = 492	N = 2,170	N = 495

However, the Irish are no less successful or hopeful economically than WASP Americans (Table 37).

Nor is there much difference between Irish and WASPs in their values and attitudes toward their jobs (Table 38). Jews are more likely to stress "responsibility" in a job and a little less likely to say they will get their major life satisfaction from their careers. The Irish are less likely to emphasize "control" over their own work and the Jews more likely to stress "intellectual" occupational values. In terms of occupational values and attitudes, then, there is much more similarity than diversity among the three groups.

Religious differences (Table 39) are considerable. The Irish and the Jews are substantially more likely to remain loyal to their religions than are WASPs; and 77 per cent of the Irish go to church every week (higher than the Catholic national average) while only 29 per cent of the Protestants and 4 per cent of the Jews attend church weekly.

Given the fact that the three ethnic groups have rather different patterns of occupational choice, the most appropriate comparisons would be among those who have entered the same general professional field. Table 40 provides some extraordinarily interesting information about Irish, WASP, and Jewish young people who have entered the fields of science and engineering. Forty per cent

197

TABLE 38

OCCUPATIONAL VALUES AND ATTITUDES OF IRISH,
WASP, AND JEWISH YOUNG PEOPLE

	Percentages		
	Irish	WASP	Jewish
"Very Important" in job			
Responsibility	55	63	55
Variety	68	67	64
Control over own work	43	58	54
Control over others' work	19	17	15
Challenge	72	76	77
Career will be major source of life satisfaction	25	17	22
Occupational values			
"Intellectual"	42	53	43
"People"	57	57	51
"Security"	11	13	15

TABLE 39

RELIGIOUS AFFILIATION AND BEHAVIOR AMONG IRISH,
WASP, AND JEWISH YOUNG PEOPLE

	Percentages		
	Irish	WASP	Jewish
Same religion as that in which they were raised	94	76	92
Weekly church attendance	77	29	4

of the Irish have Ph.D.'s, as opposed to about 25 per cent of the
Jews and 20 per cent of the WASPs. Fifty-eight per cent of the
Irish work in an academic or research setting, as do 30 per cent
of the Jews and 24 per cent of the WASPs. There is little difference between the Irish and the Jews in income; both are ahead
of the WASPs. The Jews are substantially more sympathetic with

TABLE 40

CAREER ATTITUDES AND BEHAVIOR OF IRISH,
WASP, AND JEWISH SCIENTISTS AND ENGINEERS

	Percentages		
	Irish	WASP	Jewish
Ph.D.	43	19	27
Employed by college or university	58	24	30
Earning more than $15,000	56	39	59
Expecting more than $20,000 in five years	58	24	60
High on pro-militancy index	32	20	51
High on anti-expert index	3	15	16
High on reading index	32	15	25
High on arts index	25	17	35
High on "intellectual"	75	47	64
"people"	23	14	20
"security"	5	14	12
Same religion as in childhood	90	70	98
Weekly church attendance	73	44	10
	N = 40	N = 295	N = 27

student and black militancy than the Irish scientists, but the Irish in their turn display more sympathy than the WASPs.

The Irish are the least likely (only 3 per cent) to have a high score on an "anti-science" index. They are more likely than the Jews and the WASPs to have a high score on an index measuring the amount of reading they do, though lower than the Jews on an index measuring artistic activity. They are the most likely to subscribe to "intellectual" occupational values and least likely (only 5 per cent) to be concerned about "security" in their jobs. There is, finally, virtually no difference between the Irish scientists and the other Irish (Table 39) in their church affiliation and Mass attendance.

One must conclude from Table 40 that on most measures of "scholarship" or "intellectuality" the young Irish are ahead of the young Jews. One could almost say that as a group the young Irish scientists display an enthusiastic commitment to scholarship and intellectualism. We have no measures of the quality of their work, but in terms of quantity the Irish are clearly ahead of white Protestants and certainly not behind the Jews.

Peter Berger has suggested that we might be going through a "circulation of elites" of the sort described by the social theorist Pareto. The sons and daughters of the Jewish and WASP well-to-do are joining the counterculture and leaving behind the square technological society. As they devote themselves to the "greening of America," Berger notes, only half-jokingly, "the sons and daughters of the ethnics may be involved in a 'bluing of America' " —they may be replacing Jews and WASPs in the key positions which control society and keep it moving. If Yale is unwilling to run the country any more, says Berger, Fordham will be only too happy to take over.

A number of Jewish scholars have suggested to me that the Jews are not going to be able to continue their central, if not dominant, role in the cultural life of the country because so many of their gifted young people are "tuning out." As one colleague put it, "The Irish will become the Jews of the *fin de siècle.*" Well, maybe. I'm inclined to be skeptical about the extent or permanence of youthful Jewish involvement in the counterculture. Nevertheless, while the young scientists described in these pages are too old—twenty-eight on the average when we interviewed them—to be candidates for the counterculture, they do present some evidence that the Irish are waiting in the wings of American science and will be only too happy to take over.

What will happen to the young American Irish? What will become of young people who, if our impressions and data are correct, have superabundant qualities of vitality and creative ability locked up within extraordinarily powerful mechanisms of self-distrust? I am neither sure nor hopeful. A few fortunate young men and young women may be immune from the effects of a childhood experience that was basically repressive. These should have, I think, lives of extraordinary creativity and happiness. The only thing is, I don't know any of them. A few others have been so effectively maimed psychologically that all they are capable of are lives of dull mediocrity. Through long and painful therapeutic processes, some others may be able to unlock their vast talents; but most, I fear, will live lives of noisy desperation, availing themselves of all the mechanisms of self-destruction that the Irish have traditionally made available for themselves—drink, obesity, temper tantrums, unending quarrels. Now we can add to the list those newer forms of drug-induced destruction and the typically American suburban means of slow suicide, migraine headaches, bleeding ulcers, high blood pressure, and early coronaries. It is not a very hopeful picture, but I will confess that I am aware of very little evidence that one should be hopeful on the subject of the children of the Irish upper middle class.

One of the more interesting and tragic aspects of this decline of the American Irish is the relationships between the children of the postwar lower to upper middle class and their own children. The young people I know are sophisticated enough psychologically to be aware of the mistakes their parents made in raising them; they are thus quite conscious of the possibility of making mistakes with their own children. Yet the destruction of their self-confidence has left them with very little confidence in their ability to be mothers and fathers (to say nothing of their ability to be husbands and wives). As one young mother has put it, "We are afraid of our children. We have this brand-new human being in our house, and we know that what we do to it is going to have a tremendous impact on the rest of its life; but we don't know what to do. We don't want to imitate our own parents and be too harsh, yet we understand that if we're too soft we make another whole set of mistakes. So, as a result, we don't do much of anything at all, and it doesn't take long before a child gets the idea that we are afraid of him. He's puzzled and uneasy about those fears, so he does the only obvious and easy thing—he exploits them. What do you do with a child who knows that you're afraid of him?"

And what do you do for a parent who has so little confidence in his own selfhood that he is afraid of an infant? The world of the young Irish-American is filled with all kinds of demons and monsters, more frightening and more malicious than the leprechauns, the banshees, and the pookies of the past. Now it turns out that some of the monsters are really "little people," though not the ones in Irish mythology; the "little people" are his own children.

If the kids turned into leprechauns I wouldn't much mind, for the world can do with more of them; but I am afraid they will turn into howling banshees—or their functional equivalent—and of those we have more than a sufficiency.

11.

The Irish Politician

*A man who will not be loyal to his friends will
never be loyal to an idea.*
                    Young Irish-American Politician

A few months ago my normally uneventful social life was enlivened by parties on two successive nights. One was with a group of relatively young University of Chicago social scientists, and the other was with a group of middle-aged Irish lawyer-politicians. Both parties were delightful. Each group held political and social postures similar to my own. But the difference between the two groups was striking—and it was not just that the lawyers had substantially higher incomes. Their intellectual styles were totally different. The conversation of the university people involved a considerable display of wide erudition, an attempt to achieve balanced, nuanced, and comprehensive judgments, a strong effort to see all sides of the issue, and frequent attempts to argue a position not really one's own, in order to make a contribution to the development of a subtle and balanced perspective.

At the lawyer's party, one leaped from insight to insight, from striking phrase to striking phrase, from pragmatic judgment to devastating comment with dizzying speed. The lawyers seemed more interested in dazzling their adversaries than in making what the intellectuals would have considered balanced judgments. Instead of circling around an issue, the legal style would dart instantly to the core of the problem, shake it as a cat does a mouse, and then summarize it in a few quick phrases which indicated not merely the fundamental nature of the problem but also the kind of action that ought to be taken tomorrow morning.

It is not my intention to try to make an abstract judgment about which style is superior. My lawyer friends would do very poorly at a research center, and my social science friends would get routed before a jury. Should they ever confront one another, the outcome would depend entirely on the area of confrontation. If the issue was the analysis of the complexities of social problems, the university scholars would win in a walk; if the issue was practical problems, particularly winning an election, the lawyers would cream the intellectuals, even though some of them are political scientists. Even if they shared the same goal, which I think they did, in these particular instances, working together in harness for very long would likely be a considerable strain on both sides of the relationship. If they were in opposition, it would almost be inevitable that the intellectuals would decide the lawyers were impossibly corrupt and immoral, only interested in political power, and the lawyers would assume that the intellectuals knew absolutely nothing about the realities of political power. (To use a quote attributed to the mayor of Chicago, "Those experts, they don't know nothin'.")

I am reminded of a remark made by my colleague Professor Arthur Mann, the biographer of Mayor Fiorello LaGuardia, "It is the fashion for intellectuals to write the biographies of politicians, and in doing so, they are apt to criticize the politicians for not having the skills of intellectuals. I often wonder what would happen if politicians should write the biographies of intellectuals; presumably they would criticize intellectuals for not having the skills of politicians."[1]

---

1. My colleagues Emmet Larkin and Sean O'Connor have suggested to me that there are two roots of the Irish-American political style. One may be found in the Gaelic customary legal tradition, and the other is in the British parliamentary system of the late eighteenth and early nineteenth centuries. Both these strains meet in the person of Daniel O'Connell, perhaps the greatest of Irish politicians.

By O'Connell's time there were several hundred thousand Catholic voters in Ireland by virtue of the law which permitted "forty shilling freeholders" to vote. Many of these had been enfranchised by their landlords who, characteristic of those involved in British politics of the time, thought of the vote

One of the problems in understanding the political style of the American Irish is that most of those who comment in serious journals lack sympathy and fail to understand the style from the inside. The Irish developed and continue to practice the style of ethnic politics. They see no relevance for their work in the concerns of the intellectual, and are not inclined even to listen to him. There are very few people like Daniel Patrick Moynihan who stand between the two groups, and they are likely to find themselves suspected by both. It is a pity, because the two perspectives need one another. The pure pragmatism of the Irish politician has no appeal for the young, and he is not well equipped to respond to

---

as a property which could be bought and sold. O'Connell, with the support of the Church, won these votes away from the landlords and built a political organization, which, like all British parliamentary organizations of the time, was based on patronage and personal loyalty. In addition to being a "Whig magnifico" (Professor Larkin's phrase) with thirty-six seats at his command, O'Connell was also a west-of-Ireland, Irish-speaking landlord, deeply involved in the ancient Brehon law. Brehon law was, in Father O'Connor's words, a law without law enforcement. Order was maintained by a combination of subtle, informal controls (especially ridicule) and strong networks of personal loyalty. The Irish, in other words, were able to play the British parliamentary game with great skill because there were elements in their own tradition which prepared them for that game. British politics underwent many reforms in the later nineteenth century, but the American Irish discovered a political system which was very like what they had left behind, and with much more room to maneuver in. They came to the United States with considerable political skills that were admirably suited to the politics of the cities. Many of the other immigrant groups, on the other hand, had no experience with electoral politics until they came to this shore. The Irish were only too willing to teach them the game—at the price of taking over the O'Connell role of honest broker between two political systems.

Professor Larkin has pointed out to me that the Famine Irish had not been greatly affected by either the educational revolution begun in Ireland by the national school system (1830) or by the devotional revolution which was barely underway by the time of the Famine. Thus they were uneducated and lacking in a cultural heritage around which they could focus their lives. (In Larkin's theory, the devotional revolution provided a substitute heritage for the Gaelic language and culture which was moribund in most of the country by the early part of the nineteenth century.) It is also quite likely that many of them spoke little if any English, since the Irish language was still strong in the very western counties from which most of the Famine immigrants came. The nativist stereotypes were not pure fiction. The first great wave (unlike the slower migration of mostly shopkeepers and small landholders) included many uneducated, undisciplined, hard-drinking, pugnacious, half-starved peasants. The immigrants who came after 1860 were a very different group, but the stereotype by then was firmly fixed in the American mind—and residues of it still remain.

205

the complex aspirations of poor minority groups. On the other hand, the ideological moralism of the intellectuals rarely, if ever, wins elections—at least not outside New York City. At this point, communication between the two groups seems extremely unlikely. The intelligentsia flails merrily away at Richard J. Daley without ever bothering to try to understand, or even asking whether it is worth understanding, why he keeps on winning elections. And the mayor, in his turn, continues to pile up popular landslides without bothering to ask whether the experts, for all their ineptitude, might be saying something worthwhile.

The Irish are not the only practitioners of ethnic politics, though it can scarcely be denied that they have great skills in this particular kind of urban coalition-building. Before any Irish reader gets too cocky about the political skills of his people, he should remember that the most effective ethnic political organization in the country, that of Chicago, was put together not by an Irishman but by a Czech, Anton Cermak. Cermak accomplished that feat largely because he was powerful enough to knock contentious Irish heads together; the Irish seemed to enjoy fighting among themselves more than against their proper opponents—the Republicans, of course.

The masters of ethnic politics are not intellectuals; they probably do not know of the existence of *The Village Voice*. They are not adept at articulating abstract ideas. Their insight into the city and what makes it tick is not phrased in slick social science terminology. Any attempt to state their model of the political process in formal terms is bound to lose something of the vigor and flavor of the original. On the other hand, while intellectual types may find the poor diction and malapropisms of some of the ethnic politicians vastly amusing, their amusement should not blind them to the fact that the best politicians have an intuitive grasp of the city that would make the most skillful social scientist look naive.

The first assumption of ethnic politics is that the city is composed of various groups—national, racial, economic, religious. It is the politician's role to act as a broker among these groups, arranging and rearranging power and resources in such a way as to prevent one group from becoming so unhappy with the balance that it will leave the system. He arranges (usually indirectly, informally, and

almost always gradually) among the various power elements
within the city compromises that these elements could not achieve
by direct negotiation among themselves. Without great fanfare,
Irish aldermen or congressmen are slowly phased out, to be replaced by Poles and then blacks. Does the organization slate a
black congressman to represent Cicero and Berwyn? It surely does,
but it doesn't issue press releases claiming that it is engaged in
revolution.

The "balanced" ticket is a symbol of this power brokerage game.
The politicians know that their city is composed of immigrant
groups still adjusting to American society, and these minorities are
jealous of their positions and sensitive to slights. To exclude any
one group from its "place" on the ticket is to insult and offend. If
you tell an ethnic politician that in one state the Democratic slate
is made up of three Jews and a black, and that the party still expects to get the Irish and Italian vote, he will simply not believe
you. And if you tell him that in another state a Unitarian minister
with an Irish name and an ideological liberal background heads a
slate on which, for the first time in many years, there are no Irish
Catholics, he will assume that the Irish vote will go Republican
and wonder who is responsible for such an inept decision.

He would certainly not be surprised by the post-election comment of a New York liberal, "We—the reformers—all wanted a
statewide primary. We got it and it gave us a ticket so unbalanced
ethnically and geographically that we didn't have a chance. This is
a pluralistic society—Italians vote as Italians, Irish as Irish—that's
the way it is. What haunts us is that the old bosses would never
have let this happen." But while he would agree, the ethnic politician would wonder why such a self-evident comment even had to
be made.

Nor would he be able to understand why some would consider
the balancing of power and piece-of-the-pie demands to be immoral.
The model of the new politics—enthusiastic college students from
"out of the neighborhood," vigorous ideological liberalism, passionate moral self-righteousness—would baffle him. The ethnic politician knows that in most districts of his city this model will simply
not win elections.

In his frame of reference you can't afford to lose one economic or racial or ethnic group. If you win an election at the price of turning off one such segment and setting the others against this scapegoat group, you're simply asking for trouble. No political leader can afford to lose a major group from his consensus, however self-righteous it may be. For he will find it difficult to govern without this group and even more difficult to be reelected.

No matter how you feel personally, you cannot afford to denounce any group explicitly, or even implicitly, or to let them feel excluded. Nor can you indulge in the luxury of telling them that they ought to feel guilty or that they are bigots. You win support for your policies and your candidates by obtaining consent, not by moralistic denunciations.

The ethnic politician also realizes that most people are not ideologues. He may be mildly amused by John Kenneth Galbraith's crusade for ideological purity in the Democratic party, but he knew long before Amitai Etzioni's brilliant article in *Trans-Action* that most people are quite "inconsistent" in their political attitudes— they are "liberal" on some issues and "conservative" on others. Furthermore, the ethnic politician realizes that for all the attention they get on the media, self-appointed "spokesmen" usually represent only themselves and a tiny band of friends. While ideological debates and "spokesmen" are a nuisance, they need be taken seriously only when they develop a capacity to deliver votes. Most citizens are not interested in ideology, but are moved by more concrete and pressing matters—jobs, sidewalks, garbage removal, streets, transportation, housing, access to the government to get assistance when needed. The vast network of precinct captains is not merely, or even principally, a downward channel of communication designed to convey voting instructions. It is also a technique—frequently more effective than public opinion polling—for determining what is on people's minds and providing them with a feeling of access to the system.

Why do you slate an obvious liberal like Adlai Stevenson at a time when the pundits are all persuaded that there is a realignment or a shift to the right or a backlash? Partly you may do it because you don't read the pundits, but partly because your instincts and

208

your organization say that Adlai is a winner. Why are you undismayed when a smooth advertising firm, relying on poll data and White House advice, turns out clever ads suggesting your candidate is "soft" on student radicals? Mostly because your instincts and your organization tell you that the student issue is not all that important and Adlai is still a winner. And why do you rejoice when the vice-president arrives on the scene as part of the realignment strategy and accuses Adlai of disgracing his father's name? Because you know your voters well enough to know that they are not going to be realigned by such foolishness and will certainly resent such an attack on someone about whom they have already made up their minds. Now you know he is a winner.

In other words, since he has far better data available to him and far greater faith in the relative consistency of voters, the ethnic politician is undismayed by the trends that columnists, commentators, and editorial writers in liberal journals think they see.

The ethnic politician is well aware of the voter's unpredictability, the strain toward bigotry, the extreme sensitivity to slights, the fear, the impatience with all politicians. But he also realizes that there is a strain toward rationality, openness, and trust and a sympathy for social reform, and that, in his better moments, John Q. Voter is capable of civility, intelligence, and generosity. Thus the ethnic politician is not too surprised when he rises to heights. Presiding over an organization is like conducting a symphony orchestra composed of gifted malcontents: you have good nights and bad nights (though I doubt that the ethnic politician would use the image). In other words, the appeal is to the voter's fears and his idealism, his selfishness and his integrity; and the politician hopes that he has become skillful in the art of blending them. Explicit philosophical assumptions about the nature of man are not considered, but implicitly it is assumed that he is a complicated and fragmented character and that politics requires dealing with complexity and fragmentation.

The ethnic politician is not opposed to social progress. His slogan that social progress is good politics is neither phony nor cynical but simply a statement of political reality as he sees it. His personal orientations may be either liberal or conservative, but they are irrelevant. He knows that if he is too conservative the balance will not shift rapidly enough to keep up with the changing state of his city, and if he is too liberal he may attempt to force change on the city before there is a broad enough consensus. In the '30s he supports the trade unions and in the '60s the black demand for power, but he supports both demands in ways that will not drive other groups out of his coalition. Such gradualism pleases neither spokesmen nor Official Liberals, but the ethnic politician argues that if he pleased either, the minority groups would not get more, but rather nothing, because the majority would turn to other and more reactionary leaders. In such an approach, there may be a tendency to move too slowly, especially if the organization has poor communication links with minority groups. However, the political leader is much less sanguine than his academic critic about the ability of any leadership to correct most social problems in a brief period of time.

Liberal candidates are by no means anathema to the ethnic politician. He knows that there is a strong liberal strain in his electorate, and that an articulate and intelligent liberal can have strong voter appeal. The liberal must be able to win, of course; he must want to win (frequently a difficulty for many American liberals); and he must not forget who helped him win. Furthermore, he must realize that he and his fellows cannot claim a monopoly on all offices. From the point of view of the ethnic politician, liberalism is good politics, especially when he can find a liberal who is willing to admit that politics can be good liberalism.

While his critics contend that patronage holds the organization together, the ethnic politician knows that loyalty is more important than jobs. The mockery to which Arthur Goldberg was subjected by those who thrust him into the political limelight in New York would be unthinkable to an ethnic politician. You stand by your own, even if they have made mistakes or grown a bit too old. You wait patiently in line until it is your turn to be slated. You accept the decisions of the organization with good grace, and work for the success of the ticket, even though you are personally disappointed. You do so because you are convinced that there is no other way to engage in politics; the alternative is what New York Democrats are currently calling "Balkanization."

In his book *The Irish and the Irish Politician,* Edward Levine tells the story of Nineteenth Ward Committeeman John Duffy, who supported Martin Kennelly against Daley in 1955 because of the loyalty that Duffy's mentor, Thomas Nash, felt for Kennelly. According to Levine, Daley is reputed to have said, "If I were Duffy, I would bolt." Later Duffy became the organization's president of the County Board and worked closely with the mayor. There is a nice etiquette required of those who must balance loyalties, but the phrase "Do what you have to do" is fully understood by the ethnic politicians. Levine quotes an Irish municipal official as saying, "The only criterion of success in politics is success. Right? Not with the Irish. There are all sorts of guys out of office who did the right thing in the right way or the wrong thing in the right way. You must be loyal to your friends . . . Sometimes you've got to 'stand up' even if it means going down."[2]

When he hears from an ideological liberal that this is clannishness, the ethnic politican is puzzled. What are the alternatives? To quote one of Levine's informants, "The only thing you have in politics is your word. Break your word and you're dead. The most successful politician is the politician who kept his word."[3] But if he is puzzled by the failure of the liberal to understand this truism, the ethnic politician would probably be astonished that such New Left political theorists as John Schaar are demanding the same kind of personal fealty from their political leaders. The ethnic leader and the hippie guru may have more in common than they realize.

There are obvious faults in such a political model in addition to those which are inevitable in any political model: its very flexibility and amorphousness may make dishonesty and corruption somewhat easier than the so-called reform models of politics. But ethnic systems are much less corrupt in most American cities than they have been in the past, and ethnic politicians have no monopoly on

2. Edward Levine, *The Irish and the Irish Politician* (Notre Dame, Ind.: University of Notre Dame Press, 1966).
3. *Ibid.,* p. 183.

corruption. Nor is the charge that the ethnic system is not open to the major forces of social change a valid one. Quite the contrary, if the system is working properly, social change is precisely what it is open to, though it distinguishes between actual social change and that announced by spokesmen and academic theorists.

There are three critical weaknesses, however:

1. The responsiveness of the system to groups depends to some extent on how well organized and articulate a given group is. The ethnic politician does not readily spot a situation where a given group may need his help in organizing itself and articulating its demands.

2. Small yet potentially explosive groups can be overlooked. The basic problem at root of the 1968 turmoil in Chicago was that the organization had little experience with the youth culture and was unprepared to deal with it. It learned quickly, and there have been no repetitions of the scene in front of the Conrad Hilton Hotel, but the mistake of playing into the hands of the radicals was a function of the fact that until the convention, youth culture was not seen as a serious problem.

3. While the ethnic politician is not likely to be swayed by the moralism, the dogmatism, and the perfectionism of the academic, his own proclivity for a concrete and instinctual style makes it hard for him to communicate with the intellectual and make use of the intellectual's important contribution to the political process—in particular, the intellectual's ability to spot long-range trends and problems. Most of the older ethnic politicians, for example, have not yet learned how to cope with television.

However, the point is not that the system has no weaknesses or that the organization (wherever it may be) makes no mistakes. It is rather that the system must be approached from the inside if it is going to be understood. Seen from the inside, it may have something important to say about politics and social reform in the United States.

It is difficult to write such a chapter for non-Chicago readers. The mere mention of "Irish politicians" erects a barrier in certain segments of American society which is hard to pierce. The liberal is frankly disgusted by ethnic politics. For him, the system is immoral and corrupt or, to use Mr. Goldberg's word, cheap. He may want to ponder the thought that the alternative is Nelson Rockefeller and James Buckley till the year 2000.

And the radical may feel that ethnic politics are part of the Establishment, which must be overthrown in "the revolution"— whether it be the peaceful revolution of Consciousness III or something more bloody. He may want to ponder the fact that even after the revolution he will have to contend with the same social groups in the large city, and if he does not come up with a better method, he will either have to fall back on the ethnic strategy or maintain a very efficient secret police and a very large system of concentration camps.

It has been said so frequently that it is almost a cliché: Chicago is the last of the cities with an ethnic political organization, and Mayor Daley is the last of the big city bosses. Sometimes I suspect this means that he is the last of the Irish political bosses, and those who celebrate the demise of machine politics are in fact celebrating the demise of the Irish politician. This may well be a matter of personal taste, but it also could be argued persuasively that in a society as disparate and conflict-prone as ours, a master of the art of building political coalitions plays an extremely important social role. The country can ill afford to do without him.

David Martin, writing in *Dissent,* has some particularly powerful words to say about the vocation of a politician, and even though the words were not deliberately framed to describe an Irish politician, they still are an appropriate description of what the Irish political style looks like at its best.

> The politician can be a man who wears a mask over his humanity in order the better to serve that humanity. Admittedly it is often an orthodox, conventional mask: yet it could be that behind the disguise lies more humanity than in those who affect no disguises, whose appearance of open-hearted innocence depends on the proclivity for unmasking other people. In any case, many people accept the disciplines that require a mask in their certain limited area of their life, say, their profession, but are able to relax into simple humanity in every other sphere of their life; others have no imperative need for masks in any area of their lives, perhaps because they

have chosen just those areas of social life where the discipline of social relations can be lax and easy, where few exigencies constrict and few responsibilities congeal. The politician, however, has chosen a role where exigency and responsibility demand a mask at nearly all times.

Consider the following proposition: that the highest moral responsibility could conceivably reside in a civil servant or a politician at the ministry of defense, who uses the coolest rational calculation to tread that narrow edge which is marginally closer to survival than all the alternatives. Once such a man has chosen a policy, he is within certain limits committed to it and indeed knows in advance that what he has chosen may acquire a momentum that will control him. He knows it includes certain costs, may in extreme circumstances begin to include further costs that may be appalling, but when that stage has been reached are probably (but not certainly) less appalling than the alternative costs. Perhaps such a man is a *kind* of genuine human being: willing to accept what it will be like to live with himself and with the obloquy of those not in his shoes should the worst happen.

As the consequences of his choice accumulate, he becomes totally immersed in fending off the worst, and this may mean the death of his personality; nothing but a public life and an "insane" commitment to politics. Not even the relief of an autobiographical exposition of his motives is open to him: he can only advise and act. Whatever he does now will acquire no honor in the world of those easily achieved martyrdoms undertaken in "progressive" causes. Indeed he may have to face the obloquy of seeming to acquiesce in and abet just such a martyrdom. This kind of man accepts the need for painful struggle and refuses to inveigh easily against the structures of reality, but instead employs the highest rational cunning to play those structures as far as they can be played: this is both a creative act of his own *and* an encounter with a strange, alien, recalcitrant otherness.

His highest achievement will be a tiny victory, his normal achievement just to survive. This he will never be able just to explain, and may have to accept the mortification of having to claim that a tiny victory was a great one. He may even acquire a reputation among the cognoscenti for naive reasoning and dishonest appeals, simply because the public neither wishes to know his actual reasons nor would be willing to face the stark alternative involved in that reasoning. It may even be that he is a man of the highest intelligence who must accept the contempt of an intelligentsia which has never tried to understand why he must appear stupid in public and appear ignorant of what he may know better than anyone. Perhaps such a man has some claim to his humanity and ours.[4]

As far as I am concerned, the question is not whether Richard J. Daley is the last of the Irish politicians; presumably whatever successors he may have will be more presentable on television and more skillful in using the mass media, and probably more adept at making the grand symbolic gesture so dearly beloved by liberal intellectuals. I am concerned with whether there will be any Irish politicians at all, for it is by no means certain that the younger generation of American Irish are particularly interested in politics, or particularly willing to use the political adroitness which may be as much a part of their child-rearing experience as their propensity to alcoholism, or that they will be able to build new coalitions, to cope with the new problems of American society. The old style of ethnic politician, by his lights and according to his goals, performed brilliantly; the new style of Irish politician may not perform at all. Or, even worse, he may be far more interested in moral victories than in real ones.

4. David Martin, "R. D. Laing: Psychiatry & Apocalypse," *Dissent* (June 1971), pp. 250–251.

12.

The Irishman as
Conservative

One of the great myths of "pop" social science in the United States is that the Catholic population in general and the Irish Catholic population in particular is conservative. This label is applied in an absolute rather than a relative sense. We are never told whom the Irish are more conservative than—just that they are conservative. If one asks on what matters they are more conservative, one is told that they are more likely to be anti-Communist, to favor censorship, and to oppose abortion laws—a reply delivered in a tone of voice which definitely settles the issue. That abortion is a critical issue in American life cannot be denied, though who is liberal and who is conservative on that question depends generally on who is defining the terms. As for anti-Communism and censorship, there is precious little evidence to justify the assertion that Catholics are on the far right of either issue. It has, after all, been seventeen years since Senator Joseph McCarthy, and it is time to invoke the statute of limitations on behalf of the Irish—particularly since the advent of another McCarthy.[1] I have heard it said that Eugene McCarthy is less Irish, in some way or another, than the Kennedys, which is only another way of saying

_____

1. One would think that Joe McCarthy was the only Irishman to serve in the U.S. Congress, to judge from those who argue that he was typical of Irish conservatism. Apparently we are to get no credit for David I. Walsh, James Murray, Thomas Walsh, Brien McMahon, John Tolan, or Raymond McKeough—to say nothing of Mike Mansfield.

216

that he failed to fit the stereotypes of some East Coast intellectuals. Senator Eugene McCarthy's image of Midwest Irish populism is at least as valid a part of the Irish-American heritage as the pragmatic urban politics of the Kennedys. Indeed, the Eugene McCarthy brand of Irish liberalism, reaching back to such men as Patrick Ford, John Ireland, John Ryan, and William Onahan, has played a decisive role in the formation of considerable numbers of liberal Catholic clergy and laity throughout the Middle West. In Chicago, particularly, a vigorous stand on race, labor, and religious reform is more than a half-century old. If there ever is a systematic and comprehensive attempt to study the history of the American Irish, the Middle Western liberal populism, of which Eugene McCarthy is one of the more famous and tragic exemplars, deserves to be examined in great detail.

To those who accuse the Irish of being conservative, one might reply by pointing to the Irish contribution to the development of the labor movement, particularly such men as Terrence Powderly and "Black John" Mitchell (of the United Mine Workers of America, not of the Justice Department), and the long string of Irish "labor priests." However, the union movement is not in good repute with academic liberals, and George Meany is dismissed as some sort of rightist hobgoblin—though surely organized labor is the largest and most powerful component of the liberal coalition; it has voted solidly in favor of labor reform measures for the last several decades. One notes that the Irish have traditionally voted Democratic, yet we are told that they are conservative Democrats, and what's more, they are becoming Republicans as they move to the suburbs. There are, of course, no data to support the latter assertion, and we still don't have any criteria to establish the substantive content of the label "conservative." My personal suspicion is that it means the Irish are not like Jews, and that Jews are the only ones in American society who have any claim to the label "liberal" (except for those elite WASP establishmentarians who so mightily enjoy the game of flailing away at the Establishment).

When the critics of Irish conservativism are forced to specify operational measures, they aver that the Irish are both racist and hawks, against integration and in favor of the war in Vietnam. This

TABLE 41

SCORE ON SCALE MEASURING SYMPATHY FOR POLITICAL
MILITANCY: JUNE 1961 COLLEGE GRADUATES RESPONDING IN 1968
(SCALE: 0 - 18)

All	9.5	(4,324)
Jews	11.9	(100)
Catholics		
Irish	10.6	(269)
German	9.2	(280)
Polish	10.5	(54)
Italian	8.3	(168)

TABLE 42

SCORE ON POLITICAL MILITANCY SCALE WITH NUMBER
OF YEARS IN GRADUATE SCHOOL HELD CONSTANT

	Under one year		One or two years		Three or more years	
All alumni	7.8	(1,803)	9.9	(1,211)	11.5	(1,316)
Jews	10.3	(29)	10.9	(21)	13.2	(50)
Catholics						
Irish	8.6	(92)	11.4	(70)	11.9	(107)
German	8.5	(160)	8.9	(44)	10.8	(84)
Polish	9.4	(20)	10.4	(15)	11.7	(19)
Italian	6.4	(73)	9.7	(49)	9.8	(46)

at least provides us with attitudes which survey research can measure.

The first set of data are based on NORC's ongoing study of the 1961 college graduates. A six-item scale was composed from data collected from these students in 1968, measuring sympathy for student and black militancy. We can see in Tables 41 and 42[2] that the Irish not only had more sympathy for militancy than any of

---

2. Tables 41 and 42 appear in Andrew M. Greeley's *Coalition Politics,* to be published.

the other Catholic groups, they also had higher scores on the pro-militancy scale than the national population. They were surpassed only by the Jews.

Furthermore, as long ago as 1967 (Table 43), in a national sample conducted by NORC to measure attitudes on the war, the American Irish (combined here with Germans) were second only to Jews and blacks on a scale designed to measure "dovism." It is also interesting, incidentally, to observe in Table 43 that there is little support for the myth of the white ethnic hawk racist from as long ago as 1967. Catholic ethnic groups are no less likely to be on the dove end of the scale than anyone else in American society.

Another survey conducted in 1970 was designed to measure, on a seven-item scale, the sympathy of major American ethnic groups toward integration. As we can see in Table 44, the Irish-Catholic pro-integration score was the second highest in the country, lower only than the Jewish score. Even in the North, it is very considerably ahead of the Anglo-Saxon pro-integration score. In addition, on a question measuring support for open housing legislation (Table 45),[3] all the Catholic ethnic groups except the Slavic had greater sympathy for open housing than did white Protestants. The Irish were slightly behind the German Catholics on this question, but still ahead of the WASPs.

As for turning away from the Democratic party, we note in Table 46 that among June 1961 college graduates, only Polish Jews, Polish Catholics, and blacks are more likely to assert that they are Democrats than are Irish Catholics. Only 30 per cent of the Irish would describe themselves as Republicans. (In other research we have demonstrated that, at least among the 1961 graduates, the independents are more liberal than either the Democrats or the Republicans. In Table 47[4] we see that more than half the Catholic Irish who graduated from college in 1961 are likely to think of themselves as liberal, less than the blacks, Jews, or Poles but still more than the other American religio-ethnic groups.

---

3. Tables 44 and 45 appear in Andrew M. Greeley's *Coalition Politics,* to be published.

4. Tables 46 and 47 appear in the Appendix of Andrew M. Greeley's *Why Can't They Be Like Us?* (New York: Dutton, 1971).

TABLE 43

ATTITUDES TOWARD VIETNAM WAR

	Percentage "dove" on Vietnam*
WASP	17
Italian	26
Jewish	48
Western European Catholics (including Irish and German)	29

*Proportion on "peace end" of five-item Vietnam scale administered to national sample in 1967. Size of sample, 3,000.

TABLE 44

MEAN SCORES ON PRO-INTEGRATION SCALE
BY REGION AND RELIGIO-ETHNICITY, 1970
(RANGE: 0 - 7)

	All	North		South	
WASP	3.71	4.68	(220)	2.61	(197)
German Protestant	4.42	4.67	(137)	3.41	(34)
Scandinavian Protestant	4.41	4.72	(29)	2.60	(—)
Other Protestant	4.03	4.51	(107)	3.09	(54)
Irish Catholic	5.02	5.02	(48)	5.00	(—)
German Catholic	4.62	4.85	(41)	3.00	(—)
South European Catholic	4.41	4.34	(38)	—	*
Slavic Catholic	4.41	4.37	(43)	—	*
Other Catholic	4.38	4.84	(116)	2.04	(23)
Other	4.54	5.05	(98)	2.38	(23)
Jewish	5.79	5.79	(24)	—	*

*One respondent or less.

The National Opinion Research Center is currently engaged in a project to study ethnic voting behavior and social, including political, attitudes during the last two decades. Pending the completion of that study, one must be content with the relatively frag-

TABLE 45

WOULD YOU FAVOR OR OPPOSE MAKING IT AGAINST THE LAW
TO REFUSE TO SELL OR RENT HOUSES
AND APARTMENTS TO NEGROES? (1970)
NON-SOUTH

	Percentages in favor
Protestants	
WASP	26
German	17
Scandinavian	27
Catholics	
Irish	29
German	32
Southern European	30
Slavic	17
Jews	46

mentary data presented in this chapter. It is worth emphasizing once again, however, that on matters of both peace and race the Irish are on most measures more liberal than any other American Gentile ethnic group. The conservative Irish are imaginary, at least so far as NORC's statistical evidence is concerned.

Whence comes the image that they are conservative? First of all, some Irish are unquestionably conservative, as are some members of every American ethnic group including the Jews. Second, by definition, in the minds of some members of America's intellectual elite, the words "Catholic" and "reactionary" are equated. The only way for the Irish to cease to be conservative is for them to cease being Catholic. Catholicism is presumed to be an unenlightened religion, rooted in the reactionary past and opposed in principle to social progress. It does no good to argue against this ideological reasoning or to show that in many countries of the world (not excluding Ireland), Catholics have taken progressive, liberal, radical, and even revolutionary political stances. If you are Catholic, they say, you really can't be radical; by definition radicalism or

TABLE 46

POLITICAL AFFILIATION BY FATHER'S ETHNIC BACKGROUND

(Percentages for June 1961 college graduates)

Political Affiliation	Protestant				Catholic				Jewish		Black
	English	Irish	German	Scandinavian	Irish	German	Italian	Polish	German	Polish	
Democrat	25	28	21	22	41	37	37	48	36	49	80
GOP	48	45	56	49	30	35	38	24	21	14	—
Independent	24	22	25	25	26	23	31	26	40	34	17
New Left	1	2	2	2	2	1	1	0	1	1	1
Other	2	3	6	2	1	4	3	0	2	2	1
Weighted number of responses	1,775	304	1,059	360	366	336	199	111	60	333	76

liberalism requires that you be either Marxist or atheist or both.

It is also asserted that the Irish have supported conservative political candidates. This usually means that they are not always enthusiastic about those candidates that Establishment-liberalism decrees to be morally and intellectually superior. They may not support those sides of the political issue which current liberal fashion demands. In other words, since the Irish approach to

TABLE 47

PERCENTAGE LIBERAL, IN RANK ORDER,
FOR JUNE 1961 COLLEGE GRADUATES

Rank Order by religion and ethnicity	Percentage
Black	83
German Jew	82
Polish Jew	69
Catholic Pole	62
Catholic Italian	56
Catholic Irish	55
Protestant Irish	53
Protestant Scandinavian	51
Protestant English	49
Protestant German	45
Catholic German	44

politics is more likely to be pragmatic than ideological, they are necessarily conservative. Apparently if one is willing to go down to glorious defeat on an impossible issue he will have the honor of being called a liberal, and if he is content with a modest victory in support of a political program that is possible, he is termed conservative.

Yet the Irish keep right on voting for the more liberal candidates in national elections. NORC data show that in the 1968 election there was little Irish support for George Wallace and more support for Hubert Humphrey than among any other white Gentile ethnic group.

To continue piling up the data probably would be a waste of time. The Irish may be as liberal as, if not more so than, the rest of the American Gentile population on questions of race and war. They may have voted for liberal Democratic presidential candidates for four decades, but they are still not liberal and never will be in the minds of those whose own definition of "liberal" is the only one that counts. For the only way the Irish could possibly stop being conservative is to stop being Irish.

13.

Irish and Black

On practically all available indicators, the American Irish are second only to the American Jews in their support for integrationist positions on racial questions. Furthermore, the lead of the Irish over all the other Gentile groups cannot be explained simply in terms of the superior Irish social-class position. Yet anyone wno knows anything about the American Irish must feel somewhat ill at ease with these findings. By comparative standards, it appears that the Irish are not very bigoted, yet given their tradition of revolution and their own experience as an oppressed people, it seems legitimate to wonder why the Irish are not more militant in their pursuit of racial justice, and why so many are hesitant and suspicious in dealing with blacks.

To put the matter even more concretely, if the analysis of Glazer and Moynihan in their revised edition of *Beyond the Melting Pot*[1] is correct, the Irish lost political power to the Jews in New York City precisely because the latter were better able to identify with the aspirations of the black and Puerto Rican minorities in that city. By the strictest rules of pragmatic politics, the Irish were beaten at their own game. Their blind spot on the racial issue caused them to lose that most precious of Irish commodities, political power.

Any casual survey of the Irish in American social history shows that every accusation made against more recent immigrant groups

---

1. Nathan Glazer and Patrick Moynihan, *Beyond the Melting Pot,* 2nd ed. (Cambridge, Mass.: MIT Press, 1970, paperback).

in the large cities was made against the Irish first: they were lazy, shiftless, dirty, savage. As early as the Revolutionary War, there were considerable doubts as to whether you could trust an Irish soldier:

> . . . The Irish soldiers abounded in our armies, and have fought in some of our battles; but sir, they have only fought as they were commanded, they have never led in any skirmish that I know of, and if they had known how to do anything but fight, they would never have been commanded to fight some of the battles that are the glory of our annals. It is vain for them or their friends to say anything of their patriotism and love of their adopted country—they needed the bounty . . . and risked their lives for that.[2]

Native Americans felt strongly about the new arrivals. The good Reverend Williams Alger said:

> When this naked mass of unkempt and priest-ridden degradation, bruised with abuse, festering with ignorance, inflamed with rancors, elated with blind expectations has sprung upon this continent . . . shall we . . . give this monstrous multitude instantaneous possession of every political prerogative, letting it storm our ballot-boxes with its drift of mad votes, and fill our offices with its unnaturalized fanatics?[3]

Harper's Magazine took particular delight in publishing the apelike caricatures prevalent in the nineteenth century, and pointed out how criminal the Irish were:

> They [the Irish] have so behaved themselves that nearly 75% of our criminals are Irish, that fully 75% of the crimes of violence committed among us are the work of Irishmen, that the system of universal suffrage in large cities has fallen into discredit through the incapacity of the Irish for self-government. . . .[4]

---

2. Sister Marie Leonore Fell, *The Foundations of Nativism in American Textbooks, 1783–1860* (Washington, D.C., Catholic University of America Press, 1942), p. 170. I am grateful to Daniel Patrick Moynihan for bringing this passage to my attention.

3. *Ibid.,* p. 171.

4. Quoted in Leonard Patrick O'Connor Wibberley, *The Coming of the Green* (New York: Henry Holt, 1958), p. 49.

Irish revolutionary organizations such as the Fenians (bent on freeing Ireland) and the Mollie Maguires (bent on vengeance for unlivable conditions in the coal fields) were cited as evidence of the inhuman savagery of the Irish. Everyone knew, of course, that the Irish couldn't hold their liquor, and the Irish "athletic clubs," such as the notorious Regan Colts in Chicago, had at least as bad a press (for the same reasons) as did their successors in Chicago—the Blackstone Rangers youth gang (recently renamed the Black P Stone Nation).

The Five Points district in New York was not a safe place to walk through at night, or even in the middle of the day. The Irish volunteer fire associations usually spent more time fighting each other than putting out fires, and the bloody, vicious draft riots in New York City during the Civil War (which dwarf all urban violence since then) were fundamentally a revolt of the Irish rabble.

Despite the strong similarities between the Irish experience and that of American blacks, few American Irish are willing to consider even for a moment the possibility that the black quest for dignity and freedom in the United States demands their enthusiastic support.

There are, however, a number of positive things that can be said about the Irish attitude toward blacks.

1. As the data presented earlier indicate, the Irish are less likely to be anti-black than is any other ethnic immigrant group, and this difference seems to persist when most relevant background variables are held constant. The Irish are not unprejudiced; they are simply less prejudiced, if our data are to be believed, than the other groups. Much further research will be necessary to explain this phenomenon before one could hypothesize that their mastery of the language and political success have given the Irish a stronger base of security from which to view other immigrants to American cities. Again, I do not assert that the Irish are not prejudiced. Anyone who has lived his life in the Irish-American community knows they are. They are simply less prejudiced than other groups.

2. Apparently the Irish have long since left behind the tendency to fight or riot when their neighborhoods were threatened with black immigration. The last Irish race riot was the 1919 riot in Chicago

(though there was a minor reprise in the 1950 Peoria Street riot in that same city). While the Southern and Eastern European groups stubbornly resist—and occasionally with violence—black immigration, the Irish tendency is to shrug one's shoulders and move to another neighborhood.

3. The Irish are also not very likely to engage in obviously racist behavior or to join in obviously racist organizations. The various anti-black militant groups in Northern American cities lack Irish leadership and, generally speaking, Irish membership. One very militant community organization on the southwest side of Chicago is presided over by a suspended Irish priest, but the strength of the membership is Eastern and Southern European rather than Celtic.

4. Among Catholics, and particularly among the Catholic clergy, the most enthusiastic interracialists are Irish, even though they may not speak for a majority of their colleagues. Slavic and Latin names are virtually invisible in the ranks of the Catholic leaders enthusiastically sympathetic to the cause of blacks.

5. In some cities the Irish political leadership has actively supported the development of black political leadership. Although it is true that the fall from power of the Irish in New York City can in part be explained by the failure of the Irish to respond sympathetically to the problems of the blacks, New York is not typical in this respect. As one moderately militant black leader in Chicago said to me, "I'm sticking with the organization, because for all its faults I don't see any other system likely to get as much for us as it can. They don't get for everybody everything that they want, but they do get enough to keep most groups happy most of the time, and that's the only way we're going to move ahead in this city."

In other words, this black leader saw progress inside the system as largely a matter of cooperation between blacks and the Irish minority which acts as a power broker among the ethnic populations in the city. One may disagree with his conclusion and argue that blacks should wreck the system or work outside it. However, at this point, in this city, it is clear that the vast majority of blacks are willing to bet on working within the system. With two United States Congress seats and as many as fifteen aldermen, to say nothing of a host of other elected and appointed jobs, blacks have something to show for their efforts.[5] The willingness to slate black candidates in something resembling their proportion in the total population is characteristic of Irish political pragmatism. Some observers from the inside of Irish politics claim that there is a good deal more sympathy toward blacks than might commonly be supposed. They contend that it is necessary to understand the rhetoric and the vocabulary, particularly of the old-time political leaders, to understand that while they may not use the approved categories of liberal ideology, their substantive positions are rather more pro- than anti-black.

There may be some validity in this assertion, though one would need to know much more about the mysterious internal world of Irish politics to be sure. Yet I remember talking to one grizzled and tough—and very wealthy—general contractor about the pressure that he was receiving from his well-to-do friends to provide summer employment for their sons on college vacation. Quoth the contractor, "There aren't that many jobs this summer, and if I hired all those kids I'd have to lay off some of my regular people who have families. You can't fire a family man even if he happens to be a nigger."

Young priest that I was at the time, I was horrified by what I thought was an obviously racist comment, but upon reflection I'm not so sure. The man had employed black laborers in an industry which at that time was not conspicuous for its eagerness to provide jobs for blacks, and while his choice of language left something to be desired, he made it clear that he was not going to discriminate against his black employees even under pressure from his close friends to do so. His categories of expression may have been inadequate but his behavior could not be faulted.

The above is the positive side of the balance sheet. It is stated first so that the judgments implied in the negative side to follow will not be seen as one-sided condemnations:

---

5. One of the ironies of the 1970 election in Cook County was that Cicero and Berwyn, the most blatantly white suburbs in the county, are represented in the United States Congress by a black. Conveniently for the organization, the gentleman has a name which sounds Irish. There were, you can be sure, no pictures of him in campaign posters in Cicero or Berwyn.

1. Despite all the qualifications listed above, it still must be said that the Irish, with their own splendid and ancient revolutionary tradition, have not been nearly so sympathetic with the black cause as one might have expected. Those who produced the Regan Colts ought to be able to understand the Blackstone Rangers. Those who produced the Mollie Maguires ought to be able to understand the Black Panthers. Those whose forebears were in the thick of the New York riots of 1863 and the Chicago riots of 1919 ought to understand the forces at the root of urban violence. And those today who honor Bernadette Devlin ought to sympathize with Julian Bond. Perhaps, as I suggested earlier, the respectable American Irish have forgotten their own past; this is convenient for them, but from any moral point of view it is quite unacceptable.

2. The Irish political leadership, for all its pragmatic skills (and this holds true for Chicago where Irish pragmatic skills are most skillful and most pragmatic), still does not seem to be able to understand the new black militancy. While that militancy's public manifestations are limited to a small handful of TV spokesmen, it still represents the smoldering sentiments of one part of the personalities of many blacks, particularly the younger ones. A pragmatic political leadership ought to be able to respond better to the restlessness of the young blacks than the Irish political leadership in American cities has been able to do. In this respect, they have not necessarily discriminated against blacks only. They don't seem to be able to understand the restlessness of the young whites either, including their own offspring. I cannot escape the impression that in both cases the older and middle-aged Irish political leaders are not trying very hard. By their own standards, this lack of effort to understand the new restlessness is a grave mistake.

3. As the first of the non-Anglo-Saxon immigrant groups, the Irish (with the possible exception of the Jews) have been most successful in adjusting to the American environment, and it would seem that they ought to have been uniquely able to dream visions of what American cities could have become, but they have been too busy with their golf and cocktails at the country club.

In my judgment, there is no way to escape the fact that in the Irish personality there is a powerful strain of dislike of the blacks. It may not rear its head as overt prejudice, it may not lead to political or occupational discrimination, it may coexist with a commitment to equality in American life; but it is still there. If my argument about Irish self-hatred is correct, this prejudice may be seen as a result of the fact that the black is a convenient inkblot into which the Irishman may project his dissatisfactions with himself. Furthermore, the blacks are not so threatening to the Irish as to the more recent immigrant groups; perhaps the Irish are not yet secure enough in their upper-middle-class status. It is also possible that we are dealing with residual suspicion and distrust of those who are different from us, and the Irish feeling toward blacks may not be substantially different from the way many WASPs feel about the Irish. Finally, with their own past record of shrewd and pragmatic political and social advancement, the Irish may be less tolerant toward other groups whose cultural background does not equip them quite so well for the competitive struggle in American society.

And yet it is my impression that all these explanations fail to explain fully the distrust, fear, and dislike for blacks which is latent in many Irish personalities. If I were a black, I would be ill at ease in dealing with an Irishman. He's not going to hit me; he's not going to insult me; he's not going to cheat me. He is likely to approve of my desire for better housing, education, and occupation. He may even be willing to vote for me in an election (at least more so than other American ethnics); yet deep down inside I'm willing to bet that he doesn't like me and is afraid of me, but I can't quite understand why.

Perhaps he can't either.

14.

Profile of a "Changing" Irish Neighborhood

Integration came to Beverly, and what most of the citizens had feared for a quarter-century finally occurred. One would like to be able to say that the integration was peaceful. There were no bombs or fires, to be sure, but two of the front windows of the house into which the successful black public relations consultant had moved were smashed. Most people in Beverly disapproved of the violence, even such a small manifestation, for violence in Beverly, particularly in that exclusive section called "the Ravine," was scarcely appropriate to the neighborhood's image. "There will be no violence here," people had been saying for years, and indeed, with the exception of the two broken windows, the arrival of a black face in the Ravine was a relatively quiet affair. There is not likely to be much violence, but whether there will be panic remains to be seen. On this subject the citizens of Beverly are divided. Some vigorously insist that their neighborhood, of all neighborhoods, will not be swept by panic following black in-migration. Others assert that they are going to move as quickly as they can to some place where they will be "safe" from seeing another neighborhood go down the drain. Ironically, one of the "safe" places mentioned is Flossmoor, the home of the federal judge who recently ordered public housing to be built in many of Chicago's all-white neighborhoods.

In a recent article in the *New Republic,* a Chicago newspaperman dismissed the opposition to the judge's order as opposition of those who did not want to live near black people. The tension in Beverly, then, as it faces the long-dreaded integration, is very simple: some/many/most (make your own choice) of the people there do not want to live with blacks. The American Civil Liberties Union, liberal journalists, and federal judges solve the problem by forcing integration.

The explanation that the white citizens of Beverly and other Chicago communities don't want to live with black people has a certain plausibility, because even if there was not another black within a hundred miles, there are unquestionably some people in Beverly who would not want a black face next door or down the street. But the changing neighborhood syndrome is far more complicated than mere racial prejudice; its roots will be found ultimately in the dual housing market created by widespread racial prejudice. The simple-minded "white ethnic bigot" model does not apply to the problem of racial change in Beverly. Considerable numbers, perhaps even a majority, of those who live there would rather keep it an all-white neighborhood, but the overwhelming majority of them are not bigots in the sense that bigotry is the all-controlling force in their lives. If there were some way to integrate Beverly whereby the appearance of the first black face did not set into motion a chain of causal events turning the neighborhood completely black, most of those who presently live there would not move. Some of them are bigots, some few are free from prejudice, but the majority are men and women of mixed motivations. Their response to black in-migration is not merely prejudice, it is also fear. While some of the fears may be unrealistic, many of them are all too real. It may enhance a feeling of moral self-righteousness among the liberal community to dismiss all Beverly-ites as racists and bigots, but such an explanation has little to do with the complexities of reality and nothing to do with finding solutions to the problems of changing neighborhoods.

Beverly is by no means a lower-middle-class or working-class community of the sort usually faced with the problem of changing neighborhoods. On the contrary, it is a neighborhood with the second highest real estate evaluation in the city of Chicago and has the highest median education level within the city limits. It has curving, tree-lined streets, carefully landscaped and tended lawns, attractive Dutch colonial, Georgian, and modern houses, and even hills and valleys—something rare for Chicago. It is surrounded on three sides by natural boundaries—a country club, a forest preserve, and two sets of railroad tracks. Beverly is cut off from the rest of Chicago and, since its beginning seventy years ago, has had the atmosphere of a small suburban town. The eastern half of the neighborhood was built up before the Great Depression, in substantial part before the First World War, and was settled mostly by well-to-do Protestants, many of them executives in the stockyards five miles to the north. The western half of the neighborhood was constructed immediately after the Second World War and is inhabited by well-to-do Irish Catholic business and professional men. Beverly has always sent a Democrat to the City Council of Chicago; it has voted Democratic in exactly one presidential election—1960. Most of the Protestant aristocracy is gone, and the Beverly Country Club is now carefully proportioned so that it is half Catholic and half Protestant. The Catholic population is still mostly Irish, though successful professional men of Polish, German, and Italian ethnic groups have also settled in the community.

The Catholics are generally new rich, having made their money in the years following the Second World War. Almost all Beverly's young people go to college, and a few staff members of a nearby Catholic college provide the nucleus of its small liberal intellectual segment. Many other parishioners of Christ the King Church, while neither liberal nor intellectual in the strict sense of the words, are reasonably well educated and sophisticated professionals with a distaste for violence and a reluctance to quit their neighborhood. In addition, many of the young people who were born and raised in Beverly in the years since 1940 have returned to raise their own families. At one recent meeting of Christ the King's first-grade parents and teachers, three-quarters of the parents had themselves attended first grade there. The people of Beverly, then, are not exactly universalists. The atmosphere of the Catholic segment of the community was neatly summed up when the son of a prominent M.D. chose to go to Harvard for his undergraduate training (before going to medical school, of course). The word went about the neighborhood, "Why did he go to Harvard? He had already been accepted at Notre Dame."

The people of Beverly are not ignoramuses or hard-hat slobs of the sort that certain liberal media identify with the words "white ethnic." Some of them have Ph.D.'s, and many of their children are in the process of obtaining advanced degrees. In addition to doctors and lawyers, journalists, and writers, an occasional poet and artist live there. One of Beverly's most prominent citizens occupies a sub-Cabinet position in Washington, and there is a college president in the neighborhood. The young people flocked to the volunteer organizations in the early '60s and joined the Peace Corps by the score. While they are not exactly the SDS type, they worked vigorously for Robert Kennedy and Eugene McCarthy.

Beverly ought to be able to cope with black in-migration more effectively than most neighborhoods. Its citizens are more sophisticated, they have more money and the mobility that goes with it, and they are deeply committed to their neighborhood. The community itself is not physically obsolete, its people are competent at developing organizations, they are not likely to be victimized by blockbusters, and they have access to those points in the legal and political system that are required to protect the neighborhood from massive zoning violations.

And yet Beverly is in grave jeopardy. In fact, its chances of surviving very long as an integrated neighborhood are at best dubious, and before 1980 it is altogether possible that it will be as much a part of the black ghetto as the communities to the north and east of it. This will be a tragedy for the city, for the black community, and for the white people who are so deeply attached to their colorful and lovely neighborhood.

If Beverly can't survive, the obvious question is, can any neighborhood?

I must admit that I do not feel impartial about Beverly. I worked in it for the first ten years of my life as a priest, and it got into my bloodstream, probably never to be purged. For a Catholic priest (at least of the variety trained before the Council), the first parish is like first love for an adolescent, something that you really never quite get over, particularly when the relationship lasts for a decade. But if I am not impartial, at least I am ambivalent. Seventeen years ago this summer, I first ventured forth on its shady streets to take the parish census. I found that many of the local folk were obsessed by the racial question even though at that time the boundaries of the black ghetto were still far away. Virtually every project I launched with the young people of Christ the King parish was interpreted by some parishioner as part of my scheme for racial integration—since it was supposed that all young clergy were *ipso facto* integrationists. I remember, for example, the vast controversy stirred up by the fact that the St. Ignatius band, which came to play for our teen-age dances, had a Negro saxophonist. A public library branch for Ninety-fifth Street was vetoed for fear that blacks would use it. A parish gym was vetoed on the grounds that blacks would play in it. It used to be said, and only with some exaggeration, that the Beverly-ites would like to roll up their sidewalks at night for fear blacks would walk on them. The shopping plaza at Ninety-fifth and Western was vigorously denounced because black people actually shopped there, and Grand Beach, where the Beverly-ites migrated for the summer, was the place where mysterious busloads of blacks were alleged to appear in the dark of night to lay plans for the conquest of that bastion of Irish summer respectability.

No, indeed, I am not likely to deceive myself about the absence of prejudice in Beverly, nor am I likely to forget how much hatred was turned on me because I was assumed to be pro-integrationist.[1]

Nor am I likely to forget that ten years ago the pastor and most of the lay leaders of the parish torpedoed the attempt of a Saul Alinsky organization to anticipate the problem that they face today. In retrospect, I doubt that the Alinsky organization would have

---

1. Incidentally, it was also assumed that all young priests were the social inferiors of the people in Beverly. The parishioners of Christ the King were being extremely generous to the upwardly mobile young cleric by accepting him as one of their own. This was a presumption that never yielded to fact, and that I was of the same social class as most of them was simply beyond belief.

been successful, but it certainly would not have done any harm, and it might possibly have helped to develop a regionwide response to the problem of racial change. However, the assumption in Beverly was that any such organization was part of the Church's plot to take their community away from them.

While I am under no illusions about the enlightenment of Beverly-ites, I think I can understand their fears—and I also understand that the sophisticated university intellectual world in which I have lived since I left Beverly is no less narrow, only it takes different forms—forms that are likely to be immune from attack in those journals whose function it is to sit in moral judgment on the rest of society.

Beverly is afraid. It is afraid of change, change of any sort—political, social, religious, economic. In this respect Beverly is probably no different from any human community. Despite Alvin Toffler, most human beings and most human communities are extremely resistant to the unfamiliar. (Just try to get a curriculum change in a college department, if you have any doubts about that assertion.) But there are special dimensions to the fear of change in Beverly. The older citizens are the new rich who grew up during the Great Depression and the Second World War and have never really recovered from those experiences. They feel they have earned comfort, affluence, and respectability in their community by long years of hard work.[2] They are not secure in their hard-won success and their even harder-won respectability, and the memories of the Great Depression still linger.

The younger generation does not remember the Great Depression; yet it has been touched by that awesome event, for all through its childhood it was filled with the fear of failure and the need to strive. It was also warned that, never having been tested in the crucible of the Depression, it might not have the vigor and strength

---

2. Work hard many of them certainly did, but their economic success, at least in substantial part, is the result of the fact that they happened to be around in 1945 when the American economy went on a quarter-century-long binge of prosperity. The Irish new rich in Beverly, in other words, were very lucky—a phenomenon they will bitterly deny, assuming, as must all new rich (indeed all the rest of us for that matter), that their success was the result of their own hard work and inner excellence.

of the preceding generation. The children of Beverly have very fragile egos and vast amounts of self-hatred. To cope with the world is difficult enough for them, but to cope with change is even more difficult. In business, politics, economics, both the younger and the older generations of Beverly may be flexible and even innovative, but their homes and neighborhood are bastions of security that are threatened by the prospect of change. Even if they are in sympathy with the innovations in their church, the parish church still represents a stronghold of continuity in their lives. One is prepared to admit that for the lower middle class and working class, home, family, neighborhood, and community are indispensable extensions of the personality; a threat to them is a threat to the personality itself. Such identification is less accepted in the upper middle class. In other words, it is all right for the working class to be concerned about social turf, but why should the organization man who could easily be plucked up and placed down a thousand miles away be concerned about it? Indeed, is not the notion of social turf outmoded?

Such questions may make sense if one views the world from the perspective of the college professor who must move every three or four years, or the corporation executive who would rather be in New York than anywhere else (indeed, for whom any other place is but an extension of New York). It is part of the peculiar social geography of those of us who engage in high-level worrying about American society that we seem unaware that there are members of the American upper middle class and lower upper class other than college professors, professional journalists, and corporation bureaucrats. Successful small businessmen, independent professionals, executives of local corporations are all part of an upper middle class that is more local than cosmopolitan; and when this local class is but one or two steps away from the immigrant ghetto, the stability of one's own social turf is still extremely important. The denizens of the "temporary society" are relatively few in number. The idea of having ground of one's own on which to stand is not merely a peculiarity of the urban ethnic group; it has been part of the American ethos since Thomas Jefferson's vision of a yeoman citizenry. The immense suburban proliferation after the Second

World War is sufficient evidence, if any more is required, that the dream of a place of one's own in a community of one's own is irresistible in American society, even if it flies in the face of all the canons of economic and social rationality.

The citizens of Beverly are afraid of change, particularly change that is perceived as threatening their turf: their homes, their schools, their churches, their playgrounds, their streets, their friendship groups. Is this a realistic fear? The journalists and the lawyers who support the ACLU may dismiss it as absurd; social turf is not a reality and therefore concern about it is stupid. The needs of the new rich for personal, emotional, and geographic security are "middle class" and hence reprehensible. Desire to protect one's community is reactionary, an obstacle to social change and to the improvement of the conditions of the poor and the oppressed, and is therefore culpable. On almost any ground imaginable, the liberal elites will dismiss the fear of change in Beverly as neurotic, unrealistic, stupid—and therefore not to be taken seriously. More might be said: since the middle class is immoral and corrupt and guilty of racist bigotry, it is appropriate for it to be punished. To deprive this despicable middle class of the personal security to which it so desperately clings is an act of high virtue. If the affection of the bourgeoisie for their social turf is to be considered at all, it should be taken away from them as just punishment for their sinfulness.

So be it! But one should not be surprised if this despicable, guilty, neurotic, reactionary middle class chooses to fight back. For even if better and wiser men tell the citizens of Beverly that their fears are unreal, they have considerable historical precedent for insisting that those who gainsay fear simply do not know what they are talking about. Indeed, no man is likely to give up his fear because someone says to him, "If you weren't guilty and immoral and sick you would realize there is nothing to be afraid of."

In other words, whether social turf ought to be important to people or not, it is important to the citizens of Beverly—and to most Americans. We cannot ignore the classic dictim of W. I. Thomas: that when people define something as real, the definition itself is a reality with which we must deal.

Whatever is to be said about the fear of change, the threat of financial loss is a reality which cannot be denied. A considerable literature exists showing that, in the long run, housing values go up after black in-migration, but there is no doubt that in the short run they go down, and even in Beverly few families are likely to be able to afford two homes. The blockbusters—that is to say, those real estate men who grow rich from their skill at spreading panic at the time of racial change—may be less successful in Beverly. They will not be able to call people on the telephone and ask them if they have seen the face of their neighbor. They will not be able to cheat elderly people out of the only roof they can possibly put over their heads. They will not be able to go up and down the streets playing on people's fears. They will not even be able to use some blacks as their agents in creating panic in the neighborhood. They will not be able to escape the penalties of the law for endeavoring to spread panic—though if the truth be told, the penalties are light enough and enforcement rare enough.

The panic merchants will not be successful in Beverly—not because they won't try but because Beverly-ites are too sophisticated. Nevertheless, the housing market is already soft in Beverly, in part because the black ghetto is edging ever closer, in part because of the economic recession. Property values are not what they once were, and Beverly is no longer a "desirable" neighborhood. Serious financial losses as a result of neighborhood change may not be incurred by too many Beverly-ites; yet if the neighborhood collapses in the face of black in-migration, there will be some financial loss as people hasten to get rid of their homes before it is "too late." This loss must be incurred at a time when the small-business and professional men, who are the core of Beverly, find themselves in financial straits. Furthermore, many of the Beverly-ites have been through the changing-neighborhood experience before, and they know that he who waits till the bitter end is likely to suffer the worst loss. Hence panic in the face of racial change has become almost an ingrained response. A man may one day vigorously and articulately proclaim that he is never going to desert his neighborhood and the next day dispose of his house on the grounds that he had to cut his losses for the good of his wife and children.

Nor is the fear of crime and violence unrealistic. Even though the American liberal audience may at last have some notion that crime is a serious problem in American society, it has shown little inclination to face the obvious fact of the correlation between race and crime. If we say that the crime rate will go up in Beverly with black in-migration, we run the risk of having Professor William Ryan denounce us for "blaming the victim." One must not therefore assert that black people commit crimes, because black people have been victims in the past. To say that there are black criminals (even those who prey on other blacks) is somehow to make oneself guilty of blaming the victim. Apparently the white victim of black crime ought to rejoice that he has been given the opportunity to expiate the sins of racism that he and his ancestors have committed.

Unfortunately, the citizen of Beverly does not have quite the moral integrity of Professor Ryan. He may not be willing to accept an increase in the amount of murder, rape, and burglary in his neighborhood as just punishment for the sins of the white race. To tell the Beverly-ites that most blacks are not criminals would be to state something they would not deny, but it only takes one or two stabbing murders (such as occurred in Beverly's sister neighborhood, South Shore) to create an atmosphere of intense fear that no community can long survive. Professor Ryan and his colleagues will, one assumes, argue that the Beverly-ites ought to be aware of how much fear there is in the black community. Some may know this and some may not; yet there are few of us who will not get ourselves out of a situation of terror. It is certainly very true that only a tiny minority of blacks are criminals, but it only takes a tiny minority to create terror; it only takes one man to creep through your window and stick a knife into you, and only one man to fire a sawed-off shotgun into your child's stomach. The fear in white neighborhoods at the time of black in-migration may be excessive, but, again, terror does not decrease simply because pious liberals arrive on the scene to announce that it is excessive.

There is also apprehension about the schools. The vast amount of ink spilled in liberal journals on the subject does not modify the fact that when the population of a given school exceeds a certain proportion of blacks, the school deteriorates as an educational institution and becomes a custodial institution. Nor can the fact be obscured that after a certain point of in-migration, it becomes anywhere from slightly to very dangerous to be a white child in such a school. One must quickly assert that this does not mean blacks are inferior or that most blacks engage in classroom violence. It is to assert that in the present condition of American society, the schools are not able to cope with the educational problems experienced by children of minority groups. The citizen of Beverly may be lectured on the failure of the public schools to meet the needs of the poor and he may agree completely. He may admit further that only a handful of teen-agers are responsible for the reigns of terror that occur in many junior and senior high schools, but it does not alter the fact that he perceives his child's education and physical safety to be in jeopardy when the school becomes mostly black. You may assure him that there is a strong possibility that nothing will happen to his child, but few of us are willing to commit our children's well-being to strong possibilities. You may also tell him that there are black children who are being exposed to danger and to second-rate education in the public schools, but you will find it difficult to persuade him that he is bound thereby in conscience to leave his child in a school where the education is poor and the physical risks are high.

In other words, most of the arguments against moving out of Beverly say, in effect, that you should be willing to expose yourself to dangers, financial loss, and poor education for your children because injustices have been done and are being done to black people in other neighborhoods. This may be a form of argumentation that has appeal for some sophisticated liberals (though I notice that the University of Chicago Laboratory School is very crowded), but it is not, I think, successful among most human beings at the present state of the evolution of the race.

There is a certain tragic dimension in the Beverly situation. The blacks who move into the community are exercising the inalienable American right of trying to improve the homes in which they will raise their families, and the whites who panic at the thought of black in-migration are also exercising the inalienable American right of being concerned about their homes, families, and neighbor-

241

hoods. For me, the pathos of the situation is particularly clear, because the black man who first moved into the Ravine happened to be someone I know rather well. He would, if given half a chance, fit very nicely indeed into Beverly society. That he and my Beverly friends should be in conflict is intolerable, yet the nature of the real estate situation in Chicago makes this conflict inevitable.

There are two real estate markets in Chicago, a black one and a white one. In the absence of a situation where black men can buy homes anywhere they wish in the metropolitan region, the black community must necessarily expand by the process of slowly annexing block after block. The choice is between an open real estate market and changing neighborhoods. Even in an open-market situation, there would be some neighborhood changes on the fringes of those parts of the city which had the heaviest concentrations of minority population. Some neighborhoods, particularly obsolescent ones, would inevitably change, but attractive, single-family, stable communities like Beverly could be integrated easily and permanently if the pressures along the fringes of the black ghetto were decreased by the creation of an authentic open market in the metropolitan region. For many neighborhoods on the fringe of the ghetto, that open market would come too late to prevent complete change, but this is surely not true of Beverly, given the very high real estate values there. I used to say in my days in Beverly, "If you people are really interested in saving this community, you should do everything possible to see that there are a few blacks in Glencoe, Kenilworth, Winnetka, Flossmoor, and Palos." They used to look at me with bafflement; then (at least in some cases) light would dawn, "You mean that then there would be no place else to run to?"

Not only would there be no place else to run to, there would also be options for blacks, for many of whom the changing-neighborhood experience is every bit as painful as for whites.

As my friend Anthony Downs has pointed out, the only solution is diffusion of minority groups throughout the whole metropolitan region by a system of subsidized quota integrations, and if constitutional changes are necessary to accomplish quota integrations, let there be constitutional changes. In other words, it ought to be government policy to reward with a vast variety of subsidies those communities which agree to zoning and construction that make it possible for a certain limited proportion of minority groups to move in. Even fifteen years ago, long before the threat was imminent, many people in Beverly would have accepted—some enthusiastically— the idea of a certain proportion of black people on their streets.

It is impossible to establish a quota in Beverly unless there is one Flossmoor, Palos, Park Ridge, and other neighborhoods and communities in the metropolitan region. At this point in time, Beverly is in no position to announce suddenly its conversion to the principle of subsidized quota integration. And if the truth be told, there does not seem to be widespread enthusiasm or support for the idea in the liberal community either. Arranging neat racial balances in classrooms by moving children around in buses and plunking public housing down in neighborhoods where it is bound to cause controversy seem to be much more satisfying to the liberal zealot than thinking in terms of systematic solutions on a metropolitan scale.

There can be no doubt that there are immense legal, political, social, and moral obstacles to subsidized quota integrations in a metropolitan area. Solutions of this sort would involve systematic government intervention of a kind most Americans would suspect —and that precisely at a time when skepticism about the malignity of government intervention is already very high at all points on the political spectrum. The problems of housing and race are so complicated, immense, and deeply rooted in the history of the land that only systematic, coordinated, long-range policy commitments on the part of the federal government can possibly create even the beginnings of a solution.[3]

The point is that few neighborhoods, not even one as affluent and sophisticated as Beverly, can solve their own problems. If you happen to have a major university available, as Hyde Park did, it may be possible to create a subsidized quota integration in one

---

3. There would have to be corresponding trust in both the black and white communities. Yet one must understand the skepticism of black political leaders who would view the diffusion of minority groups throughout a metropolitan region as, in fact, a scheme to take potential political power away from the minority groups. The fear is legitimate and it deserves some kind of practical response.

neighborhood, in effect; but there are not too many such neighborhoods in Chicago, or elsewhere. It is remotely possible that a large religious body like the Roman Catholic Church could be powerful enough to make important beginnings in metropolitan integration. Unfortunately, the Catholic Church exists today in a state of organizational chaos near collapse and is scarcely able to face its own internal problems, much less have any influence on the rest of the city.

It is pathetic to see the frantic efforts of a threatened neighborhood to save itself. I recently heard two young priests describe to a group of seminarians how they were facing the problem of racial in-migration. One young man insisted that what his community faced was a "religious problem"; that he and his fellow clergyman in the community were attempting to persuade their parishioners that it was a matter of religious obligation both to welcome the blacks and not to run. The other priest, more activist in his orientation, observed that in their neighborhood they weren't merely talking about religious problems, they were also engaged in fighting the blockbusters and getting zoning and housing enforcement.

I confess that I was appalled. These two young men seemed to be ignorant of the dynamics of the dual real estate market, and they also seemed completely unaware that similar efforts have been disastrously unsuccessful in threatened neighborhoods over the last fifteen years. And yet I suppose I cannot blame them, for they felt that something had to be done, and there was really nothing much else for them to do.

This is the tragedy of it all. At this point in time, nothing much can be done in Beverly. Ten, fifteen, twenty years ago, had the politically influential citizens of Beverly enough vision to realize that something had to be done to break the dual real estate market, perhaps their neighborhood could have been saved. As it is now it may survive, but only by chance. There may not be enough blacks able to buy homes in Beverly. The peculiar dynamics of ghetto expansion may move in other directions. The younger generation may, more out of individual stubbornness than organized virtue, simply refuse to move. The political influence of some Beverly-ites may assure intensive police protection and special educational programs. All kinds of frantic efforts at community organization are likely, but I have the sinking feeling that they will do more harm than good. The parish priest will take a strong stand in favor of racial justice, but unless he turns out to be a charismatic genius, he is not likely to be able to hold the community together in the face of its present crisis. I would estimate the chances of Beverly's survival as a more or less permanently integrated neighborhood to be moderate at best; they depend almost entirely on things that happen in Washington and Springfield, in the City Hall and County buildings, and in the federal courts. If the Beverly-ites are smart, they will lean on Mr. Nixon and his Secretary of Housing and Urban Development to do everything in their power to integrate the upper-middle-class suburbs beyond the city limits. Such pressure would be woefully belated, but would indicate a grasp of the realities of the situation that has been singularly absent in Beverly in bygone years.

There will be many worried, intense conversations on the veranda or in the locker rooms of the country club, in back of church on Sunday morning, on the Rock Island train going into the Loop, at the evening bridge and cocktail parties, or on the shore at Grand Beach. All these conversations have been heard before, but the difference is that the question is no longer will *they* come, or when will they come? Now it is, they are here, what next? And all my ambivalence returns, for the Beverly-ites have got themselves into a big mess—of their own creation in part; and from the depths of my morose Irish personality a vindictive little voice says, "They wouldn't listen. It serves them right."

The people of Beverly are not totally responsible: they did not bring slaves to America; they did not exploit blacks for hundreds of years, they did not create racial prejudice, or the dual housing market. The problem in which they are enmeshed is one created not so much by their bigotry as by a complicated, disgraceful, and messy history. The hand of history sits heavy indeed on that doomed neighborhood, which for all its mistakes, failings, and weaknesses still has about it much that is lovely and good.

So there is another little voice, equally Celtic, which cries, "Damn it all, they deserve better!"

15.

The South Side Irish
Since the Death of Studs

I remembered enough about the story of Studs Lonigan[1] not to want to read it again. I knew it would force me to think once more about a problem that is too painfully close to me, both as a priest and as a human being—the tragedy of the Irish. Yet when one comes off the Chicago Skyway onto Indiana Avenue and stops at the traffic light across from St. Anselm's Church (built by Father Gilhooley to "save the neighborhood"), the ghosts of the Irish past rise up to protest.

Two blocks farther down Indiana on the corner of Fifty-eighth is the place where Levin's drugstore (now a liquor store) stood. One can walk down the street and see where Helen Shires lived. In the playhouse which was behind it, she and Studs had long and confidential talks. Next door is the gray home with the front porch from which Studs's beloved Lucy Scanlon waved him a kiss.

A block over on Fifty-eighth and Michigan is the "Carter" playground, across from which was the three-flat building that Paddy Lonigan purchased in full confidence that the neighborhood could be saved. One need only drive a few streets to the east to come upon Washington Park where Studs and Lucy spent an afternoon sitting in the tree sharing their adolescent affection. Nearby is the football field where Studs and the Fifty-ninth Street Cardinals brutally stopped the brilliant running of "Jewboy" Schwartz. Be-

---

1. See James T. Farrell, *Studs Lonigan* (New York: Vanguard, 1935).

246

yond the park is the alley between Kenwood and Kimbark where Studs's attempted robbery ended in low comedy. And south of the University of Chicago is the drugstore on Seventy-first and Jeffrey where Studs, his brother Marty, and some of their friends from the "old neighborhood" bemoaned the passing of the community between Fifty-seventh and Fifty-eighth on Indiana.

Even if one does not know the Studs Lonigan story, one still drives down these streets with the sense that many ghosts out of the Irish past are lurking in those buildings. Rejecting these ghosts, one is forced eventually to pick up James T. Farrell's trilogy and learn what it was like to be a young Irish Catholic in St. Anselm's between 1915 and 1930.

His life ended when the nurse placed the white sheet over Studs's face as his mother sobbed hysterically, but I'm sure I would have known him if his life had been different: if he had had the courage to declare his love to Lucy Scanlon, if he had not destroyed his health at Weary Reilly's orgy, if he had not put his money in Insull stock, Studs would have survived the Depression somehow or other. His fortunes would have turned in the late '30s and the early '40s. His father's painting business would have been transformed into a "decorating contractor" firm. Studs would have made a good deal of money during and immediately after the war and would have invested it wisely before he was fifty. He would have bought a home in Beverly and moved to Christ the King Parish, finding at Ninety-third and Hoyne a community where the old loyalties of Fifty-eighth and Indiana could be born again.

He would have joined Beverly Country Club and eventually become chairman of its greens committee. His children would have attended Christ the King school and I would have played basketball in the schoolyard with the younger ones. Although Studs and Lucy would never have joined CFM or Cana, they would still be active members of the parish. He certainly would have been president of the St. Vincent de Paul Society. She would have served a term as head of the Women's Altar Guild. They would have had a summer home at Grand Beach and their oldest children, now in their late thirties or early forties, would move back to Christ the King to raise their children in the neighborhood which they loved so much and perhaps to assert that they would stay in Beverly even if it should become integrated.

Studs would not have appreciated the "new Church." When Jack Hotchkin and I tried to introduce dialogue Mass and hymn-singing he would have, I fear, dismissed us as brash, radical young men. And yet when it became clear that the pastor was supporting such changes, indeed in the name of the Second Vatican Council, Studs would have enthusiastically accepted them. By now I think he would be dead, for he was entirely too choleric a person to live to be nearly seventy. He would have been buried with full honors from Christ the King Church to Holy Sepulchre Cemetery, with the pastor having praised him as a loyal parishioner, a fine father and husband, a distinguished citizen—perhaps with passing remarks as to how enthusiastic he had been in organizing the fund-raising drive which made the beautiful parish church possible.

Yes, indeed, Studs Lonigan, I know you well. What a shame we never met.

Much has changed from Fifty-seventh and Indiana to Ninety-third and Hoyne. The young Irish of Beverly and Grand Beach spend relatively little time hanging out in front of drugstores; rather they drive up and down Longwood Drive in their convertibles. Only rarely do they feel the need to demonstrate their masculinity by physical pummeling. It is not necessary for their parents to insist that they go through high school and college (as Paddy and Mary Lonigan unsuccessfully insisted). They drink as much, if not more, and are as frightened of sex, if not more.

Physically, the world of Ninety-third and Hoyne is vastly different. Studs could never have dreamed of a neighborhood with broad, landscaped, and neatly manicured lawns, curving streets, Georgian and Dutch colonial homes, and shiny Cadillac cars. If the merciful heavenly Father should permit Studs Lonigan to visit Beverly for a day to see how his nieces and nephews really lived, he would marvel at the great changes that had occurred among the South Side Irish.

If one is asked how the South Side Irish have changed since the death of Studs Lonigan, the answer is they haven't changed at all. The veneer may be different, but they are as bent on their own destruction as were Studs and all his friends who preceded him to the grave. Studs Lonigan was not destroyed by booze, nor women, nor the disastrous New Year's Eve party, nor by pneumonia. He destroyed himself. Dubious about his masculinity, harassed by his mother, nagged by his sisters, lacking a confident father to imitate, and paralyzed by guilt, Studs was already bent on self-destruction when he graduated from St. Anselm's in 1916. His deep prejudices against "smokes" and "kikes," his noisy bravado, his violence with women, and, above all, his passion for John Barleycorn all served to protect a small and insecure sense of self. Studs Lonigan loathed himself, and his whole life was a systematic effort to punish himself for his own worthlessness. His low self-esteem prevented him from going to high school, and destroyed his relationship with Lucy Scanlon. One suspects that James Farrell is inclined to blame the Church for Studs' self-loathing. Clearly his pastor, Father Gilhooley, and the missionary Jesuit, Father Shannon, did not preach a gospel which augmented confidence in one's manhood; but on the evidence presented in the trilogy, it was not Gilhooley and Shannon who destroyed Studs but his mother and father—his mother with her enervating sweetness, her punitive religious devotion, her blind insistence that Stud's problem was whether he ought to be a priest, and his father whose aloof and reserved exterior hid the fatal weakness which put him in a speakeasy at Sixty-third and Michigan roaring drunk when his son lay dying. The Irish male is not permitted much self-confidence or self-respect by his parents, and thus he has very little to pass on to his own children.

None of this has changed. The site has moved from Fifty-eighth and Indiana to Beverly, but the self-loathing and self-destruction continues. South Side Irish—a marvelously gifted and creative people—have been bent on destroying themselves for three-quarters of a century. It looks as though they are beginning to succeed.

Last year the NBC program *First Tuesday* presented an appalling report on corporal punishment in the Irish schools. One watched in dismay as priests, brothers, and lay people seemed to delight in disciplinary tactics which preserved order and respectability at the price of destroying the integrity and dignity of children. The American Irish are far more sophisticated. We don't have to beat our children. Studs Lonigan's father hit him but once, yet his mother and father still controlled him and ruined his life. Even if his self-destruction was a form of punishing them, it took place within the constraints they had established, and he punished them at the price of killing himself.

Studs survived most of his friends. By the time he died at the age of twenty-nine, Paulie Haggerty, Arnold Sheehan, Shrimp Haggerty, Tommy Doyle, Slug Mason, and Hank Webber were already dead, and Weary Reilly was in jail as a rapist. In Beverly we were much more sophisticated. There were some suicides, and at least one brilliant and gifted young man is presently behind bars in the Cook County jail. Self-destruction now can be extended from thirty years to fifty or sixty or even seventy, but it goes on just the same. The South Side Irishman is a creature of fear and anxiety, from which he escapes only by slowly destroying himself.

He is fearful of his masculinity, no more able to relate with firmness and tenderness to a woman as a human being than Studs was to Lucy Scanlon or later to Catherine Banahan. His idea of sexuality is limited to the kind of fantasies which led Studs to sleep with the Jewish matron in South Shore. He is wary of self-revelation, of risking his real self in any human relationship, lest his emptiness be perceived. He is dreadfully afraid of being different. His mother's central moral principle, "What will people say?", has practically destroyed his capacity for risk-taking. And the judgment spoken by his brothers and sisters, "Who do you think you are?", is enough to banish even the slightest temptation to nonconformity. He is uncertain of his own emotions and the irrational powers which, he dimly perceives, reside in the depths of his personality. But if his anger is ever given full vent, he is afraid that he will kill and destroy—especially the parents about whom he feels so ambivalent.

He is afraid of failure and thus leads a narrow, constrained, restricted life, which, while it guarantees that he will not fail, also prevents him from achieving the success that his talents and creativity would make possible. Like his predecessor Studs Lonigan, a contemporary South Side Irish male is the master of romance daydreaming, and, like Studs, he even understands vaguely that he has the capacities to make the daydreams come true. To put the matter bluntly, the Irishman will not and cannot be himself because his mother won't let him.

One suspects that it is not only the nieces and nephews of Studs Lonigan who are beset by strong self-destructive urges. Some see the tragedy of the Kennedy family as hideous coincidence, others see it as an ugly fate; but one who knows the Irish is inclined to suspect that the clan Kennedy, like so many other Irish clans, is damned by its own self-destructive instincts.

Self-hatred is not uniquely Irish, as any reader of American Jewish fiction knows. It is worth observing that while the Jews don't have a monopoly on self-hatred; at least they have been able to talk about it and turn it to literary profit. The Irish cannot even do that. Studs Lonigan is an Irish Portnoy.

The Jewish mother encourages her children to overachievement so that she may be proud of them. The Irish mother encourages underachievement, in order that she may continue to dominate them. One knows all too many Irish families made up of old maids and bachelors (some of them priests and nuns) who are completely dominated by a tiny, frigid, ailing old woman whose virtue everyone proclaims and praises (and she drove her husband to kill himself with drink thirty years before). No matter how old her children are, she is still the center of their lives, and any outside interest, be it career or potential spouse, that is seen as a threat to her control must be demolished.

Elizabeth Cullinan in her brilliant novel, *House of Gold,* describes just such a woman and the zombies whose lives she dominates. Not all Irish families, of course, are such a caricature of matriarchy, but the reaction of Mrs. Lonigan to Studs's fiancée, when Studs lay dying of pneumonia, is characteristically Irish. The Irish mother hides behind the mask of respectability and religious piety, but when the chips are down her desperate need for control emerges in all its ugliness. She will not permit her husband or sons to be men, and it is therefore quite impossible for her to be a woman. One can find no better summary of the tragedy of the South Side Irish than the concluding chapter of the Lonigan trilogy: Studs dying of pneumonia at twenty-nine (his health ruined by a

251

drunken brawl), his mother viciously denouncing his fiancée, his sister planning the abortion of his unborn child, and his father and brother noisily drunk—and, of course, the representative of Christianity giving the "last rites."

Despite the handicap of an underachievement syndrome, the Irish are the most succesful of the Catholic immigrant groups, and they have reached the American Protestant population in social and economic achievement. With a few breaks, Studs Lonigan would not have died in 1929 and would have moved into the upper 5 per cent of American wage earners. But he would have carried his self-loathing to the grave, along with the narrowness which seems to be an inevitable by-product of self-hatred.

Yet it is to be feared that the course for the South Side Irish is downward. While Thomas Aquinas Foran may be a far more sophisticated (and more liberal) version of Richard Daley, one looks in vain for any newer versions of the same men among the young Irish lawyers in their thirties and late twenties. The young Irish clergymen who make up the young priests' caucus do not in combination have as much charisma or political insight as Monsignor John Egan has in his little finger. Most serious of all, the artists, the poets, and the storytellers are nowhere to be seen. What happens to the Irish when they've lost their capacity for storytelling? Where are the Jimmy Farrells of the 1970s? Who will celebrate the agony and the glories of Christ the King the way Jim Farrell celebrated St. Anselm's? Is there no one left among the South Side Irish who can see visions? Are there no young men or women who, looking over the fairways of Beverly Country Club, are transported by some ancestral daemon back to the peat bogs where leprechauns and banshees frolic in the mist? It is their imagination that has kept this most distressful people going for a thousand years and more. What will happen to them when they have lost it?

I do not believe that they have lost it. There was not just one Jim Farrell in Christ the King, but at least a score. And the social and human reality of which they are part is a richer and more complicated one than that over which Farrell agonized. The creative genius of the Irish is not gone. It has merely been effectively repressed. The difference between James T. Farrell and his successors is that he (and his alter-ego, Danny O'Neill) was able to break away from the paralyzing respectability of St. Anselm's. His potential followers in Christ the King are as effectively caught as was Studs Lonigan.

For the South Side Irish have learned how to cope effectively even with the University of Chicago. O'Neill (and James T. Farrell) could walk down Fifty-ninth Street from Indiana Avenue to Cottage Grove and enter a new world, a world where it was possible, even praiseworthy, to be a novelist. The Beverly Irish can attend law school, or business school, or medical school, or even the sociology department of the University of Chicago without ever leaving their own world. The trauma of the Great Depression, the dizzying affluence of the postwar years, the possibility, nay, the likelihood of "the good life" have all led to a *decrease* in the possibility of the young South Side Irishman setting words on paper. Jim Farrell could leave Fifty-eighth and Indiana behind more easily than his counterpart in the 1960s could leave Ninety-third and Hoyne behind. Now there is much more to leave behind, and also much more reason to fear that words on paper represent one's most fundamental self, the self which can be utterly demolished by the taunting words, "Who do you think you are?"

I remember visiting a South Side Irish pre-med student (the son of a famous physician) at an elite American university. Every inch of shelf space in his room was crammed with English literature. We spoke of nothing all afternoon except fiction and poetry. He showed me some of his own work, which was both very funny and quite good. Finally, I asked him why, since his whole life seemed almost obsessed with literature, he was majoring in biochemistry. He shrugged his shoulders cynically. "The old man and the old lady are paying the bills. I gotta do what they want."

Compared to this young man, Studs Lonigan got off easy.

Why are there no writers among the Beverly Irish? The answer is simple enough. Their mothers are far more effective at stopping them than was Danny O'Neill's.

Is the fantastic energy of the Irish immigrant thrust diminishing? Is it in fact being drowned in a country club martini glass? Is this generation of South Side Irish the last one to have the creative mark? If they repress it, is there any chance of its being passed on to their children? I am inclined to think that Beverly is indeed the end of the road for the South Side Irish. They will not get another chance. I am not suggesting that they will sink back into poverty; quite the contrary. They will be "successful" doctors, lawyers, and businessmen, living lives of noisy suburban desperation quite indistinguishable from their WASP neighbors. Many will even think that this assimilation represents social progress. There are others, however, who will lament the passing from the scene of the James Farrells, the John O'Haras, the F. Scott Fitzgeralds, the Edwin O'Connors, and the J. F. Powerses. And at least a few of us will lament that Beverly will not leave behind it a last will and testament like the *Studs Lonigan* trilogy. Beverly is both more fascinating and more tragic than Fifty-eighth and Indiana. But such a testament is not likely ever to appear, for, after all, what would people say?

The South Side Irish, then, will not disappear. Something far worse will happen. They will become dull. The present generation will destroy itself, indeed perhaps more effectively than Studs and his friends destroyed themselves—though it will take longer. The self-destruction may end then but, alas, nothing much worthwhile will be left.

Ah, Jim Farrell, you were born thirty years too soon; for if you had come into this world at Ninety-third and Hoyne in the late '30s, you would have found the *Gotterdammerung* of the South Side Irish even more fascinating than Indiana Avenue between Fifty-seventh and Fifty-eighth streets.

But then, I suspect you would never have set a word on paper.

16.

A Balance Sheet

If the fundamental theme of this book is correct, we are nearing the final solution of the Irish problem: the American Irish will disappear, not into concentration camps, but rather into upper-middle-class suburbs. They have made it into American society, but at the price of repressing their past and denying their future. It may well be that, given the historical circumstances, such an outcome was inevitable. It may even be, as editorial writers in both the *Christian Century* and the *National Observer* suggested in their comments on an article of mine, that this outcome is admirable. Probably because of biases of my own, however, I am inclined to think that it is tragic.

Let us attempt a balance sheet, stating the assets and liabilities of the American Irish. They came in large numbers before any other immigrant group, with the exception of the Germans and their Scotch-Irish neighbors. They spoke the language and understood, more or less, the culture of an Anglo-Saxon country. They had political and organizational skills which enabled them to amass certain kinds of power rather early in the game. They were able to appropriate key positions for themselves in the polity and in their church. Their power in both the Church and city politics is waning, but their influence is still far out of proportion to their actual numbers in the Catholic ethnic population. They have been moderately successful at resisting attempts by more recent Catholic arrivals to replace them, though, as Moynihan and Glazer point out, they were completely unsuccessful in resisting the Jewish quest for political power in New York City.

Their early arrival, their skills with the language, their political and religious power all enabled the Irish Catholics to acculturate to American society more quickly than any other group but the Jews. Indeed, they have acculturated so effectively that if there are any major differences between them and northern urban WASPs, these are rarely acknowledged explicitly on either side of the dividing line. The Irish may be "different," but neither they nor the WASPs are inclined to mention the differences very often.

If one is convinced that the most appropriate goal for American culture is the homogenization of the various components of the total population into one relatively WASP-like group, then the story of the American Irish is a great success.

The melting pot theory, at least in its more sophisticated manifestations, expects the various immigrant groups to contribute something of their own to the host culture, and in turn to assimilate most of the characteristics of that culture. These theorists note that the Irish contribution to American society seems limited to St. Patrick's Day and the Clancy Brothers.

On the other hand, if the commitment is a philosophy somewhere between assimilation and complete cultural pluralism, the disappearance of the American Irish might be viewed with less enthusiasm. There are contributions to the national life and culture that the American Irish could have made which have not been made. The all too brief Kennedy years might raise in the minds of even the strictest WASP assimilationist the possibility that there is something in the Irish style worth preserving.

There are also some liabilities in the history of the American Irish which must be honestly acknowledged. There is no great wealth in the American Irish community, with the exception of a relatively few rich families such as the Kennedy clan. There is almost no intellectual tradition, and that which seemed to be emerging at the end of the 1950s seems to have been aborted by the trauma to the Catholic Church of the Second Vatican Council and the disastrous reign of Paul VI. The Irish, for all their political success, are not too visible in the upper levels of the large business corporations—despite Mr. Roche's long administration at General Motors. Nor have they had much influence in the upper echelons of higher education; the new president of Columbia University, William J. McGill, is the first Catholic to occupy the presidency of a major university. (The WASP stranglehold on such positions is evidenced by the fact that the president of Columbia and the president of the University of Chicago are the only non-WASPs, so far as I am aware, ever to preside over a major American university. We used to have to be content with bragging that some of the university presidents were married to Catholics.) While there are more than enough Irish Catholics in the Senate and the House of Representatives, I have the impression that they are underrepresented on the staffs of Congressmen, and probably also underrepresented in the intellectual positions of state and national bureaucratic agencies, save for police or investigative organizations like the Federal Bureau of Investigation, the Secret Service, or other governmental institutions where a large supply of lawyers is needed.

Nor do the Irish have any positions in the mass media comparable with the decisive roles Jews play in the media. But one can say more. Despite the success of their assimilation, I have the impression that the Irish are viewed with some suspicion in precisely these areas in which they are underrepresented—although not as much suspicion as is reserved for the Poles or the Italians. The Irish will eventually become more accepted in the worlds of academia, the media, and the intellectual bureaucracies—not as quickly or as dramatically as the Jews, but they will get there. In short, the assimilation process, while fundamentally successful, has yet to be completed.

While the American Irish have accomplished basically what they set out to do one hundred years ago, there is still a good deal of restless energy in their ranks, manifesting itself in the continued problem with alcohol and, if my impressions are correct, the powerful self-defeating neuroses to be found in many of the Irish youth. Having made it, at least more or less, the Irish now find themselves looking for new challenges. With no knowledge of, or interest in, their own heritage, they really have no idea what the next goal ought to be. The challenge of immigration seems to have released tremendous vitalities in the American Irish communities, which persist even though practically all of the goals of the immigrant community have been achieved.

The American Irish had the shortest way to come of any of the immigrant groups—for all the impoverishment of the Famine, the Atlantic crossing, and the early years in the slums. With the exception of the Jews, they have achieved the most remarkable success of any immigrant group. The only thing they have lost is their explicit sense of distinction as a group and their consciousness of a heritage—and, necessarily, any consciousness of goals for the future.

What remains for us, then? Football games, cocktail parties, college education for our children, trips to Hong Kong, and dim regrets for lost opportunities whose nature we don't fully understand? A rather sorry end when one stops to think about it, but then it is not really much different from the end of most Americans.

Has the rest of American society been deprived of anything? Most Americans would probably say not, for the Irish did not bring very much with them except their Church, their drink, and their damnable political corruption. Yet I am told that even on the dullest day in the chambers of the U.S. Senate, when Edward Kennedy arrives on the floor there is excitement in the galleries; and despite all the scandal and tragedy which surround that poor young man's life, at this writing he is among registered Democrats the most popular candidate for the presidency in 1972. Camelot was, after all, a Celtic city, and the Kennedys, for all their Harvard education, are still unquestionably and irrevocably Irish. Perhaps some Americans might ask the inevitable question: are there any more like them around? My obviously biased response—based, alas, on no empirical data—would be, "You bet your life there are!" And if things were what they should be, the Kennedy years would not be the end of the story of the American Irish, but only the beginning.

If cultural heritage means anything at all, there are two contributions which the Irish could have made to American culture. First of all, that fierce faith in life, institutionalized in Catholicism but not completely contained in it, which kept the Irish going through a thousand years of oppression should have offered variety, vitality, and spice to the life of the larger American culture. Second, an equally fierce passion for freedom, which made it impossible for the Irish to quit until they finally became free, ought to be at the very core of American social reform. Had they obtained freedom for themselves, one would like to think that the Irish would now busy themselves with obtaining freedom for others. Vitality and freedom —combined with wit and the ability to tell a tale—this was the genius of the Kennedy years, which, for all their imperfections, still represented an interlude of bright hope that American political life desperately needed. Again, it may be my own biases, but I think it will be regrettable if future Camelots are assimilated out of existence before the walls are even built.

If I had my way, what would I like to see on the agenda for the next twenty or thirty years of the American Irish experience?

In the Church I should like to see the growth of democracy combined with a more sophisticated and nuanced version of the profound convictions of the past. What I think will happen, however, is anarchy and a shallow ecumenism, empty of any substantive content.

I should like to see poets and novelists singing hymns and telling stories of vision and laughter, men and women sympathetic with their own past and with the struggle for freedom of other American groups whose songs and tales could stir the minds and hearts of men the way political clichés cannot possibly do. But what I think will happen will be that most of the singers and storytellers will remain silent, and those who do speak out will alternate between self-hatred and self-pity.

I should like to see more scholars who will become expert in the vast range of disciplines, some of whom will help gather together, for understanding if not for admiration, the pieces of their own heritage. What I think we will get is one group of scholars expert in their own disciplines but quite unconcerned with their heritage and another group of quasi-scholars who will continue the Irish Catholic liberal tradition of compulsive self-criticism.

I should like to see political leadership that would combine the sophisticated and explicitly Catholic viewpoint of Eugene McCarthy with the powerful will to win of the Kennedy clan, the unquestionable ward and precinct skills of Richard Daley with the laughter and wit of Jimmy Breslin. What we *will* get, I think, is one group of politicians who continue to practice the precinct skills without any sense that political realities are changing and another group of self-proclaimed liberals for whom moral victories are more important than real ones.

I would like, finally, to see the rank and file of the American Irish a little more conscious of who they are and where they came from, a little more encouraging of the creativity of their children, and a little more confident of their own position in American life. To put the matter more simply, having made it in American society, I wish the Irish would begin to enjoy their success instead of feeling guilty about it.

What we will get, however, is the successful Irish professional man and his wife, different from the rest of Americans only in that their guilt feelings are stronger and their annual consumption of alcohol higher: men and women who are still to some extent prisoners of a heritage they don't understand and of whose existence they are unaware.

I do not think that my hopes are at all utopian. As a matter of fact, if the Kennedy years had not ended so tragically, I think these modest hopes might have translated themselves into expectations with a good chance for fulfillment. I must say I see absolutely nothing in either the present condition of the United States or the American Irish to make me particularly hopeful for any Irish contribution in the years ahead. Daniel Patrick Moynihan, in a poignant and unforgettable interlude on television the day of John Kennedy's death, commented, "We may laugh again, but we'll never be young again." One perhaps can say more: we're not doing much laughing and our children are born middle-aged.

We've made it all right, but at a price—a price which includes giving up several years of our lives. In a brilliant nine-year study of nutrition and heart disease in Ireland and the United States, Professors Frederick J. Stare of Harvard and W. J. E. Jessop of Trinity College, Dublin, compared American Irishmen with their brothers who had not migrated from Ireland. It turned out that the hearts of the Irish were from two to six times more healthy than their American brothers. Even though there were more calories and more fat in the Irish diet, the Irish brothers had lower blood pressure and lower cholesterol in their bloodstreams. The hearts of the Irish brothers looked fifteen to twenty-eight years younger than their American counterparts.

The two scholars see a nutritional component in the phenomenon —particularly less calcium in the Irish diet—but their principal explanation is that the Irish go in for physical exercise much more than their American counterparts. They have to, for their living depends upon it, but it seems to me they also like to. In either case the Irish brothers are much less likely to be overweight, and here may be the main reason for their longer lives.

But there is another factor too. In Stare's words, "It's nothing you can weigh or graph, but whether you can measure it or not it's there. I mean the Irish attitude. When you survey a great many people, you can't help noticing that there's a hopefulness, a courage they get from trust in God. I believe this is a factor in their health. I can't prove, of course, that the uncomplaining, looking-on-the-bright-side attitude of the Irish stems from their faith, but it's there. I think it may have a bearing on their hearts, and I think Americans could add this lesson to the others our study offers."[1]

Oh yes, the rate of heart disease is going up in Ireland in recent years. They're beginning to make it just like their American cousins.

God help us all. . . .

---

1. Quoted in Mary McSherry, "Why Some Men Live Longer," *Woman's Day,* October 1971, p. 113. See also Frederick J. Stare, "Epidemiologic Factors Related to Heart Disease," *World Review of Nutrition and Dietetics,* Vol. 12 (1970), 1–42.

17.

An Epitaph for the Irish

Not so long ago I was wandering through the halls of a progressive Catholic women's college with a young woman I know and noticed a sign announcing that the Irish Club was to meet that afternoon.

"Are you a member of the club, Peggy?" I asked.

"A member? I'm the president!"

"And what do you do at your meetings?"

"Why, we plan the St. Patrick's Night Ball."

"Peg, have you ever heard of the Easter Rising?" She had not.

"And, Peg, what about the Sinn Fein?" She thought it might be Chinese.

"And, what's the Irish Republican Army?" As a loyal Cook County Democrat she wanted no part of it.

Finally: "Peg, who is Eamon de Valera?"

"Oh, I know! He's the Jewish man who's mayor of Dublin."

And so the last of the American Irish fade away into the mist.

The American Irish are in a most unusual position. For the first time in the history of American society it is legitimate to be an ethnic. Black pride has become acceptable, even obligatory, for American blacks. The Chicanos and the American Indians are right behind them proclaiming pride in their traditions. If black is beautiful, and if red is beautiful, the children and grandchildren of the immigrants are asking why they should not think the same way. Polish is beautiful, Hungarian is beautiful, Italian is beautiful,

Greek is beautiful; in Chicago even Luxembourg is beautiful. One may not only be publicly proud of one's heritage on certain days of the year, one can be proud every day of the year. Nay, increasingly, one *must* be proud. He who does not have any racial or ethnic tradition to fall back upon is forced to stand by in shamed silence. If you are neither black nor ethnic how can you be part of the black-ethnic dialogue? One confidently expects the dawn of the day when some New England prophet will announce that Yankee is beautiful.

In the midst of all this resurgence of ethnic pride, the state of the Irish is distressful (to use their word), indeed. At long last it would be legitimate for them to act like they were Irish.

Only they've forgotten how.

The legitimation of ethnicity came too late for the American Irish. They are the only European immigrant group to have over-acculturated. They stopped being Irish the day before it became all right to be Irish. The WASPs won the battle to convert the Irish into WASPs, just before the announcement came that permanent peace had been made with ethnic diversity. Daniel Patrick Moynihan makes the lonely hegira from Washington to Cambridge with the melancholy thought that he and Richard J. Daley are the last of the American Irish.

Some will argue that the Irish have never been more powerful. All kinds of citizens, whose Celtic origins are problematic at best, will sport green emblems on the seventeenth of March (even though the Roman Church threw St. Patrick off the calendar—for which God forgive the Curia—together with St. Christopher). Richard M. Nixon goes to Ireland in search of his roots. Gaelic names have become part of the common pool of names that American mothers impose upon their children: Brian, Kevin, Maureen, Sheila, Eileen stopped being exclusive Irish property a generation ago; now Sean, Seamus, Moira, and Deidre get attached to Polish, Jewish, black, and even Oriental faces. Only Liam and Phionna have not yet been expropriated (and when I hear of a Liam Levy, I will know it is the end). The Clancy Brothers and the Irish Rovers will set hippie feet stomping in packed concert halls. Tens of thousands of Saxons,

Africans, Teutons, Semites, Slavs, and Latins will march down Fifth Avenue and proclaim the glories of the Emerald Isle. And there's even Bernadette Devlin.

So much of the nation seems to have become Irish. Only it's too late because there's nothing left. Characteristically, the Irish quit just before they won.

The political star fades. If there is another Catholic president in the near future he is likely to be Polish. Mr. Moynihan and his colleague, Mr. Glazer, have documented the fall of the Irish from political power in New York City. Unless one counts Mr. Buckley (and west of the Alleghenies we'd rather not), the Irish have vanished from office and even from election slates in New York. Mayor Lee is gone from New Haven; Boston has a Yankee mayor; and few doubt that Richard Daley will be the last of the breed.

The voice of the storyteller is mute. The O'Connors, Flannery and Edwin, are dead. J. F. Powers stands in his store-front window in St. Cloud and dreams of a church which exists no more. Fitzgerald has become the object of scholarship and Jim Farrell dreams still of Fifty-seventh and Indiana, but no one is interested. There are no entertainers to replace Cagney or O'Brien or Crosby; and Notre Dame has an Armenian coach and a Methodist quarterback.

Even in the Church the Irish power wanes. Boston is Portuguese, Philadelphia is Polish, Brooklyn is Italian, and the U.S. Catholic Conference in Washington is presided over by another Italian. Seventeen per cent of American Catholics are Irish, as are 35 per cent of the priests and 50 per cent of the bishops; but the young Irish are no longer flocking to the seminaries. The Irish Catholic intellectuals vie with one another to see who can reject his own past with more enthusiasm, and the clergy and people drift apart as the former get caught up in a painful identity crisis and the latter permit the respect of old to be transmuted into contempt. The hierarchy, apparently lacking the political skills of their civil counterparts, can no longer keep their priests in line; and Irish priests and bishops have little time to ecumene with their separated Protestant brothers (formerly heretics) because they are so busy fighting each other.

The Irish young buried their political hopes with Robert Kennedy. The flags of Camelot are furled, never more to dance merrily in the brisk spring breezes. Young men slide their permanently unfinished novels into their brief cases as they board the commuter train, and their matrons leave half-written poems in Buick glove compartments when they drive to the country club.

The Irish sun was shining brightly in the heavens at the beginning of the 1960s. Mr. Moynihan could write with pardonable pride of the President of the United States and the Prime Minister of the United Kingdom standing on a yacht in front of a life preserver marked "Honey Fitz—U.S.A." The "Honey Fitz" is gone and in a few years no one will even remember who he was; all we will have left from the glory days of the early '60s are memories—and tragic ones at that.

The Irish have finally proved to the WASPs that they could become respectable. But they paid a price: they are no longer Irish. What does it take to be Irish? A distinguished American sociologist of Florentine extraction once observed to me, "The Irish don't have a cultural heritage; they don't have a unique cuisine or an art or a family structure. They're just lower-middle-class WASPs with a political style and a religious faith of their own."

But a religious faith and a political style are not all that bad as a heritage. (I even believe that I made a fairly nasty comment to my colleague that I was unaware that the Italians had either.) In fact, they have done rather well for a millennium and a half; the only trouble is that the American Irish are in the process of losing both.

The nineteenth-century myth about the Irish was that they were dreamers, mystics, brawlers, political pragmatists, and far too committed to their other-worldly faith to become good Americans. Some of the twentieth-century Irish self-critics have elaborated on this theme to argue that Irish Catholics were too other-worldly to achieve economic success in American society, too Catholic to become good intellectuals, and too pragmatic to be good Democratic liberals.

The implicit standard for these judgments (and in Mr. Moynihan's case the standard is quite explicit) is set by the achievements of New York Jews. The Irish are not as "successful," not as "liberal," and not as "intellectual" as the New York Jews (though they recently displayed that they are still somewhat better at winning elections). However, they are more successful, more liberal, and more intellectual than just about anyone else in sight—and the data to support this statement are overwhelming. In fact, on various measures of the achievement syndrome called the Protestant ethic, the Irish Catholics score higher than anyone else—save the Jews.

Where indeed are the mystics to be found, the dreamers who look into the mists and see visions of splendid new worlds—with or without the aid of a mug of "The Creature" which nineteenth-century cartoons invariably placed in Paddy's hand? Surely not in the Roman Church of the Irish-American variety. The bishop and the parish priest have become the standard American corporation types —though somewhat pre–Harvard Business School in their style. As manifested in such journals as the *Commonweal,* the intellectuals are no more interested in being mystics or dreamers than are their role models on the *New York Review of Books.* The young Irish clergy are trying their best to act like Methodists and in the process have finally yielded to the WASPs on those twin bugaboos of nineteenth-century Protestantism, the parochial school and clerical celibacy.

The most serious political failure of the Irish results not from an excess of pragmatism but from not being pragmatic enough. Even if they didn't have a revolutionary tradition of their own, even if the Blackstone Rangers do not call to mind the Regan Colts and the Black Panthers do not look like the Mollie Maguires (though in truth the Panthers are much more moderate), even if Bernadette Devlin is not the Julian Bond of Ulster, the Irish, on the most pragmatic of political grounds, should have identified with the aspirations of the blacks and Spanish-speaking in American society. This failure of the most elementary political intelligence allowed the alliance of Jewish and Yankee liberals to sweep the Irish from political power in New York—and then, of course, put Mr. Buckley in the United States Senate.

This mistake, being duplicated in some fashion or the other in many other American cities, has been avoided in Chicago for the time being. But after Daley, what? The problem is not so much that the mayor will be succeeded by someone who is not concerned about the problems of blacks but that a new generation of Irish will appear on the scene that is not seriously concerned about politics at all. As one young Irish ideologue put it—having successfully learned to imitate the style of American liberalism—"All Daley is interested in is winning elections." The alternative to winning elections is losing them; and since it has been clearly demonstrated that WASP and Jewish Democrats would sooner lose elections than win, the Irish were the only winners left in the party. After a thousand years of losing in the Old Country, the American Irish were once quite hungry to win. Now they are not hungry and can permit themselves the luxury of self-righteous defeat. So the young Irish amateur politicians (nothing is more immoral than a professional politician; he belongs to a "machine") proclaim Adam Walinsky and Allard Lowenstein their heroes and switch allegiance from McCarthy to McGovern as they sally forth in search of more windmills.

A Jewish colleague once observed to me, "The big difference between the Jews and the Irish is that we know we have a self-hatred problem and take it into account. You don't even know you have the problem." So the American Jewish novelist turns his self-hatred to literary and financial profit, and the American Irish novelist doesn't write at all.

How did it all happen? The Irish were seduced by the possibility of respectability. A millennium of oppression by a foreign invader would work havoc with even the strongest of national egos—and there is no particular evidence in Irish history to indicate that emotional security was ever one of their notable assets. Though obviously not so severe, British oppression of the Irish is somewhat analogous to white tyranny of American blacks. The Clancy Brothers lyric which proclaims

> *When we at last are civilized,*
> *Won't Mother England be surprised!*

is more than just a joke. It manifests the mixture of envy, hatred, admiration, and need to imitate which every subject people displays toward its masters. The Irish could be dreamers, mystics, prophets, pragmatists, and occasionally even saints when no other alternative was available.

In this land of the free, the "Mick" was told there was no reason why he couldn't succeed, no reason why he couldn't be respectable, no reason why he couldn't even be President of the United States— so long as he went to Harvard. Respectability was his for the asking, so long as he was willing to settle down to the serious business of becoming just like everyone else. The temptation proved irresistible. You could sit by the bog and dream, so long as respectability was not a real possibility. But in the United States, the Irishman finally found an opportunity to be accepted—not fully, of course—by the "real world" of the Anglo-Saxon. Aided and abetted by his mother and his priest, he set out to prove definitively that he was just as good as anyone else, if not a little bit better. Unfortunately, he succeeded.

But respectability has always meant something very lower middle class to an Irishman, even if he owns a steel mill. His concept of respectability is shaped by the narrow parochialism of the lace curtain—probably because most of his aristocrats long since went over to the enemy. The sad truth is that the Irish new rich do not really know how to spend their money, and their idea of class and style rarely exceeds flying to Dallas to watch Notre Dame play in the Cotton Bowl. In Chicago it is not merely that they do not go to Orchestra Hall, but they do not know that it exists. Respectability does not mean aristocratic responsibility for culture and the arts; it means that you act in such a way that no one will dare to say, "Who do you think you are?" Such an attitude spares most Irish communities Mercedes 600s—or even 300s—but it also means that a young person who wants to be a poet or an artist is packed off to the local psychiatrist.

The primary agent of this seduction by respectability is the Irish mother. The Jewish mother may kill her children with kindness (if the novelists are accurate reporters). The Irish mother manipulates her children by starving them for affection. The Jewish mother may, according to her sons who write about her, say, "Eat your chicken soup; it's good for you." But the Irish mother announces, "There is not enough chicken soup to go around; and if you don't love Mother enough, you'll go to bed hungry."

There is no need for women's liberation in Ireland. The mothers have been running the country for centuries—together with the clergy, who, in their turn, are dominated by their mothers and housekeepers. When a real chance for respectability arrived, the Irish matriarch wasted no time in setting her male off in hot pursuit. If his enthusiasm seemed to flag, she set him in motion once again with her most powerful weapon, "What will people say?"

And so the WASPs won. Seduced by the bright glitter of respectability and egged on by their mothers, the Irish have become just like everyone else, and the parades on St. Patrick's Day are monuments to lost possibilities, of which few people in the parades are aware.

Yet one is permitted to sit by the side of the peat bog, stare into the mist, and think of all the things that might have been.

What if American Catholicism had been presided over by more Irishmen like John England, who democratized his diocese in 1825, or John Ireland, who preached and practiced ecumenism in 1890— long before even the word was invented?

What if there had been mystics or poets or storytellers who, long ago, could have raised for all Americans the question of whether technological and economic success was really enough?

What if there had been a few Irish political leaders who could have realized how much the Irish had in common with more recent migrants to the city and allied themselves with the poor and the oppressed, not so much for losing elections as for winning them?

What if John Kennedy had not been shot?

What if one white immigrant group had been able to keep alive some of the wild passion of its tribal days, a passion which suburban culture abhors but desperately needs? What, in other words, would have happened if the Irish had hung on to not only their souls but also their "Soul"?

And yet . . . on the South Side of Chicago a toddler named Liam does battle with a Burmese cat while his red-haired mother sits at a kitchen table and scrawls poetry on a yellow note pad:

THAT MOST DISTRESSFUL NATION

I shall not to you give, my son, a heritage of
    splintered dreams
that slushed down the sink with stale beer and
    squeezed out tears of pain
for all the years that might have been if I had
    lived
instead of killing dead my heart and ours, bit by
    bit,
with breaking rage and chunks of sorrow,
passion which guilt turned sour and then, misunderstanding
took my soul and crashed it in the night.
I shall not go desperate dying into life.
The enemy that dare to take the sea's surge from our eyes
I shall defy and drag to hell and back and shake the
    skull of suicide
which says the gift will be ungiven and the hope denied.
No, for we shall sing, my son, and eat the sweets of
    victory.
Lie peaceful down your head
This hunger will not be quieted, nor ever fully fed
Not before we hold the stars and until then,
we'll go a'brawling and wooing life
there're fights to be fought and battles won
But never in the name of life direct our own undoing
Nor allow while we breathe that Life should be undone!

So maybe the Irish haven't been tamed at all. . . .

270

Index

INDEX

Nudity, aversion to, 104

Oakboys, 30
O'Brien, Patrick, 264
O'Brien, Thaddeus, 96
O'Casey, Sean, 56
Occupations of Irish-Americans, 123–124, 195–200; attitudes toward, 151–152, 195–197; in Beverly, 234; in the early years, 120–121; in early 1900s, 185; in 1930s, 182–183
O'Connell, Daniel, 31, 32
O'Connor, Edwin, 57, 124, 254, 264
O'Connor, Flannery, 52, 57, 124, 264
O'Connor, Sean, 46
O Cuiv, Dr. Brian, 78
Office of Education, U.S., 3
O'Hara, John, 52, 124, 254
Onahan, William, 217
O'Neill, Eugene, 124
O'Neill, Hugh, 17
O'Neill, Owen Roe, 17, 26
Organizations: racist, 227; revolutionary, 33, 226, 266 (*see also* Irish Republican Army); vigilante, 30–31
O'Sullivan, Jeremiah, 68
Ownership, in Ireland, restrictions on, 28, 35

Pain, Irish response to, 20, 109
Palos, Illinois, 242, 243
Papalism, 84, 63–64, 81
Parents: relationship of, to children, 163–166. *See also* Families; Fathers; Mothers.
Parishes: Americanization of, 90–91; importance of, 87–89, 90–91, 125, 237
Park Ridge, Illinois, 242
Parliament: Catholics forbidden in, 27; early Irish, 18
Parnell, Charles, 32–33
Parsons, Talcott, 96
Patronage, 210
Paul VI, Pope, 256
Peace Corps, Irish-Americans in, 124, 234
Peel, Sir Robert, 36
Peep o'Day Boys, 30–31
Penal Laws, 11, 18, 20, 27–34

Penance, 68
Perceval, Richard, 129–130
Permissiveness, sexual, 167–169
Persecution, of priests, 81. *See also* Penal Laws.
Philadelphia, Polish Catholics in, 264
Philadelphia, Here I Come (Friel), 191–192
Pilgrimages, religious, 68–69
Plunkett, Blessed Oliver, 130, 135
Pluralism, cultural, 256
Poetry: Anglo-Irish, 50; Celtic, 48–52; need for, 269
Policemen, Irish, 11
Polish: Catholics, 264; immigrants, 179; Jews, 219
Polish Peasant in Europe and America (Thomas and Znaniecki), 5
Politics: blacks in, 227–228; in Chicago, 226–267; ethnic, 206–213, 224; ethnic, weaknesses of, 212; Irish, 5, 30, 203–215, 258; Irish, decline of, 195; Irish, development of, 46–48; Irish, future of, 258, 259–260, 264; Irish, as a heritage, 265; new, 207; role of clergy in, 85, 87; structure of, in Celtic Ireland, 44–48; study of, 123–124
Pollard, H. B. C., 19
Polygamy, 79–80
Pookahs, 72
Poor Law Act, 35
Population, Ireland's, 24, 25; control of, 113; effect of Great Famine on, 34, 36, 38–39; increase in, before Great Famine, 83; recent increase in, 39
Populism, 217
Portuguese, 264
Poverty: in Ireland, 28–29, 34–35; of Irish immigrants, 37, 40, 120
Powderly, Terrence, 217
Powers, J. F., 6, 52, 57, 124, 254, 264
Prayers, ancient monastic, 69–70
Presbyterians, in Ulster, 30
Pride, ethnic, 262–263, 269
Priests. *See* Clergy.
Progress, social, and politics, 209, 211
Prosperity: Irish attitude toward, 184–185. *See also* Status, rising.
Protestant Church of Ireland, 28–29

Protestant ethic, 266
Protestants: in Ireland, 18, 20; migration of, 31; opposition of, to Irish immigrants, 84, 118–119; relationship of clergy with, 264; socialization with, 183; in Ulster, aligned with Catholics, 30. *See also* WASPs.
Psychology, study of, 124
Psychology Today, 105

Racism, 5, 216. *See also* Bigotry; Blacks, Irish-American attitudes toward; Riots, race.
Radicalism, and ethnic politics, 212–213
Rebellion, Irish, 17–18, 19–23; during Penal era, 30–31
Red men, 72
Reform, religious, need for, 67, 78–80
Reformation, rejection of, by Irish Catholics, 70–71, 80–82, 84
Regan Colts, 226, 229, 266
Religion: of the Celts, 14; effect of rising status on, 125–126; ethnic differences in, 197–200; importance of, 62, 84; and superstition, 71. *See also* Catholicism.
Renaissance, 15
Rents, during Penal era, 28
Research: on ethnic characteristics, 145–177; lack of, on families, 116; on political attitudes, 218–223
Respectability, importance of, 42, 112–113, 127–128, 154–155, 189–190, 250, 253, 267–269
Revolution: of '98, 15. *See also* Organizations, revolutionary; Rebellion.
Ribbonmen, 31
Ridgeboys, 30
Ridicule, 57, 107–108, 250
Riots, race, 226–227, 229
Risk-taking, aversion to, 189–190, 192–193, 194, 250
Rockefeller, Nelson, 213
Rockites, 31
Rule (St. Columbanus), 68
Russell, Lord John, 35
Ryan, John, 217
Ryan, William, 240

St. Angela parish (Chicago), 182–185
St. Anselm's parish (Chicago), 246
St. Boniface, 68
St. Brendan, 54–55, 68, 77–78
St. Charles Borromeo rectory, 180
St. Columbanus, 64, 65, 68–69
St. Gabriel's parish (Chicago), 181
St. Lawrence parish (Chicago), 181
St. Leo's parish (Chicago), 181
St. Patrick, 64, 263
St. Patrick's Day, 256, 263–264, 269
Sarsfield, Patrick, 17
Scandinavians, personality characteristics of, 146–147, 148, 151, 152, 159–160, 167–169
Schaar, John, 211
Scholars, future Irish, 259
Schools: integration of, 240–241; in Ireland, discipline in, 249–250; parochial, 5, 32, 87–88, 91, 121, 268
Sciences, Irish-Americans in, 200; compared with Jews and WASPs in, 197–200; lack of, 123, 124
Scotland, 15
"Scots-Irish," 31, 255
Scuthian, 54–55, 77, 78
Security. *See* Change, fear of; Self-confidence; Status, rising.
Self-confidence: ethnic differences in, 148, 160–161, 162; lack of, among Irish-Americans, 127–128, 189–190, 192–194, 201, 236; lack of, among Irish youth, 236–237, 249
Self-defeat: of Irish youth, 257. *See also* Risk-taking, aversion to; Self-confidence, lack of.
Self-depreciation, 147, 160–161
Self-destruction: Irish propensity for, 250, 251, 254; forms of, 200–201; of Studs Lonigan, 249; within Kennedy family, 251
Self-exile, as penance, 68–69
Senior, Nassau, 36
Sermons (St. Columbanus), 68
Sex: effect of religion on attitudes toward, 105–106; extramarital, 115; humor about, 55; marital, 103, 114–115; perceived dangers of, 102; repression of, 101–106, 167–174, 248, 250; repression of, and alcoholism, 133; sexual puri-

A Note on the Author

Andrew M. Greeley is Director of the Center for the Study of American Pluralism, National Opinion Research Center, University of Chicago. Born in Oak Park, Illinois, he has lived in Chicago all of his life. He studied at St. Mary of the Lake Seminary, was ordained a priest, and later studied sociology at the University of Chicago, where he received a Ph.D. Father Greeley is a past president of the Catholic Sociological Society and a member of the editorial board of *Sociological Analysis*. His other books include *Why Can't They Be Like Us?*, *The Catholic Experience*, and *Priests in the United States: Reflections on a Survey*.